Geoffrey Ashe was born in London and lived for some years in Canada, where he attended the University of British Columbia. Returning to England, he studied at Trinity College, Cambridge, where he took a First in the English Tripos and was awarded an essay prize by the historian G.M. Trevelyan, at that time Master of the college. Most of his numerous books are on historical and mythological topics, especially the Arthurian legend, and he was secretary of the committee that excavated Cadbury Castle, the reputed original of Camelot. Geoffrey Ashe has held visiting professorships at several American and Canadian universities. He lives in Glastonbury, a focal point of British legend.

D0038848

THE BOOK OF PROPHECY
From Ancient Greece to the Modern Day

GEOFFREY ASHE

ORION

An Orion paperback

First published in Great Britain in 1999
by Blandford, a division of
The Orion Publishing Group Ltd
This paperback edition published in 2002
by Orion books Ltd,
Orion House, 5 Upper St Martin's Lane,
London WC2H 9EA

Revised and updated
Copyright © Geoffrey Ashe 1999, 2002

A CIP catalogue record for this book
is available from the British Library.

ISBN 0 75284 847 X

Typeset by Deltatype Ltd, Birkenhead, Merseyside

Printed and bound in Great Britain by
Clays Ltd, St Ives plc

Contents

Preface

In its primary sense, prophecy means inspired utterance. A mortal is speaking with more than mortal knowledge or insight, perhaps of future events, but not necessarily. Foretelling the future, however, is what the word has generally come to mean, and that is what this book is about. It happened to take shape at a time when prophecy was beginning to enjoy a vogue because of the approach of the year 2000. For that reason, I think it important at the outset to say what it is *not* about.

It is not about what may be called rational forecasting or intelligent anticipation. Over the past century and more, a vast amount of this has been going on. Political journalists, economic prognosticators, statisticians and scientists assess what they see as current trends and project them into the years ahead. Science-fiction authors have been doing much the same with freer and bolder imaginative flights.

One justification for looking at other sorts of prediction is that the rational kind have not been all that successful. Between about 1965 and 1975 'Futurology' was actually masquerading as a science. It no longer does. Two predictions at the dawn of the twentieth century might have come to serve as warnings. In 1901 Wilbur Wright said to his brother Orville that 'man would not fly for fifty years'. Two years later those same brothers made the first flight. Science-fiction foreshadowers have scored rather higher than the more pretentious kind, yet H.G. Wells, the doyen of all science-fiction predictors in English, wrote: 'Aeronautics will never come into play as a serious mode of transport and communication.'

In 1980 David Wallechinsky, Amy Wallace and Irving Wallace brought out *The Book of Predictions*, in which they assembled a huge array of invited forecasts by a variety of experts and imaginative authors. There has been time to test many of these. A few have turned out right; hundreds haven't. One particular issue has proved to be crucial. Listing reasons for the decline of Futurology, Nicholas Rescher writes:

> The inability of American 'intelligence' specialists to forecast the downfall of Communism in the former USSR and its satellites was another major cause for disillusionment.

That failure was paralleled in *The Book of Predictions*. One of its rational predictors did foretell the break-up of the Soviet Union and the end of Soviet Communism, a decade or so before it happened; but most of the others thought Communism would soon conquer most of the world.

On this great issue, moreover, virtually all the experts were outdone by a Portuguese village visionary who was no sort of an expert at all. For me, that has been a motive for at least casting an impartial eye on *non*-rational prediction (or paranormal prediction, if 'non-rational' is a loaded term): on supposed cases of knowledge of what is to come through clairvoyance, dreaming, astrology, contact with informative spirits or communication from supernatural beings. The story ranges over many centuries. Among its *dramatis personae* are Greek priestesses, Hebrew prophets and Tibetan lamas. In medieval Europe the first major manifestation outside religion was the entry of Merlin as a literary figure. In his prophetic role he is ancestral to an immense company of seers. While the volume of nonsense has been prodigious, it remains a reasonable exercise to sift the data and see what can be picked out as deserving attention. If it emerges that nothing can, and all alleged prophecy can be explained away, that in itself will be a step forward.

My concern is always to establish the facts. Taken together, they do seem to carry a certain weight and to point in a certain direction, but I will say at once that I don't think clichés such as 'prophetic vision' or 'seeing the future' are of much help with them. They call for a mental adaptation that is much less obvious.

A prophet who exemplifies some of the problems is Nostradamus. He lived in sixteenth-century France and wrote 942 four-line stanzas of verse, most of them predictive and most of them cryptic. He has attracted all too much notice. The mass of writing about him has been so wishful, pro or con, that it has obscured the facts. Some commentators have made resolute attempts to debunk him completely. Others have maintained that he foretold many things that he certainly did not foretell – the rise of Hitler, nuclear weapons, the assassination of President Kennedy. On the one hand, the attacks are inadequately informed and misrepresent him; on the other, the wild claims depend on such far-fetched interpretations that they discredit him. Actually, the facts about Nostradamus are more interesting than either side realizes, and I have done my best to disentangle them. The results may be unwelcome to both sides.

I make no apology for giving considerable space to Jewish and Christian scripture. In Western society, the idea of prophecy as prediction is due to the Bible more than anything else; to the Bible and, it must be added, to misunderstandings of it. A few of these are included. If some have an air of comic relief, it can't be helped, and they must not divert attention from those prophecies that are impressive from any point of view and that may shed light on prophecy outside the Bible. The facts, I hasten to add, don't support Fundamentalism any more than they support total rejection. (Biblical quotations in this book are from the Revised Standard Version, abbreviated as RSV, except in one or two places where another translation seems to me to bring out the meaning better.)

The greater biblical prophets, such as Isaiah and Jeremiah, raise an important question, and one aim of this inquiry is to answer it. They are exceptional figures, who rise above their human setting and are often in opposition. Their God singles them out and speaks to them and through them. That applies when they make predictions – perhaps especially then – and the implied view of prophecy has remained, on the whole, the norm: it is the gift of a minority, probably quite a small minority. Even when it is done by a technique such as astrology, the technique cannot be used by everyone equally: a successful astrologer is a special person, an expert in the art. Even prophetic journalists, such as the late Jeane Dixon, are supposed to be 'psychic'. This assumption – an elitist assumption, if anyone cares to call it so – needs to be examined in the light of any positive evidence that may emerge. If the thing happens at all, is it in fact exceptional, does it happen only for exceptional people?

The assumption was challenged several decades ago, on the basis of research that may now look old-fashioned and inadequate but has been echoed since. A British aircraft designer, J.W. Dunne, set it forth in 1927 in a book entitled *An Experiment with Time*. Reflecting on some personal experiences, he began to suspect that entirely ordinary people have anticipatory dreams, only they forget them or don't recognize the fulfilment when it comes. He recorded several of his own and kept a look-out for fulfilments which seemed to happen. He believed that waking mental events might have the same time-jumping quality, but dreams remained his chief concern. Friends of his tried. What emerged was not prevision of complete experiences, but prevision of bits of them, sometimes taking the form of isolated images or images differently grouped.

An artist, for instance, dreamed of a lifeboat painted red and blue, standing on green turf with a net draped over it. Next day he saw a boat painted red and blue like a lifeboat, similarly pointed at both ends and standing on turf. It was not, in fact, a lifeboat, and there was no net. But some distance away he saw another boat that did have a net draped over it. A cousin of Dunne's dreamed that she met a German woman in a public garden. She recalled that this person wore a black skirt with a black-and-white striped blouse and had a distinctive hairstyle. Soon afterwards she stayed at a hotel and was told that another woman staying there, thought to be German, had aroused curiosity. She met this guest in the hotel grounds, with much the same appearance as in the dream, but the setting was different.

Dunne's most systematic experience is described in a later

edition of his book. He enlisted six volunteers who recorded their dreams as fully as they could, over an agreed period, and he did it himself over the same period. Out of a total of eighty-eight dreams, twenty could be construed as anticipating future images in the dreamers' lives, always or nearly always with some kind of scrambling or distortion. Dunne's book was a best-seller, and dream diaries became fashionable. A similar study was carried out during 1969–70 as part of the programme of a dream laboratory at the Maimonides Community Mental Health Center in Brooklyn, New York, and positive results were reported. Dunne himself was convinced not only that precognition was real but that it was not extraordinary. Questions he raised are still living ones. *If* it happens, *what* happens, *how* does it happen? He formed a theory of multiple time according to which the dream consciousness can reflect happenings on another track, so to speak, at points not reached by the waking consciousness. J.B. Priestley flirted with Dunne's ideas in his plays and kept interest alive in a non-fiction work, *Man and Time*.

In this book I consider Dunne's findings, with comparable cases of more recent date, but I return to Dunne only after surveying prophecy in general. Only in the long perspective can such cases be evaluated and fitted into a theory – if the facts demand a theory.

One last point. Are we going to end up with any forecasts for the immediate or nearer future? I have not come across any that seem clear and impressive enough to mention. Some may ask, 'What about prophecies in the Bible?' The answer will become apparent. Attention has been drawn to alleged 'Mayan Prophecies', which are based on an ancient Central American calendar and are supposed to portend cataclysms in 2012. Well, maybe. But I am not in the predictive business myself.

Chapter One

Priestesses and Star-gazers

Prophecy, I repeat, originally means *inspired utterance*, which raises the question, inspired by whom? Supposedly, by a god or goddess or spirit or, at any rate, by some unseen being other than the person inspired. That person became in a sense the being's voice. A prophet was a 'forthteller', not a 'foreteller'. At first prophecy did not imply predicting the future, and in Islam it still does not. Muhammad is The Prophet because Allah spoke through him and he proclaimed Allah's will, not because Allah made forecasts through him. But long ago, in a variety of cultures and countries, prophecy took on a predictive meaning because of a belief that the being who inspired could reveal things to come, enabling the recipient to foretell them.

There is a difference here from divination. From time immemorial people have sought knowledge, including knowledge of the future, by magical methods. They have looked for guidance and omens in the flight of birds, in the entrails of sacrificial animals, in the fall of dice and of cards. Omens are of innumerable kinds. But an omen is not a message. It simply happens. It works, if it does, for no definable reason. A correct forecast based on it may owe something to insight on the diviner's part, as in successful fortune-telling. But no gods, goddesses or spirits need be involved – not even imaginary ones.

A place called Dodona, in the northwest of ancient Greece, had a very old oracle, and the way in which it functioned marks a transition between divination and prophecy. Dodona centred on an oak tree sacred to Zeus, the chief of the Olympian gods. Anyone who came to consult the oracle was given a thin strip of lead and told to write on it a question in a form allowing a yes-or-no answer. The strip was rolled up and the inquirer's name or an identifying number was scratched on the back. A priestess dropped the strips in a jar and took them out one by one, simultaneously drawing a lot for the one taken out, probably a bean coloured black or white. The colour of the bean showed whether the answer was 'yes' or 'no'. Hundreds of these lead strips have been found on the site. Most of the inquiries on them concern personal problems. Gerioton asks whether he should marry; Cleotas wonders whether to go into sheep-farming. Questions about the future include a troubled one from Leontios: will his son recover from an illness?

This was divination performed in a sanctuary on a regular basis, under a god's auspices. Zeus was presumed to be responsible for the yes-or-no answers. But he did not communicate beyond that, he did not inspire. In Greece, the god who did inspire was Apollo. It was mainly because of him that prophecy left divination behind.

Apollo was the most Greek of deities, yet he was not a native of Greece. Before he was known there, he was worshipped in Asia Minor with his sister, Artemis. Elements from much further afield probably went into his making. His nucleus, so to speak, may have been a god of Asian shamans who went into states of ecstasy and received communications from him; a god carried westward and southward by folk-migrations. Wherever Apollo's cult came from, some form of it reached Greece together with his sister's towards 1200BC. A new myth was created giving them a Greek birthplace on the island of Delos, and a kinship with Zeus's Olympians. Apollo became civilized and multiple, annexing the functions of other gods. He was the patron of healing, music and mathematics, but a more primitive and irrational part of him, his role as a dispenser of inspiration, never died. He acquired shrines in various places and spoke through priestesses, women being more receptive than men. In particular, he occupied Delphi near Mount Parnassus.

Before Apollo the place may have been sacred to the Earth Goddess. According to legend, her daughter, Themis, maintained an oracle here and gave significant dreams to visitors who slept in the precinct. There was even a guardian dragon; Apollo slew it and took possession. Delphi was a charged and magical spot. The most potent thing in the temple was the *omphalos*, a stone marking the centre or 'navel' of the Earth, then regarded as a disc. The point had reputedly been determined by two eagles, who flew inwards from opposite points on the circumference and met at Delphi.

When Apollo was there first, the oracle could be consulted on only one day a year, his birthday. Later it could be consulted on the seventh day of any month when he was in residence. He was not in residence all the time, however, and for three months of every year he left another god, Dionysus, to look after the temple, although not to give oracular messages, and went off to stay with the Hyperboreans, a mysterious northern nation said to have helped him to establish himself at Delphi. This northern connection is one of the clues to far-off, maybe shamanic antecedents.

Consulting the oracle was by no means a casual undertaking, and even on a permitted day, simply dropping in was forbidden. There was a moral prerequisite: the inquirer was expected to be without guilt. Sometimes owners of slaves set them free as a meritorious act. Consultation, moreover, was expensive. The minimum basic charge was the equivalent of two days' wages, and to this had to be added the cost of travel and offerings. Apollo spoke through a priestess called the Pythia, who first underwent a ritual purification in the nearby Castalian spring. Accounts of her further preparations differ. Perhaps she chewed laurel leaves, associated with inspiration. Perhaps she burned them, or burned hemp or bay leaves (sacred to Apollo) and inhaled the fumes. A tripod is mentioned. Either she sat on it herself or it was supposed to be the seat of the god. When he took control of her, making her a kind of medium, the inquirer could ask a question. She did not reply directly and might have been incomprehensible if she had. A priest took down the god's message verbatim and translated it into normal language, often in hexameter verse. In that form it could be written and carried away.

Under Apollo's regime, Delphi was revered. It was the single sanctuary shared by all Greece, the focus of union among its city-states. The temple complex housed an art gallery with pictures and sculptures from all quarters, and poets and musicians gathered there to present their works. The city-states sent envoys to ask for guidance, not only on immediate issues but on matters of policy. So far as can be judged, Apollo's advice was moderate and conciliatory. Athenians claimed that he had dictated some of their laws. Spartans claimed that their entire constitution was based on messages from him. In several cities officials called exegetes, attached to the government, discussed the meaning and application of his rulings. He counselled Greeks who were planning to found colonies overseas, and most colonies had temples dedicated to him. Plato, in the *Republic*, seeks to found a social system on pure philosophic reason, yet even he says 'the greatest and finest and most important of legislative acts' – those establishing the republic's religion – should be entrusted to Apollo. 'For he is the national expositor who explains these things to all men from his seat at the navel of the Earth.'

All of this was 'inspired utterance', with nothing in it about the future, but some who consulted the oracle wanted to know what *would* happen, especially what the consequences would be if they did such-and-such. They asked Apollo because he had foreknowledge. That had been proved in a traditional case when he granted it to a mortal. The legend was none too creditable. Just before the Trojan War, he had had sexual designs on Cassandra, a daughter of Priam, king of Troy. He promised that if she complied, he would confer the gift of prophecy on her. She accepted the gift and then had second thoughts. Apollo asked for one kiss, and when their mouths were close, hers apparently being open, he spat in it. She kept the gift of prophecy but henceforth nobody would believe her.

When the Greeks besieged Troy, she foretold its fall without effect. Shakespeare introduces her briefly in *Troilus and Cressida*. While Priam and his sons are debating whether to continue the war or restore Helen to her husband and end it, Cassandra enters, 'raving, with her hair about her ears' (as we shall see, a symptom), and predicts the doom of Troy unless Helen is returned. Hector is willing to listen, but Troilus dismisses her 'brain-sick raptures', and the war goes on. In legend, the Trojans had a last chance when they manoeuvred the Wooden Horse into their gateway with Greek warriors hidden inside it. Cassandra warned of what would happen if they brought it into the city and was ignored as usual. The Greeks emerged from it at night and opened the gates to admit their comrades. Troy fell.

Cassandra's story might have raised queries about the wisdom of prophetic dealings with Apollo. The temptation, however, was too strong; questions about the future were put to him and he was willing to answer. His oracular predictions were seldom clear cut, and they could turn out to be correct in a way the inquirer failed to anticipate. Herodotus, the Greek 'Father of History', gives a famous account of such an event. In 546BC the proverbially rich Croesus, king of Lydia in Asia Minor, wanted to know his prospects in a projected campaign against Cyrus, king of the Medes and Persians. He decided to test seven oracles and sent messengers to all seven, inviting them to tell what he was doing on a certain day. The answers were to be written down and brought back to him.

On the appointed day, says Herodotus, he did something so peculiar that he judged no one could guess. He chopped up a tortoise and a lamb, put the pieces in a bronze cauldron and set it on to boil. Somehow or other the priestess at Delphi got this right, and the written answer duly came back. Convinced of her divine inspiration, Croesus put his real question. What would be the result if he proceeded with his war? He made a lavish sacrifice to Apollo and sent expensive offerings to the shrine. The answer was that if he marched against Cyrus he would destroy an empire. He also asked about the duration of his own domain and was told that Lydia would fall only when a mule ruled the Medes. Doubly reassured, he attacked, but was defeated, and Cyrus conquered Lydia. Croesus had destroyed an empire: his own. As for the mule, Cyrus was of mixed blood, with a Persian father and a Median mother. Croesus sent a delegation to Delphi to complain. The priestess, speaking in her own person, said he should have asked Apollo to clarify and not jumped to conclusions.

The paranormal prelude to this account might be thought to cast doubt on it as a whole, but the messages are not untypical. Other predictive equivoques are on record, the best known being concerned, like the Croesus message, with warfare, the subject likeliest to cause apprehension. Some depend on language and cannot be properly translated. When Pyrrhus, king of Epirus, consulted Delphi about a war against Rome, he got an answer that could mean either 'I tell you, Pyrrhus, that you can defeat the Romans' or 'I tell you, Pyrrhus, that the Romans can defeat you.'

Herodotus gives three interesting pronouncements that date from 480BC, when the Persians under Xerxes invaded Greece. Delphi informed the Spartans that either the Persians would take their city or one of its kings would die. When a small Spartan force led by King Leonidas made a celebrated stand at Thermopylae, all were killed, including Leonidas, but although the Persians advanced, they never took Sparta. It is possible, of course, that the heroic king believed in the oracle and accepted his fate, so that the prophecy created its own fulfilment.

In the same crisis a delegation from Athens consulted the oracle. The priests seem to have expected a Persian victory, or at least to have tried to insure against that result. The answer that the Athenians got was alarming. (I quote an English version in an approximation of the original metre.)

> Wretches, why tarry ye thus? Nay, flee from your houses and city,
> Flee to the ends of the earth from the circle embattled of Athens!
> Body and head are alike, nor one is stable nor other,
> Hands and feet wax faint, and whatso lieth between them
> Wasteth in darkness and gloom; for flame destroyeth the city,
> Flame and the fierce War-god, swift driver of Syrian horses.
> Many a fortress too, not thine alone, shall he shatter;
> Many a shrine of the gods he'll give to the flame for devouring;
> Sweating for fear they stand, and quaking for dread of the foeman,
> Running with gore are their roofs, foreseeing the stress of their
>   sorrow;
> Wherefore I bid you begone! Have courage to lighten your evil.

The horrified envoys tried again, threatening to camp in the sanctuary, and got a slightly more constructive response. While the Athenians were not to resist the Persian army, they should trust to a 'wood-built wall' and confront the invader in a different way. The last lines gave a geographical pointer:

Salamis, isle divine! 'tis writ that children of women
Thou shalt destroy one day, in the season of seed-time or harvest.

After much debate in Athens, it was agreed that the wood-built wall referred to a fleet, and there would be a sea-battle off the island of Salamis. If so, the lines looked ominous, yet perhaps it was the enemy who would suffer. The Athenian commander Themistocles argued that if the Athenians were going to lose, the island would have been called something like 'unfortunate Salamis', whereas the epithet 'divine' was encouraging. He carried the day, the sea-battle was fought, and the Persians were beaten.

Whatever Apollo's priestesses really said – and it may have been nonsense – any predictions that the priests extracted were either general, as in the one about the Persian invasion, or cryptic and hedged. The message would cover different contingencies, or it was a sort of riddle that might have meaning in retrospect – like the 'mule' prophecy – but was less than enlightening at the time. There seem to have been few Delphic forecasts that were right in a plain, straightforward way and with no possibility of deliberate fulfilment, as may have been the case with Leonidas. Greeks recognized this, and even gave Apollo the sobriquet 'Loxias', 'the Ambiguous'. Yet his spell persisted. It was largely because of Delphi that the Greek words for 'prophet' and 'prophecy' began to acquire a predictive meaning, though, in classical Greek, they did not go all the way.

Apollo's inspiration was not confined to his temples. Back in Asia Minor, the land from which he had crossed the Aegean, his wilder past lingered. He had freelance prophetesses called Sibyls. Historically, little is known about them. They functioned alone and without the Delphic closeness. When the god inspired them they flew into uncontrolled frenzies. The philosopher Heraclitus speaks of one of them as having a 'raving mouth, uttering things without smiles or grace'. They sound rather like the raving Cassandra, and occasionally Cassandra herself is called a Sibyl. The few sayings of theirs that are quoted are mostly vague outpourings about plagues, famines and other disasters. One such outpouring might be described as anti-clerical, voicing a dislike of Apollo's priests. The most interesting thing about these women is that they existed at all.

With the passage of time they became involved in a mythology of their own. Sibyls, preternaturally long-lived, were located not only in the homeland but in several other countries. The senior Sibyl, who was sometimes given the name Herophile, was said to have been Apollo's half-sister. She was born in the neighbourhood of Troy, before the Trojan War, and settled at Erythrae, on the coast of Asia Minor opposite the island of Chios. Hence, she was known as the Erythraean Sibyl. She lived a very long time indeed, perhaps a thousand years. Classical writers mention nine others. Persia had a Sibyl and so had Egypt. But the Erythraean remained the chief and was often referred to as if she were the only one, 'the Sibyl' pure and simple. At Erythrae, in more or less historical times, Sibylline sayings were written down and preserved. Some at least were versified as at Delphi.

Romans had great respect for another Sibyl, the Cumaean. Her home was a cave at Cumae near Naples, the site of an ancient community of Greeks. In Virgil's *Aeneid* the Trojan prince Aeneas, reaching Italy with his migrant companions after Troy's fall, consults her about their prospects in the new country. Her name is Deiphobe. Inspired by Apollo, she goes into her prophetic ecstasy.

> Her countenance and her colour changed and her hair fell in disarray. Her breast heaved and her bursting heart was wild and mad; she appeared taller and spoke in no mortal tones, for the god was nearer and the breath of his power was upon her.

Deiphobe, or Apollo speaking through her, promises that the Trojans will effect a settlement but they will have to fight for it: 'I see Tiber streaming and foaming with blood.' (This passage is the source of a modern prophecy, by a classical scholar turned politician, about immigration into Britain causing 'rivers of blood' to flow.) When the fit has passed, the Sibyl conducts Aeneas into the Underworld, where he meets the spirits of the dead and is granted a prevision of the glories of Rome, the city that the Trojans' descendants will found.

Aeneas's visit to Cumae is poetic legend, but a shrine may have existed here later, with a succession of priestesses, so that there was always a Cumaean Sibyl. In his novel *I, Claudius* Robert Graves gives a fictionalized account of the cave, its occupant and the Sibylline Books. The last, at least, were real. The story goes that in the sixth century BC the Cumaean Sibyl brought nine books of Greek verses to the Roman king, Tarquin. They may have come from the collection at Erythrae. She offered to sell them, but he refused. She destroyed three and asked the same price for the remaining six. Again he refused. When she repeated her action and offered three only, his augurs persuaded him to accept.

The Sibylline Books were kept at Rome in a stone chest, underground, with a board of priests as custodians and Greek slaves as interpreters. They were consulted in times of crisis for the advice and predictions they contained. The procedure was complicated. One method was to choose a line, write its letters vertically, and find other lines that began with those letters. The resulting acrostic was the message, which seemed usually to have advised some ritual action to propitiate the gods. Seers, genuine and otherwise, added to the collection. In 81BC it was destroyed by fire. Priests restored what they could from memory, travelled to Erythrae and elsewhere, and assembled about a thousand lines. Some of the new matter was doubtfully Sibylline, and the Emperor Augustus attempted a purge. He transferred what he approved to two gilded cases under a statue of Apollo.

Virgil believed – perhaps rightly – that these Cumaean texts included a prophecy of the return of the golden age, when the ancient god Saturn ruled the world and the virgin Astraea, Justice, dwelt among mortals. In 37BC, when Augustus was still known by his personal name Octavian and had not yet attained supremacy, Virgil published a series of poems called *Eclogues*. In the fourth of these he associates the golden age with the expected birth of a child. Most of the poem is metaphorical in its glowing imagery, but the child, a boy, seems to be literal.

Now is come the last age of the song of Cumae; the great line of the centuries begins anew. Now the Virgin returns, the reign of Saturn returns; now a new generation descends from heaven on high. Only do thou, Lucina [a goddess], smile on the birth of the child, under whom the iron brood shall first cease, and a golden race spring up throughout the world! . . .

Enter on thy high honours – the hour will soon be here – O thou dear offspring of the gods, mighty seed of a Jupiter to be! Behold the world bowing with its massive dome – earth and expanse of sea and heaven's depth! Behold, how all things exult in the age that is at hand! O that then the last days of a long life may still linger for me, with inspiration enough to tell of thy deeds! . . .

Begin, little boy, to know thy mother with a smile.

It is not clear what the poet intends by this expansion of Sibylline prophecy, and there are signs that he revised the Eclogue, in which case the original text is unknown. It is not clear, either, how this Messianic language could ever have been justified. He may be thinking of a son to be born to Octavian, or to Mark Antony, at that time still Octavian's partner in power. Both their wives were pregnant, but both the offspring turned out to be girls. The wonderful child never materialized, and in the *Aeneid*, written later, Virgil makes Augustus himself the restorer of the golden age.

The irony is that in a sense the child did materialize. Christians, noticing likenesses in the Fourth Eclogue to certain biblical passages, claimed that Virgil was divinely inspired (although unconsciously) and foretold Christ. The new religion, however, was not kind to the Cumaean Sibyl or to Apollo. Towards the end of the fourth century AD, when the Roman world had become officially Christian, Augustus's collection of verses was burned. A mass of 'Sibylline' matter survived, but, as we shall see, it was different. A few years before the incineration, Apollo had given up at Delphi. Julian, the last pagan emperor, sent emissaries to try to get a response, and they did, but it was depressing.

Tell ye the king: the carven hall is fallen in decay:
Apollo hath no chapel left, no prophesying bay,
No talking spring. The stream is dry that had so much to say.

★

Pagan Rome had her home-grown seers, although they were of a somewhat elementary kind. The most famous instance of Roman soothsaying is the warning to Julius Caesar about his assassination. Spurinna, the soothsayer who gave it, told him to beware of danger that would come not later than the Ides of March, that is, the 15th. An important meeting of the Senate was to be held on that day. The night before, Caesar and his wife had disturbing dreams. In the morning he was hesitant about leaving his house, but on learning that the senators had been waiting for some time, he decided to go. As he entered the building, Spurinna was standing by. Caesar laughed and pointed out that the Ides of March had come. Spurinna replied that they had come, but not gone. When Caesar took his seat, the conspirators, led by Brutus and Cassius, gathered round and stabbed him. This event has been cited as a perfect case of precognition. Many, however, were in the conspiracy besides the actual assassins, and leaks undoubtedly occurred. Spurinna may simply have picked up rumours.

Soothsaying continued to flourish, and so did divination from dreams, omens and the inspection of the entrails of sacrificed animals, but an increasingly sophisticated society wanted a more sophisticated technique, and found it in astrology. Belief in the old gods and goddesses was waning, but some were making an astrological comeback. The Western version of the art, which survives to this day with modifications, began in Babylon in the sixth century BC and was improved by Greek astronomers. Seven celestial bodies were designated as planets or 'wanderers' because they were not fixed from the standpoint of a human observer as the stars were. These were the Sun, the Moon and the five true planets seen without telescopes. Astrologers plotted their movements through sectors of the sky defined by the constellations of the zodiac.

Earth was at the centre of the universe – astronomy was Ptolemaic, not Copernican – and seven transparent spheres rotated around it, one outside another, each carrying a planet. The Moon's was closest, and after that in order came the spheres of Mercury, Venus, the Sun, Mars, Jupiter and Saturn, the outermost. Outside Saturn's sphere was a larger sphere bearing the stars. Outside that was an even larger one, the *primum mobile*, imparting motion inward to

spheres exerted influence on the world below, and
their varying relation to the signs of the zodiac, were
. Deities judged to be appropriate were matched to
e names Mercury, Venus and so forth are the Roman
of the divine beings who were assigned to those planets by
ast ogers. Apollo, having taken over the Sun, now had a place in
the heavens.

On the basis of the planets' positions at someone's birth, it was
supposed to be possible to draw up a horoscope and infer the
subject's character and destiny. On the basis of their projected
movements, future events, or at any rate probabilities, could be
foretold; good or bad days could be identified in advance for some
activity; and so on. Comets, being unpredictable, were a rogue
factor in the system and were thought to portend special happenings,
such as the deaths of prominent people. One that appeared after
Julius Caesar's death arrived too late to be a portent. It was
interpreted as his spirit ascending to the heavens, a convenient
adjustment.

Some Romans opposed astrology as a Greek fantasy exploited by
charlatans. Caesar took no interest in it, and the Senate passed
resolutions against it. But Augustus, as emperor, recalled the
accuracy of an astrologer he had consulted in his youth and had the
horoscope made public. His successor Tiberius took the art seriously
but wavered in his attitude. At one point he wanted to banish
astrologers from Rome. However, he kept one named Thrasyllus in
his household as a companion and confidant. Thrasyllus had a
narrow escape. At first he was not successful, and Tiberius, thinking
he had entrusted him with private matters to no purpose, was about
to push him off a cliff. Thrasyllus made a correct prediction in the
nick of time. After that Tiberius became, in the words of the
historian Suetonius, addicted to astrology.

By this time its place in society's upper echelons was secure, and it
was widespread in the Empire. The casting of horoscopes at birth
was becoming normal practice. Nero's, in AD37, caused apprehension. When he was growing up during the reign of Claudius,
Thrasyllus was still at court, and it is said that he indicated an exact
date for Claudius's death. He was proved right, but only – it is

further said – because Claudius's wife Agrippa, the mother of Nero, had resolved to poison him and understandably chose that day to do it. She then chose an astrologically propitious hour to have her son proclaimed emperor. Both Nero and his wife Poppaea developed an interest in the art and listened to another astrologer, Balbillus. When a comet was thought to threaten the emperor's death, Balbillus observed that rulers could sometimes avert their fate by killing an important subject; Nero proceeded to kill several. The emperor Vespasian, who reigned soon after him, and Vespasian's sons Titus and Domitian, were also believers.

One Roman prophecy of interest has survived from this period. It may be stretching the conception to count it, but it is more than simply a rational forecast. Its author is the Stoic philosopher Seneca (*c.*4BC–AD65), who was born in Spain, became Nero's boyhood tutor and wrote fulsome praise at his accession. Nero was not the best of advertisements for Stoic philosophy, and the ex-tutor ended up as one of his victims on a conspiracy charge.

Seneca was familiar with astrology through Balbillus's discourses, but his prophetic feat owed nothing to it. He took an interest in geography, and he wrote plays, and the two pursuits intersected. As a native of Spain he was more conscious of the Atlantic Ocean than Romans generally were, and he was one of the first to discuss circumnavigating the world. Greeks had proved it to be spherical, and made good estimates of its size. But what were the practical implications? If you sailed out west, how far would you have to go to reach Asia? An earlier Stoic, Posidonius, had suggested a distance of 7700 miles from Spain to India. Seneca was more optimistic. He reckoned that with a fair wind you could cross in a matter of days.

He assumed, as Posidonius did, that there was nothing in between. At that time the limit of the known world was Thule, a place beyond Britain, with a frozen sea a day's sail past it. Thule was discovered in the fourth century BC by the Greek explorer Pytheas. Early authors who mention it identify it with Iceland, probably correctly. At any rate 'Ultima Thule' was the end of everything. However, in a choral passage in his tragedy *Medea*, Seneca springs a surprise. The ode is about voyages going farther and farther, and builds up to a climax:

Venient annis secula seris
Quibus Oceanus vincula rerum
Laxet, et ingens pateat tellus,
Tethysque novos detegat orbes,
Nec sit terris ultima Thule.

This may be freely translated: 'The time shall come at length when Ocean will unloose the bonds he imposes, when the vast Earth will lie open, when the sea-goddess will reveal new worlds, and Thule will not be the last of lands.' In his sober geography Seneca makes the gap between Europe and Asia so narrow that he leaves no room for these new worlds. His poetry contradicts his prose. The ode could have had a climactic end without departing from his rational view. It could have said, 'The time will come when voyagers will cross the western ocean to India,' or even, 'The time will come when voyagers will sail around the world.' Seneca does otherwise. A foreign element has intruded into his thinking.

There is no real antecedent in classical literature. In his account of Atlantis, Plato refers briefly to a continent beyond it that didn't sink when Atlantis did and is presumably still there. But that is probably pure myth-making. No one before Seneca relates any such notion to real future exploration or foreshadows the discovery of . . . well, America. These lines excited Columbus, although he didn't think of 'new worlds' any more than Seneca did in prose. After reaching America, he spent the rest of his days trying to prove that it was Asia.

Chapter Two
....

Prophetic Israel

Suetonius mentions one more prophecy, as a talking point during
the reign of Nero. Another Roman historian, Tacitus, takes note
of it in much the same terms. Here is what Suetonius says:

> There had spread all over the Orient an old and established belief,
> that it was fated at that time for men coming from Judaea to rule
> the world. This prediction, referring to the Emperor of Rome, as
> afterwards appeared from the event, the people of Judaea took to
> themselves. Accordingly they revolted . . . Since to put down this
> rebellion required a considerable army with a leader of no little
> enterprise, yet one to whom so great power could be entrusted
> without risk, Vespasian was chosen for the task, both as a man of
> tried energy and as one in no wise to be feared because of the
> obscurity of his family and name . . . He took his elder son Titus
> as one of his lieutenants.

Vespasian had held a command in the invasion of Britain during
Claudius's reign, capturing more than twenty 'towns', probably
hill-forts, and carrying out the occupation of the Isle of Wight.
Nero's death in AD68 initiated a year of confusion when three
pretenders rose and fell. Vespasian was still busy fighting the revolt
in Judaea. Omens were said to point to him as the right man to
pull things together, and he won enough support from the other
army chiefs to become emperor. He returned to Rome, leaving
Titus to finish off Jerusalem. After doing so in 70, Titus followed
and worked closely with his father, in due course becoming

emperor himself. Both did well. 'Men coming from Judaea' ruled the Roman world. The prophecy was fulfilled ... apparently.

Suetonius, of course, turns it upside down. It was not truly fulfilled at all. The Jews who 'took it to themselves' had every right to it. This was their own prophecy of the Messiah, who would liberate them and give them dominion. They rose against Rome in the hope that he would come to lead them, and they fought heroically, but he never came. Jerusalem was wrecked and its Temple destroyed. It was the victors Vespasian and Titus who took the prophecy to themselves, quite illegitimately.

Belief in the Messiah was the culmination of a long prophetic tradition. Most of it, although not the last stage, can be traced in the Bible. In Christian parlance the Bible means the Old and New Testaments. The Jewish Bible is the Old Testament only and must be looked at, for the present purpose, alone. Christians reinterpreted it, and Christian doctrine affirms that the Old Testament can be properly understood only in the light of the New. Whatever the value of that claim, we must try to get (so to speak) behind it and read the Old Testament as if the New did not exist.

Its theme is the relationship between the God of Israel – Yahweh, the Eternal, the Lord – and the world and its people, especially his Chosen People, the ancient Israelites and their Jewish descendants. Why Chosen? Not because of their numbers, importance or cultural distinction, and certainly not because of a supposed racial superiority. They seem to have begun as a small grouping in a medley of Semitic tribes that roamed about the fertile crescent between the Mediterranean and Mesopotamia. Egyptian official correspondence calls some of these people 'Habiru', and 'Hebrew' may be the same word, but the Israelites can have been only a minority in the Habiru complex. 'Israel' is first on record as a national name, with no exact clue to its whereabouts, in an Egyptian inscription dated approximately 1207BC. Israelite tribes can be detected archaeologically in upland Canaan – Palestine – a little before 1000BC, using a primitive Hebrew script. The early books of the Bible, the fundamental

Torah or teaching, were slowly taking shape during the centuries after that.

Genesis, the first of these books, gives the account of the tribes' origin that was developed by their leaders. They had a common ancestor, Abraham, who lived in the Mesopotamian city of Ur, a real and important place, about a thousand years previously. His original name was Abram, but it was changed. God summoned him to leave Ur with his family and household, traverse the fertile crescent and settle in Canaan. 'Israel' was a name divinely bestowed on his grandson Jacob. Jacob's twelve sons were the ancestors of the twelve Israelite tribes.

In a crucial passage (13:14–17) God promises to give Canaan to Abraham's descendants. If he is worthy (some of the tests of his worthiness are frightful), and by implication if *they* are worthy, they will be established there with God's blessing and grow into a great, numerous and favoured people. This is the Lord's decree and his covenant. However – the narrative continues – several generations of these descendants did not live in Canaan as possessors, but in Egypt as an increasingly oppressed population. They multiplied and at last found a liberator, Moses.

Two points are vital and remain so. One is the territorial claim. The Promised Land is central to Israelite religion and to the Judaism that later evolves from it. The other point is the nature of the God who has made the gift. The first chapter of Genesis presents him as the creator of the world. That passage was written later than much of the rest and added at the beginning, but it is not a theological afterthought. God is just as much the creator in a more primitive story in the second chapter. He never figures in the Bible as a mere tribal deity among other tribal deities. In the eyes of its authors, he is always the only Higher Power to matter. Other gods have a sort of reality but an infinitely inferior reality; they are hardly more than idols, and they dwindle as Israelite ideas mature. God's decisions are, therefore, absolute and unchallenge-able, and they include the granting of the Promised Land to his Chosen People. While this grant can never be cancelled or withdrawn, it is conditional. They must live as he desires them to live and keep his commandments. Otherwise he can dispossess them, not totally and for ever, but, if he wills it, for a very long time.

The Israelite claims and prophetic hopes, leading up to the hope of the Messiah, are rooted in a unique sacred history to which Genesis is the prologue. It begins a little before the time when Israel is becoming a visible entity. To what extent this is real history is a disputed question. Quite possibly a fair amount of it is real, but the early part is not confirmed by external evidence, and while archaeology is by no means silent, its meaning is disputed likewise.

Exodus, the book following Genesis, begins with the Israelites enslaved in Egypt. God speaks to Moses, tells him the secret of his name Yahweh, 'He Is', and appoints him with his brother, Aaron, to negotiate with the Pharaoh for the release of his people so that they can return to the Promised Land. To effect this deliverance, God works tremendous miracles. He afflicts Egypt with plagues, and, when the Israelites are on their way with Egyptians in pursuit, he opens a path of escape by parting the waters of the Red Sea. After they have walked across, the waters flow back and overwhelm the Egyptians. (The Red Sea story – such a spectacular gift to Hollywood – is thought to be the result of an early misunderstanding. The location that the author intends is probably a lake called the Sea of Reeds on the Suez Canal route, which had places where a crossing on foot could be effected under temporarily favourable conditions, but would quickly have become a trap for the Egyptians' heavy chariots. The marvel would not be so much that the crossing became possible as that God made it so at the moment of the Israelites' need.)

These events confirm Moses in his leadership and in his claim to have a special relationship with God. Ascending a mountain in the isthmus of Sinai, he receives the Ten Commandments. In the existing biblical text, many further ordinances are added, making up the Mosaic Law, which still applies to Orthodox Jews. The Israelites wander in the wilderness, and very few of the original host get to the Promised Land at all. Its conquest is a task for their offspring. As for the indigenous Canaanites, God is ruthless: they should be smashed. A great Jewish scholar, Rashi (1040–1105), makes the astonishingly frank statement that the previous Genesis narrative, going back to the creation of the world, was written to justify what we might now call an attempted genocide. The God of Israel, who gave his people the Promised Land, had to be unequivocally supreme so that neither the dispossessed Canaanites nor anyone else could appeal against his decrees. It was the will of the Creator, no less, to form a special community in a special place; so Israelite occupancy was founded on an incontrovertible right. (Actually the Canaanites were not smashed or dispossessed as completely as we are led to believe, but they were very much subordinated.)

The biblical story goes on to a phase when the settled tribes are only loosely united and governed by 'judges', one of whom, it is interesting to note, is a woman – Deborah. In practice, Yahweh's reign over his people is not total. They are often tempted by the local cults of fertility-spirits, baals, and a goddess, Asherah. After some time they want to have a king, initially for leadership against enemies. The Lord speaks through the priest Samuel, warning them that they may regret it but granting their wish. Their first king is Saul, who turns out poorly. The second is David, a native of Bethlehem, who becomes an idealized prototype-monarch despite some fairly flagrant shortcomings. He makes Jerusalem his capital, with the hill of Zion at its heart. His son, Solomon, builds a temple for the Lord. Solomon's heir is a tyrant who provokes a revolt, and the northern tribes break away, forming a separate kingdom confusingly called 'Israel'. The residual southern kingdom consists mainly of the large tribal territory of Judah and bears that name.

Scripture begins to mesh with the records of other nations after the close of the tenth century BC. Thenceforward it is more and more feasible to trace a history that is factual in the normal sense There are references outside to two prominent kings in the north, Omri and Ahab, whose kingdom, with a capital at Samaria, was more opulent than Judah, but lacked its crucial assets: Jerusalem, the Temple and the royal line descended from David. Although Yahweh's cult was still practised, it lost ground. In 720BC the Assyrians conquered the northern kingdom – according to the

Bible, as a divine judgement on apostasy – and deported many thousands of its more important inhabitants. The non-deportee population became hybridized under Assyrian rule and lost all political pretensions. Judah survived, but here too there was backsliding, and for a time the Temple itself harboured very peculiar cult-objects. A scripturally approved king, Josiah, cleared them out, and in the biblical authors' eyes the southern kingdom kept an essential soundness.

The fate of the deported northerners, the Lost Tribes, has been a theme of speculation and myth. They were dispersed beyond the Euphrates and probably assimilated. The Bible, however, refers to them as still somehow in existence and destined to reappear. They have been fancifully identified with the Afghans, the Japanese and even some section of the American Indians, having doubtless crossed the Bering Strait on the ice. The British-Israel theory was launched in the late eighteenth century and had a following well into the twentieth. It was based on the assumption that because God's promises were unbreakable, a major body of his Chosen People could not have vanished without trace; they must still exist, as the Bible seemed to indicate. Moreover, God had spoken of divine favour and visible greatness. So who were the Lost Tribes? How were they disguised? How were the divine favour and visible greatness made manifest? The theory maintained that they had drifted by various routes into northwest Europe and become, essentially, the British people – predominantly the Anglo-Saxons, although a Celtic element was admitted without much enthusiasm. As long as the British Empire stood, Britain could be seen as fulfilling the main requirements. Much ingenuity was expended on tracing the British royal line back to David. Yet it is hard to avoid a suspicion that the mainstay of the theory was a pun. The word 'British', it was observed, suggests the Hebrew *b'rit ish*, meaning 'covenant man'.

Ancient Israel had its diviners and seers. Biblical writers mostly condemn the former, but sometimes approve of the latter. There is a clear contrast with other nations. Genesis, in chapters 40–41, tells the story of Abraham's great-grandson Joseph in Egypt. He correctly interprets several anticipatory dreams, including Pharaoh's, and thus attains influence at court. The dreams have no obvious meaning, and in expounding them, Joseph does not use a mantic technique, such as a magician might do. Pharaoh's magicians try without success. Joseph succeeds because the Lord inspires him, and he could not have commanded the inspiration himself. He says, 'Do not interpretations belong to God?' and 'God has revealed to Pharaoh what he is about to do.'

The writer is making a point of principle, not claiming that Joseph was a prophet. In a later part of the story it appears that Joseph does employ divination, perhaps in conformity to Egyptian custom (44:5, 15). The Bible applies the term 'prophet' to a few of its other early characters. Moses, his brother Aaron and their sister Miriam form a kind of prophetic family, although it is only to Moses that God speaks directly. A song in praise of the Lord's deeds, sung by Miriam (Exodus 15:21), may be the oldest thing in the Bible, and Deborah also sings such a song. However, they are not prophets in what becomes the distinctive Israelite sense.

We begin to glimpse this in Numbers 11:24–29, when Moses summons seventy elders, and 'the spirit of the Lord rests upon them' and they prophesy, although no details are given of what they say. Moses expresses a wish that all the Lord's people were prophets. This is an isolated episode. Full-time prophets, counterparts to Apollo's inspired women, emerge after the settlement in Canaan is well established. The word equivalent to the Greek *prophetes* is *nabi*, probably meaning a person who is called.

Israel's prophets were numerous and usually, though not always, male. Some were freelances like the Sibyls, some combined in groups or guilds with a leader. They wore garments of skin. They played musical instruments: harps, tambourines, flutes, lyres. As minstrels of Yahweh they could invite his spirit, and when it came upon them like a great wind, they passed into an ecstatic state, dancing and seeing visions. As a part of the experience – not the whole of it – they might pour out oracular chants, which were revered as divine messages and might include predictions. The excitement could be infectious. Just before the proclamation of Saul as king, he meets a band of prophets, and the spirit of the Lord descends on him too and he prophesies with them. Hence a proverbial saying, 'Is Saul also among the prophets?' expressing surprise at finding someone in unexpected company. Later, some messengers sent by Saul to look for David are similarly seized, and he himself, following them, strips off his clothes and rolls about on the ground for hours. This belief in Yahweh's overmastering power is reflected in the story of a Gentile seer named Balaam, who is hired by a Moabite king to curse the Israelites but can only bless them.

The *nabi* prophets were respected. They could live on presents and hospitality, since generosity to them was thought to bring good luck. They were not in conflict with the priests who conducted regular worship, and even kings consulted them. But out of this innocuous background a towering figure stepped forth, who started Israelite prophecy on a long divergence from Delphi.

Elijah, according to the Bible, lived in the breakaway northern kingdom during the reign of Ahab, in the ninth century BC. Ahab had married the Phoenician princess Jezebel, thought by some to have been a relative of Dido, queen of Carthage in Virgil's *Aeneid*. An elegant and strong-minded woman, she brought a new sophistication, as appears in surviving fragments of buildings and art. She also brought the cult of the Tyrian Baal, Melkart, a more formidable deity than the village baals whom the Israelites had encountered in the Promised Land. With Melkart came the goddess Asherah. Elijah confronted Ahab, proclaiming the wrath of the true God, and foretold a long drought as a sign of his displeasure. Meanwhile, Jezebel persecuted the other prophets and drove them into hiding. Few of the northerners offered much resistance to the new state religion.

Elijah challenged them with an uncompromising choice: they must make up their minds. On Mount Carmel he staged a contest in which the Lord kindled fire on an altar when Baal could not. (Rationalizations of this miracle need not detain us.) However, Jezebel hounded him and he escaped to Mount Horeb in Sinai, where, long before, Moses had conversed with Yahweh. Elijah was in despair. Then the Lord spoke to him, not in spectacular demonstrations, but in a 'still small voice'. Seven thousand of the people had not submitted to Baal, and a change would come. He must return. Ahab, urged on by Jezebel, was now engaged in seizing a vineyard belonging to Naboth, one of his subjects, an act of un-Israelite despotism. Naboth was condemned on a trumped-up charge and stoned to death. Elijah came to Ahab as he walked in the vineyard and predicted disaster for him and Jezebel.

The way in which Ahab perished confirmed the new atmosphere. A plain distinction had emerged between prophecy uttered to oblige a patron and prophecy that told truths no matter how unwelcome they were. Ahab planned an expedition to recover Ramoth-gilead from the Syrians who had captured it. He assembled a large body of *nabi* prophets and asked whether he should proceed. They chorused that Ramoth-gilead was his for the taking: 'Go up, for the Lord will deliver it into the hand of the king.' One of them put on a pair of iron horns, and quoted the Lord as promising that Ahab would 'push' his enemies. But another prophet, Micaiah, described a vision that was much less encouraging. He had seen the Lord authorize a 'lying spirit' to enter into Ahab's prophets and lure him to destruction. Ahab was angry, led his army to Ramoth-gilead and fell in battle. Jezebel survived him for several years and came to a bad end.

To reverts to the account of Elijah himself, several prophetic themes make their appearance in it. When he foretells the drought, prophecy begins to include prediction as a major element. Further, he takes a courageous stand against an authority seen as evil. This willingness to make enemies in the Lord's name is echoed in the incident of Micaiah, and the echoes continue in later prophets, who are decidedly not agreeable fortune-tellers and are far from Apollonian moderation. Elijah's career also fore-shadows the conception of a faithful remnant, which becomes prominent in Israelites' thinking about themselves. While most of the people have bowed the knee to Baal, 7000 have not. After Elijah, it gradually comes to be accepted that the Chosen People are not an indivisible bloc. Whole sections can fall away, but God's promises will always apply to those who remain. The northern tribes did fall away and were deported to Assyria. The southern ones, centred on Jerusalem, retained enough fidelity to survive, although even they underwent a sifting and separation.

Elijah is inspired like the earlier prophets, but in a more sober fashion. His speeches are straightforward, the divine communication at Horeb is quiet. He breaks the ground for prophets of a different kind, through whom the religion of Israel makes an indelible mark, and begins to be profoundly concerned with the future. In the biblical story he is taken up to heaven in a fiery chariot without death, leaving his disciple Elisha as a successor. He becomes an immortal, like King Arthur; the last of the prophetic books, Malachi, closes with the expectation of his return as the forerunner of a divine judgement.

Elijah's eloquent stance prepared the way for a series of literary prophets whose revelations were written down and became part of the canon of scripture. This is a purely Israelite phenomenon. Such a prophet was 'called' like a *nabi*; the word of the Lord came to him unbidden. He might go into an ecstasy as a *nabi* would, he might have revelatory flights of imagination, or he might see visions and dream dreams. But his experiences made sense, and he translated them into serious messages, often rendered in memorable rhetoric and poetry. Many of the prophetic utterances now had a moral nobility that surpassed the Israel of older times and was uncommon anywhere.

First of the literary prophets in date is Amos, who was active before 760. He has a special interest as the first writer to denounce oppression and unscrupulous wealth-seeking in anything approaching a left-wing style. Not that Amos or any other prophet talked revolution, but most of them were deeply critical of the irresponsible luxury of the rich and the reduction of Israel's religion to official ceremonies and sacrifices, sometimes with pagan contaminations. They did not reject Jerusalem's Temple, any more than they rejected monarchy, but they cherished a nostalgia for the simpler life of the tribes, of the shepherds and farmers and craftsmen of olden days. They longed for uncomplicated devotion to the Lord, and proclaimed that justice and mercy and charity mattered more than pompous ritual and burnt offerings.

Yahweh loved his people, yet his people were estranged from him. The prophets urged this theme in public speeches and songs. They performed symbolic actions, like shattering a pot to symbolize a city's destruction. The greatest of them, Isaiah, looked outside and talked about other nations. They attracted disciples, and to judge from the confusion in some of the existing texts, it may often have been these who committed the prophets' words to writing.

The literary prophets sometimes look to the future, and this is the main reason why 'prophecy', in the Western world, has come to have the sense of prediction. When they do, there is nothing clairvoyant about it. In fact, several of their specific forecasts are simply wrong – although even the wrongness can be interesting: there are few hedged predictions in the Delphic manner. What the prophets voice is usually best described as a reading of the situation and the way it is tending. This may be dramatic, as in recurrent forebodings about a 'Day of the Lord' when God will inflict judgement on the erring Chosen People. The prophets' insight can be impressive, but, for the present purpose, the question is whether they show more than insight, whether their language goes beyond and suggests any precognitive gift. Perhaps it does. However, this element comes into view only gradually and must be defined. What the prophets foresee is not so much a literal future as a potential future, in which certain things will be able to happen against rational expectation. This feature of their prophesying is not easy to make clear in the abstract. It emerges in the historical perspective, and when it does it can be evaluated, pro or con.

While the prophets may see the Chosen People as adrift from the Lord, even temporarily rejected by him, they also anticipate a renewal. In doing so they lay their collective finger on something that is extraordinary about ancient Israel, however explained. I would like here to pay a tribute to a neglected writer on the Bible, my great-grandfather Dr Isaac Ashe, who, in 1875, published an essay showing a perceptiveness ahead of his time. He pointed out (among much else) that comparative religion, often invoked against Israel's uniqueness, actually supports it. All the similar surrounding peoples had religions that grew naturally out of their culture and situation. Many Israelites were constantly trying to have one, to settle down comfortably with baals and goddesses and nature-worship, yet they were constantly being dragged back against the grain. The prophets and their disciples inspired a decisive number to cling to what did *not* come naturally and was *not* paralleled among the nations – the vision of a world sustained and morally ordered by the blessing of One Supreme.

Because of this, the prophets could foresee a renewal in the future when there were few signs of it in the present. It came to be linked with the conception first hinted at in Elijah's time – and taken further by Isaiah – of a remnant who would survive through all apostasies and catastrophes. These would always be the true Israel and inherit the whole divine legacy.

A major prophet who develops this idea is the sombre Jeremiah. He was distressed not only by Judah's transgressions but by the perversion of prophecy to sedative ends. Popular false prophets said 'peace, peace' when there was no peace. Jeremiah's horizon was wide and he looked around him: he had a good deal to say about Gentile countries and foretold the rise of the Chaldean power of Babylon. Its king, Nebuchadnezzar, would become God's agent for the chastisement of his people. The blow fell quickly enough. From 605 onwards Nebuchadnezzar was expanding his empire. He was willing at first to leave Judah intact as a protectorate, but its kings stupidly rebelled. In August 587 a Babylonian army besieged and took Jerusalem. Its commander, Nebuzaradan, 'burned the house of the Lord, and the king's house and all the houses of Jerusalem; every great house he burned down. And all the army of the Chaldeans . . . broke down the walls around Jerusalem' (2 Kings 25:8–10). Jeremiah himself was put in prison during the seige because his all-too-accurate prophecies were thought to show pro-Babylonian sympathies.

In this way the southern kingdom also perished and with it the Temple, whose treasures and movables were carried off to

Babylon. Judah's city-dwellers and people of consequence were led off into captivity. Nebuzaradan released Jeremiah and offered to take him to Babylon, as a guest rather than a captive, but he declined. He is said to have gone to Egypt and died there. The remaining population of Judah was an impoverished peasantry, and many migrated beyond the Babylonians' reach, leaving an almost empty country.

Yet although the prophet had seen the disaster coming, his writings show that before it happened, he was already looking beyond with hope. In a vision of two baskets of figs, good and bad, he symbolized the faithful remnant who would survive and the others who would be cast off. The deportees were the good figs. They would be purified by their sufferings in Babylon and would be freed from captivity when Babylon fell to enemies from the north, including the Medes (correct). However, it would not fall soon. They would endure penitential exile for seventy years, perhaps a symbolic period rather than a literal one, although in the upshot it was not wildly wrong, and it was destined to be remembered and to undergo a strange reassessment. When the purified remnant came home, the Lord would deal graciously with them; he would bring back the scattered northern tribes to join them; he would make a new covenant, writing his law in the hearts of his people so that they would all know him.

One prophetic book is associated with the Captivity itself. It bears the name of Ezekiel, a priest, who of course had no Temple in which to officiate. There are queries about the text, but let us call the author, or the principal author, Ezekiel. The book is more highly wrought than its predecessors. Ezekiel begins with a complicated vision of a divine chariot, believed by commentators in later times to contain profound secrets. He takes a further step in the exaltation of the holy city, by making it literally the world's centre, like Delphi, or at any rate the centre of its inhabited lands.

Thus says the Lord God: This is Jerusalem; I have set her in the centre of the nations, with countries round about her. (5:5)

...... medieval geography when the world is
...... spherical. Jerusalem is the centre of the land
...... else is ocean.

...... phets, Ezekiel rails at the people's sins, but he
...... ure restoration foretold by Jeremiah, inseparable
...... the Promised Land. Perhaps his most interesting
...... 37–39. In a famous image of dead bones coming to
life, ... shadows not only the return of the exiles of Judah but
the retu.n of the long-lost northerners and a complete resurrection of the Chosen People.

> Thus says the Lord God: Behold, I will take the people of Israel
> from the nations among which they have gone, and will gather
> them from all sides, and bring them to their own land; and I will
> make them one nation in the land . . . and they shall be no longer
> two nations, and no longer divided into two kingdoms . . . My
> servant David shall be king over them.

'David' must mean a king of the royal Davidic line. In chapters 38
and 39 Ezekiel goes into the next act, passing beyond Jeremiah.
There will be an attack on the Chosen People in their recovered
Land by 'Gog of the land of Magog', the chief prince of Meshech
and Tubal, out of 'the uttermost parts of the north', with various
allies. Ezekiel's geographic point is now more specific: the
restored Israelites will be dwelling 'at the centre of the earth'
(38:12). God will destroy the invader with pestilence, hail,
torrential rain and other weapons in the celestial armoury. This
cataclysmic defeat of Israel's enemies will manifest God's glory to
the rest of the world. After this, Ezekiel describes a sort of utopia
centred on Jerusalem.

These prophecies have never been entirely fulfilled. However,
the earlier part of the twentieth century witnessed a claim that all
of them were well on the way to fulfilment – a claim that shows
the need for caution in attempting to apply scriptural prophecy to
modern times. In the aftermath of the First World War the
aforementioned British-Israelites pointed out that, according to
their own theory, the two branches of Israel actually were being

reunited in Palestine as Ezekiel said. The country had detached from Turkey and placed under the rule of the British, allegedly the northern Israelites; while the Zionist movement, under British sponsorship, was repatriating Jews. In 1936 Edward VIII came to the throne, and he was known to his intimates as David – 'my servant David'! Everything seemed to be going well, with support, it must be added, from measurements of the Great Pyramid. The next step would be an invasion of the Middle East by Soviet Russia, 'Gog' being Stalin and 'Meshech and Tubal' being Moscow and Tobolsk. Then it all fell apart. King Edward abdicated, Soviet Russia was otherwise engaged, and in the next few decades the British Empire came to an end, so that the prophetic texts that were supposed to show Britain's Israelite character no longer applied.

To revert to realities, Jeremiah's predicted reversal came in 539, a little ahead of schedule. Cyrus, the same king of the Medes and Persians who figured in Croesus's unlucky experience with the Delphic oracle, captured Babylon and gave the exiles leave to go home. A prophet who hailed this deliverance raised Israel's prophetic tradition to a magnificent climax. His name is lost. His work, for some reason, is attached to the Book of Isaiah and forms a portion of that book beginning at chapter 40. Despite his literary greatness, we can know him only as Second Isaiah. He extols Cyrus as the anointed of the Lord, his instrument for the crushing of Babylon, and writes joyously of the triumphant return that Cyrus has made possible. With Second Isaiah, Yahweh becomes unambiguously the only God, Lord of all the earth; in due course, the prophet says, the glory of reinstated Israel will lead all peoples to acknowledge him.

The exiles who had won through were survivors of the southern kingdom of Judah, and the term 'Jew', Judahite, enters proper usage applied to this remnant which inherited the promises and the Land, plus their descendants in perpetuity. They were free to go back, as Jeremiah and Ezekiel had foretold. But many had no wish to. After forty-eight years, most of the deportees were dead, and for the younger ones born since the deportation, the Promised Land had never been home at all. Large numbers

...ylonia, where they were comfortable. ...nto other countries. This was the beginning ...pora. A fair-sized group that did return to ...Zerubbabel, a grandson of one of the last kings ...ese people made a start on a new Temple, ...eventually built, but the community had neither ...ation nor the resources to restore the city. Jerusalem re...ed semi-derelict, and Second Isaiah's hope petered out in anticlimax. Prophets still arose, but the prophetic impulse was dwindling.

Real revival began only in 445, when a Jew, Nehemiah, was cupbearer to the Persian king, Artaxerxes I (this was a more important post than it sounds, because it gave personal access to the king). In Susa, the capital, Nehemiah heard depressing reports of the condition of Jerusalem and told Artaxerxes. The city was now within the Persian domains, and the king sent Nehemiah there with authority to organize its rebuilding. In spite of much harassment, he succeeded in getting it repopulated and walled. The other outstanding figure in this phase was the priest and scribe Ezra, 'scribe' meaning an expounder of the sacred texts. Artaxerxes sent him also to Jerusalem with a commission to enforce the law of his God. Arriving with a team of assistants, he tightened up observance of the Mosaic code. According to tradition, he also made a collection of sacred writings that became the first form of the Bible. Ezra's work was the strongest single factor in establishing the Jewish people's identity. It made for more conviction and solidarity, but also for more separateness.

The situation was still rather anticlimactic. It drifted on for a long time and might have drifted on longer still if it had not been for changes in the world outside. Cyrus's successors showed goodwill, and contributed funds for the new Temple. The Jewish enclave around Jerusalem, far too small to be a Persian province or satrapy in its own right, was part of the Satrapy Beyond-the-River – that is, the Euphrates. It was simply the district of Yehud, recognized as a priestly domain, with its own treasury and coinage. The Persian connection may have influenced the emergence of new doctrines akin to tenets of the religion, Zoroastrianism, and gradually a belief grew up in resurrection of the dead or, at least, some of the dead. Ideas of life after death had been almost imperceptible in Israel before the Persian contact. Another feature of an expanding Judaism that may have reflected Persian theology was the conception of a great active power of evil, personified as Satan, a conception which is scarcely perceptible in earlier times.

Belief in a power of evil, resulting in a sharpened dramatization of history, received an immense impetus from a crisis after the end of the Persian period, a crisis that has been described as 'at once terrific and inconclusive' and that led to a new kind of prophecy. Alexander the Great conquered Persia and took over its empire. The Jews did not suffer from the change, which created a Greek-speaking 'Hellenistic' society with enlarged opportunities. Alexander's empire broke apart into fragments, ruled by dynasties descended from his army commanders, and for a long time all was well. In 175, however, Palestine was part of a Syrian kingdom under Antiochus IV, called Epiphanes, who had the very un-Greek notion of enforcing religious conformity. Exploiting a dispute about the Jewish high priesthood, he used a pro-Greek faction to impose his own nominee, who had, significantly, adopted the Greek name Menelaus. The king failed to foresee the convulsion his policy would cause with these particular subjects of his.

Menelaus killed Onias, the legitimate high priest, and his brother plundered the Temple. Antiochus ordered the cessation of the daily sacrifice. He had the Temple's lamps extinguished and, in December 167, installed a statue of Zeus. He issued edicts against the observance of the Sabbath and the circumcision of children. Some Jews acquiesced, others refused, and their refusal brought a new phenomenon into the world – martyrdom for a religious cause. The king made it a capital crime to own copies of the sacred books, yet not all were surrendered. He tried to discredit resisters by making them violate the Mosaic Law. Respected members of the community were dragged to a pagan altar and commanded to eat pork, on pain of

held out and did die by torture.
Jerusalem's wall and poured troops into
the faithful scattered into the country
ese were called Hasidim, meaning the 'pious'

policies produced a revolt, led by Judas Maccabeus,
December 164, recaptured the Temple. The daily
sac   was resumed and the lamps were lit, a triumph
commemorated to this day in Hanukkah, the Feast of Lights.
Judas died in battle, but two of his brothers carried on the
struggle. Reviving fervour revived the nation, and a successor of
Antiochus recognized Jewish independence in 142. The Maccabee territory now included most of Palestine and some country
beyond. Galilee and Edom, southeast of the Dead Sea, were
thoroughly Judaized.

Shaken by the crisis provoked by Antiochus and doubtful in an
unstable independence, reflective Jews wondered where it was all
leading. The Lord's care for his Chosen People implied that it
must be leading somewhere, but the prophets had been left
behind and their books gave no obvious guidance. Merely to
mark time was unthinkable. Prophetic thinking began to be
extended beyond its scriptural bounds, and one result was
apocalyptic literature. 'Apocalypse' means 'revelation', and this
genre took up motifs from the inspired authors and developed
them as divine secrets or mysterious doctrines. Symbolic unfold-
ings of the course of history were portrayed as leading up to a
grand conclusion.

Apocalyptic matter does just achieve a foothold in Jewish
scripture, appearing in parts of the Book of Daniel that were
written during the Antiochus crisis but fathered on a folk-hero
said to have lived in Babylon long before. The practice of
ascribing one's 'revelations' to a hallowed figure from earlier times
became normal. We find apocalyptic matter in books purportedly
written by Ezra; by Baruch, Jeremiah's secretary; by Enoch, an
ancient patriarch; even by Adam – it would be hard to get back to
anyone with more seniority. These works were excluded from

the Bible as not being inspired scripture, but they were never wholly out of touch with the prophetic tradition.

A recurrent scenario is that the pseudo-author describes a series of visions of supernal realities, which build up to a future world-transformation and a final triumph of Israel, making sense at last of all that has happened. The end is to be brought about by special and spectacular divine action, as foreshadowed by Ezekiel in the Gog episode. Gentile kingdoms will perish; Israel will endure and rise to a sublime destiny. The underlying thought is that success in human terms, as in the Maccabee revolt, will never be more than provisional. The climax and conclusion of history can come only through intervention by God, virtually ending the present world. This will involve calamities and slaughterings, and indeed some of the literature dwells so much on disaster that 'apocalypse' tends to suggest chiefly doom and still has that meaning metaphorically.

A new factor is the entry of supernatural characters. In the world of apocalypse angels are active, and so are devils. The hostility of the latter is now added to Israel's shortcomings as a reason for the disappointments of history. Satan begins to step forth openly, as does an evil dragon-monster called Beliar. The Lord, of course, will rout the demonic horde.

Some of this is already in the Book of Daniel, which is not counted as prophecy by Jews and is simply a Sacred Writing. In it, Nebuchadnezzar, king of Babylon, has a dream about a giant image with a head of gold, a body of silver above and bronze below, legs of iron and feet of iron mixed with clay. A stone 'cut out by no human hand' strikes the feet, toppling the image over and breaking it, and grows until it fills the whole earth. Daniel explains. The head is the king of Babylon himself. Afterwards – not named in the text, but identifiable – will come a Median kingdom, a Persian kingdom and a Greek kingdom, Alexander's, this last being a realm of mixed peoples that will not cohere. The stone is the supreme and everlasting kingdom of Israel, which God will found on the ruins of the others.

Later Daniel has a dream of his own, confirming Nebuchadnezzar's. He sees the successive kingdoms as four beasts. The first is like a winged lion, the second like a bear, the third like a leopard with four wings and four heads. The fourth is not described: it is 'terrible and dreadful and exceedingly strong', and it has ten horns. A 'little horn' rises among the others and plucks up three of them. It has human eyes and a mouth speaking great things. The horns are doubtless Greek kings who will reign after Alexander in parts of his empire, and the aggressive and vocal 'little horn' is Antiochus. Subsequent passages continue to attack him, going into more detail and predicting his downfall. His profanation of the Temple is described as setting up an 'abomination that makes desolate', a phrase destined to be repeated elsewhere.

By this denunciation the Book of Daniel supplies a pattern for later writers. Judaism evolves what is known as typology. Persons or events or images in scripture are valid in themselves, but can sometimes be construed as symbols of others that are yet to come . . . anticipations. Antiochus can be seen as foreshadowing future persecutors. The fourth beast and the phase of ascendant evil are taken up and given fresh meanings. Even the duration of the ordeal, three and a half years, is to be significant in other contexts.

The book has two further points of interest. I omit the lions' den, which is the best-known thing in it but irrelevant here. Daniel recalls Jeremiah's prophecy that the desolation of Jerusalem will end after seventy penitential years. But, he says, God's people do not appear to be purified. The angel Gabriel (notice the entry of an angel) explains that the real period is seventy weeks of years – that is, 70 × 7 or 490. Jerusalem will be rebuilt, but its troubles will not cease. The final week will bring slayings and destruction, and relief will not dawn until after that. Daniel is supposed to be looking ahead to Antiochus's onslaught, which the final week is presumably to witness, but it is impossible to make up 490 years between Jeremiah's prophecy and the persecution; and the text includes a verse that implies another meaning entirely, a puzzling and genuinely predictive meaning. This will be best considered in the context of Christian interpretation.

The second point of interest is that in the passage about the four beasts and their supersession by a glorified Israel, Daniel's vision goes on after the glimpse of Antiochus as the 'little horn'.

He sees the Ancient of Days, God himself, pronouncing judgement on the last of the beasts. Then another figure appears:

> Behold, with the clouds of heaven there came one like a son of man, and he came to the Ancient of Days and was presented before him.
>
> And to him was given dominion and glory and kingdom, that all peoples, nations, and languages should serve him; his dominion is an everlasting dominion, which shall not pass away, and his kingdom one that shall not be destroyed.

Here the Son of Man could be a personification of Israel. But in the Enoch book, written towards 100BC, he is clearly an individual who heads Israel rather than personifies it. He is the Righteous Elect One, a viceroy of God, who will sit enthroned, ruling all, judging all and enlightening the Gentiles.

Steps towards the Gentiles' enlightenment had already been taken. Jews were now dispersed over a large part of Alexander's former empire where the international language was Greek. They were numerous and important in Alexandria. Here, during the third century BC, the Bible had been translated into Greek by, according to tradition, a team of about seventy scholars, so that the Greek version was and is called the Septuagint from the Latin for 'seventy'. The Septuagint was a boon to the Hellenistic Jews scattered among Greek-speaking foreigners, but it was undoubtedly meant to inform Gentiles, and it enjoyed some success. Little by little, converts drifted in. This development helped to make sense of the Chosen People's long ordeal. Tobit, in the apocryphal book bearing his name, says:

> Sons of Israel, make God's name known, publish it for all the Gentiles to hear; if he has dispersed you among heathen folk who know nothing of him, it was so that you might tell them the story of his great deeds, convince them that he, and no other, is God all-powerful. (Tobit 13–14, Knox's translation)

With the conversion of Gentiles an accepted fact, as Second Isaiah had prophesied, other and more surprising attempts were made to impress them. Hellenistic Jews fabricated texts purporting to be the work of Greek authors, acknowledging the true God. The process went further. A Babylonian priest named Berosus had invented a Babylonian Sibyl and composed verses for her, endorsing Babylonian religion and mythology. About 160BC an anonymous Alexandrian Jew recast some of Berosus's matter and created a pseudo-Sibylline book in Greek that confirmed Jewish teachings. More Jewish Sibylline writings followed, foretelling the end of the age in apocalyptic style, with Jerusalem becoming the capital of a world renewed. Jews were never much interested in these effusions. Some Gentiles, however, took them seriously as productions of a real Sibyl.

About this time we at last begin to glimpse the Messiah. The temporary success of the state launched by the Maccabees encouraged a hope that it would be the nucleus of Daniel's eternal kingdom. The references to a future David in Ezekiel and elsewhere, meaning a king of Davidic lineage, hinted at a human agent in a future convulsion and the triumph of the Chosen People under his leadership. 'Messiah' means 'anointed' as a king or priest; 'Christos' is the same word in Greek. It was used in a figurative way to signify divine choice, being applied, for instance, to Cyrus as the Jews' liberator. But from about 100BC onward, many Jews were anticipating *the* Messiah, a man anointed by God as none had been before. He would be Israel's leader and final deliverer, playing a central part in the end of the age. He would be of the line of David. This was logically necessary because of a divine promise that David's royal house would never be permanently deprived of sovereignty (2 Samuel 7:16). As the conception of the Messiah expanded, more and more came to be expected of him. He would not only establish his kingdom in the Holy Land, but also 'shatter unrighteous rulers' and make his people supreme in the world. He would bring back the lost northern tribes, in keeping with the Lord's word to Ezekiel.

Apocalyptic fantasy and Messianic prophecy ran alongside each other without completely merging. It might seem obvious that the Messiah would be the same person as the apocalyptic Son of Man, yet it is not certain that any of the Jews who were looking ahead actually identified them. Both forms of hope, however, envisaged an end to the world's present condition. The Dead Sea Scrolls are documents of a Jewish community that saw itself as the true faithful remnant and expected a war of 'the sons of light and the sons of darkness'.

The Romans occupied Jerusalem in 63BC and extinguished the kingdom. They tried ruling through a sponsored monarch, Herod, but in AD6 they formed a garrisoned province of Judaea, under a governor who was responsible to the emperor. Imperial rule was bitterly resented, and the longing for the Messiah grew powerful. A fanatical political grouping, the Zealots, campaigned for an uprising. By the 60s they had become a constituted party and a force to reckon with, and a stronger national sentiment had grown up, in at least partial sympathy with them. The nationalists did not have it all their own way, however, and a pacific element argued that a fighting Messiah was a contradiction in terms, because, as a good Jew, he would have to stop fighting on the Sabbath and the enemy would win. Another group, the Christians, also rejected militancy and claimed that the Messiah had already come, in the person of their founder Jesus. His death ruled him out as the Messiah of the main hope, and so did the spiritual nature of the Christians' message. They proclaimed his resurrection and prospective return, with some success, but their time had not yet come.

In 66 provocation by the Roman authorities ignited the revolt that Vespasian was sent east to subdue. The Zealots and kindred nationalists played a leading role, some possibly cherishing a delusion that they could force God's hand, so to speak. If the Chosen People were in such an extremity, he would send the Messiah to save them. However, no Messiah appeared, and the war became a massacre. After the year 70, when Titus laid Jerusalem waste and destroyed the Temple, Judaism had no centre, but it continued to exist in various parts of the Roman world, dominated now by rabbis who presided over its local congregations, and presented and expounded its teachings.

Tragically, one of the wisest and best of these, Akiba ben Joseph, could not accept that the change was final. He sponsored the only contemporary Jew who did claim to be the Messiah, Simeon ben Koseba. 'Koseba' sounded like *kochba*, a star. Simeon could fulfil the prophecy that the Lord extorted in the remote past from the Gentile seer Balaam (Numbers 24:17): 'I see him, but not now; I behold him, but not nigh: a star shall come forth out of Jacob, and a sceptre shall rise out of Israel.' Akiba convened a gathering and anointed 'Bar-Kochba', the Son of a Star, as king. A second revolt began in 132, this time with a Messiah to lead it at last, but it was far too late. Rome crushed it, and Akiba was put to death by torture. The emperor Hadrian rebuilt Jerusalem as a predominantly pagan town with the new name of Aelia Capitolina.

The Jewish people survived in dispersal, taught never to forget their ancestral relationship with God and their corporate vocation. The hope of the Messiah endured in spite of all, although speculation about him was generally discouraged. With many, he came to be pictured as a world-enlightener rather than a leader or ruler. In modern times, some have argued that he should be seen not as a person but as a symbolic figure representing Israel's influence, not only through Judaism but through its derivative religions, Christianity and Islam, and through great Jewish individuals.

What persisted with utter tenacity, through all miseries and persecutions, was the prophetic theme of a return to Zion. Israel's identity was bound up with the Promised Land, as indeed was the Messianic hope, and it could never be relinquished. Century after century, Jews learned a fundamental creed in which scriptural texts interwove the love of God with the territorial claim. Synagogues were usually oriented towards Jerusalem, and the chief prayers were recited facing in that direction. The service included a series of benedictions, and several were focused on the ingathering of Israel. The tenth, for instance, ran thus:

Blow the great trumpet for our liberation, and lift a banner to gather our exiles, and gather us into one body from the four corners of the earth.

Blessed be thou, O Lord, who gatherest the dispersed of thy people Israel.

Likewise the fourteenth:

To Jerusalem thy city return thou in mercy and dwell in her midst as thou hast spoken, and build her speedily in our days as an everlasting structure and soon establish there the throne of David.

Blessed be thou, O Lord, the builder of Jerusalem.

As long as Jerusalem, the one-time site of the Temple, had no home for the Lord and his people and his prospective Messiah, the Jew was a mourner, and various customs kept the realization alive. When a man married, a drinking vessel was broken for sorrow at Zion's desolation. When he moved into a house, he left a patch of wall unpainted for the same reason. When he was buried, a handful of Palestinian earth, if his family could get it, was thrown into his grave. The Passover ceremony included the words 'Next year in Jerusalem'.

Modern Zionism, which actually brought about the return to the Promised Land, started as an idea in the middle nineteenth century and began to produce results during the 1880s. At first it took the shape of a quiet resettlement by Jews from Russia. They realized that Western-style assimilation into Gentile society would never work under the tsarist regime, and in any case they rejected it as an aim. Financial aid from Baron Edmond de Rothschild helped to sustain twenty-five farming communities. As a political movement, Zionism was born in 1897. Its founder Theodor Herzl (1860–1904), an Austrian journalist, was fully assimilated and assumed in his youth that all Jews could be assimilated like himself; especially as the Reform wing of Judaism seemed to be giving up on the Promised Land. However, the Dreyfus Affair in France caused an eruption of anti-Semitism and this, plus a slowly dawning awareness of Russian pogroms, convinced him that assimilation could not wholly succeed. He wrote a book, *The Jewish State* (1896), putting the case – as he saw it – for an independent country.

In 1897 Herzl assembled the First World Zionist Congress in Basle, and predicted that the Jewish state would come into existence in fifty years. His commanding presence and talent as a speaker made him an indispensable leader. However, he did not picture the state as a reconstituted Promised Land, and he had no interest in the resettlement that was already in progress. He acknowledged the ancestral Palestinian hope, but as a motive force to be harnessed, not an ideal to be realized. Zionism for Herzl was a project for creating a Jewish homeland that might be anywhere, a refuge and no more (a view of it that persisted for many years and in many minds besides his). He saw it as a relief operation, designed simply to resolve a problem. Assimilated and prosperous Jews were to stay where they were and organize the new state as a haven for the less fortunate. In that spirit he travelled about, trying to enlist support from governments.

The moment of truth came in 1903, and the prophetic legacy blew his misconceptions to pieces. He got an offer of territory in Uganda, then a British colony. To his consternation the rank-and-file Zionists were decidedly cool. Furthermore, the main opposition came from the Russians, the very people he imagined himself to be rescuing. They chose to stay in Russia and go on suffering, rather than abandon the ancient promise. Without them the Uganda plan was unworkable. He charged them with ingratitude; they charged him with betrayal. He died prematurely soon afterwards.

By then, however, Zionism had acquired its own momentum. Leadership passed to the scientist Chaim Weizmann (1874–1952), whose background in eastern Europe gave him a sounder grasp of realities. Migration to the Promised Land accelerated. Through wartime contacts with the British government Weizmann secured the Balfour Declaration, by which Britain agreed to sponsor a Jewish national home in Palestine. The ensuing process was long-drawn-out and violent. However, by a strange convergence of circumstances the State of Israel was voted into existence by the United Nations in 1947, fifty years almost to the month after Herzl's prophecy.

Familiarity after the event has obscured Zionism's original nature and the fantastic unlikelihood of its history. The movement began in what, to all qualified observers, was mystical nonsense, even in the form Herzl gave it. It made headway and succeeded against every rational expectation and against mountainous and multiple opposition. Orthodox Jews tended to take the view that repatriation must be the Messiah's work and should not be attempted as a human enterprise, while a large part of the Jewish intelligentsia regarded Herzl as insane, Weizmann as more so, and passed on the latter opinion to the British government in the hope of preventing the Balfour Declaration. Many in Germany liked to call themselves 'Germans of the Mosaic persuasion', and detested Zionists for rejecting that view of Jewishness and imperilling their social acceptance. Yet it was this enlightened, assimilationist Judaism that succumbed in horror and disillusionment. It was Zionism that went on.

Some would say that this movement, with its amazing achievements in a once-derelict land, was magnificent. Others would say that the career of the State of Israel has shown it to be a dangerous error. Still others perhaps would say that both opinions have truth in them. Evaluation is not the issue here. The point is that the thing happened, in defiance of all human probability and all rationality, not least Jewish rationality. Prophecy triumphed, even through a movement that was not essentially religious, in the normal Jewish sense.

It may be urged that Herzl's fifty-year bull's-eye was pure luck. Yet it seems curious that such luck should have occurred in this of all contexts. In practice, how many would-be rational forecasters have matched it in any context? It may also be urged that the reconstitution of Israel was not a case of successful long-term prediction, but a case of prophecy creating its own fulfilment through generations of conditioning. Perhaps; but that is not a rebuttal. Prophecy foreshadowed a state of affairs, not humanly foreseeable and never approximated in well over a thousand years, when a window would finally open and it *could* create its own fulfilment and do so against overwhelming odds.

Chapter Three

The Other Messiah

The Christian Church began as a Jewish sect, some time about AD 30. Its nucleus was a small group who shared a life-transforming experience centred on a person, Jesus of Nazareth. His teaching, his gifts as a healer, his ability to cure the demented drew followers to him. His extraordinary impact and powers of language made some of them permanent disciples, going with him wherever he went. His air of authority was such that when he spoke of a coming kingdom of God, his words carried weight. The principal disciples, called the apostles, became convinced that he was the hoped-for Messiah, 'Christ', *Christos*, the Anointed.

When he entered Jerusalem and addressed the people, a major demonstration looked imminent. However, he was condemned to death as dangerous by the Roman governor Pilate, under pressure from the Jewish establishment, and scourged and crucified without protesting or calling on his disciples to do so. The adventure seemed to have ended in despair. Then something happened. In Christian tradition it is known as the Resurrection. Whatever its nature, it restored the disciples' faith and raised it to new heights. They announced that he had returned to life. He had talked with some women in his immediate circle, then with the apostles, then with other followers. He had conquered death, and, although now definitely departed, he would return in glory to bring the present age to an end.

These events have a prophetic aspect. What needs to be understood is the full content of the Christian message. This is vital for the appreciation of one prophecy in particular, which may have implications outside Christianity.

At the earliest levels, nothing survives in writing. The Christians were a minority within the main Jewish body, spreading their wild words over a limited area. They expected Christ to return soon and establish his earthly reign. Handbooks and histories were not needed. With the belated arrival of the apostle Paul, a change set in. He had never met Jesus, and as a former pupil of Gamaliel, one of the most eminent rabbinic teachers, he had opposed the Christians. Conversion, however, gave him a convert's ardour. After a while he began urging that the Church must be more than a party within Judaism. It was for all humanity. He went on missions in Asia Minor and Greece that created Gentile Christian communities. This network involved him in correspondence. Paul's letters – the genuine ones; doubt has been cast on several – are the oldest known Christian documents.

The Roman destruction of Jerusalem in 70 was fatal to its Jewish Christian community. Henceforth the Church was predominantly Gentile: Paul had won. Also, since Christ's return was delayed, it became clear that the Church required written statements. The four Gospels that it approved, Matthew, Mark, Luke and John, drew on older materials now lost and on oral tradition. In their present form they date from the last three or four decades of the first century. Matthew, Mark and Luke give a general survey of Christ's ministry and death from much the same point of view, although with wide differences of interest and emphasis. They can be lined up in parallel columns and compared, and are referred to as the Synoptic Gospels. John goes its own way. In the Acts of the Apostles we have a record of the young Church in its formative years, after the period covered in the Gospels. Letters written by Paul and others were collected and added to the canon, as, after some time, was the Revelation attributed to John, Christ's 'beloved disciple'.

These writings are in Greek, the international language of the Roman east, and they comprise the New Testament, forming the Church's account of its own origins. The historical status of this account is too large a subject to discuss here. The Gospels, of course, do not pretend to be biographies – they are more like memoirs – but the story they develop in their different ways cannot, in its essentials, be reasonably rejected, if only because any thoroughgoing alternative is incredible. Whatever elements of legend they may contain, they could not have been invented as a whole, not in an age when imaginative fiction was hardly being written at all. There was no relevant soil for them to grow from. To argue that they are fictitious raises the question, who was responsible? It is really not to be supposed that a group of unknown creative geniuses – not just one, but several – appeared together in a vacuum, spun the Gospels out of their heads, got people to believe their story for no reason and to live by it and die for it, and vanished without trace. Much the same point was made by two unbelievers who knew plenty about the writing of fiction, H.G. Wells and Marghanita Laski. Irrespective of who 'Matthew, Mark, Luke and John' actually were, there has to be a factual basis. Early non-Christian authors supply some evidence for it, and none insinuates that it was other than factual.

Moreover, in a hostile, sometimes persecuting Palestinian milieu, the pioneer Christians could never have got away with public mendacity. If, in their preaching, they had told circumstantial tales of a Christ who was not a real person or had grossly falsified events that survivors had witnessed, their enemies would have been quick to refute and discredit them. The retort 'To begin with, your Christ never existed' would have been devastating; and nobody made it. The main externals of the story were certainly – it may be too provocative to say 'true' – irrefutable.

The word 'externals' is important, however. Strictly speaking, the theme of the early Christians – those, at least, whose opinions prevailed – was not Jesus's visible career as such but their interpretation of it. They were aware of mysteries that demanded explanation, and they explained them under the guidance (as they believed) of the Holy Spirit. Jesus had risen from the dead, but why had he been put to death in the first place, in a shameful way that repelled potential converts? The Christians' answer, based on hints understood to have been dropped by him, was that he had made himself a voluntary sacrifice, atoning for the sins of the world. Afterwards, the Resurrection demonstrated his triumph over death. All who believed, freed from the burden of their sins, could enter into beatitude with him. Belief meant far more than a verbal or intellectual assent. It meant a deep conviction, transforming their lives in keeping with his teaching.

This was the Good News, sometimes called the *kerygma*, 'proclamation'. In some Christian circles, at least, it took shape fairly rapidly, but the orthodoxy that grew from it went further. The infinite mass of iniquity required an infinite act of atonement and reconciliation. No human individual could have made such an act, but Christ could do so because he was divine as well as human, the Son of God, united with the heavenly Father of whom he spoke. Descending from heaven, he was historically and humbly made Man, sharing in the pains of the human condition. His divinity was confirmed by his working of miracles. This theology, the doctrine of the Incarnation, appears in Paul's letters and in the Gospels, most explicitly in the fourth, ascribed to John, much of which is an exposition of Christ's significance rather than a literal narrative. In the earlier phases, to talk of orthodoxy as if it were unanimous is an oversimplification. Different Christian groups had different versions of the Good News. Unofficial Gospels and other writings, the New Testament Apocrypha, existed alongside the official ones, but traditions received from people close to the beginnings carried the day. They moulded the orthodoxy that emerged and determined the nature of mainstream Christianity.

To say all this is not to make a commitment as to truth, one way or the other, or as to how far it is possible to sort out interpretation from fact. Arguably, the doctrines are interwoven so closely with the rest that they cannot be separated; arguably, the many attempts to prune them away and isolate a basic 'Historical Jesus' or 'Christ Myth' have produced only conflicting theories that, taken together, make the reality more rather than less mysterious. It is enough for the present purpose that we can say: 'This is what the Christians believed, this is what they taught.'

The Christian traditionalist is free to add: 'Yes, and they were right.'

The rabbis who governed Judaism after the fall of the Temple said no such thing. They could not accept any of it, and the Christian break with the Jews became final. Drawn to a Church that had become mainly Gentile, many pagan converts had a background of myths that made it easier for them to embrace the theology. They knew about dying gods, for instance. Christian communities scattered through the Roman Empire tried to accommodate themselves to its authority, in so far as they could do it without compromising their own convictions. One result was that the Gospel writers, in their treatment of Jesus's trial and condemnation, did what they could to avert suspicion that he was a nationalist or a rebel against Caesar. He was the Messiah, but he was not a Messiah that the Jewish establishment could ever have accepted.

That being the case, what became of the Jewish Bible, the compilation now called the Old Testament? Some Christian extremists wanted to drop it altogether. Those of the mainstream kept it, but gave it a radical reinterpretation, to show it leading up to Christ. Part of this enterprise was an attempt to prove that it prophesied him. His own authority was invoked – after the Resurrection he had expounded scriptural texts as referring to himself – but the Gospels give no record of what he said, or was said to have said, and we have to study the process in the writings of his followers. It is easiest to see this in the first of the canonical Gospels. We may call its author Matthew for convenience, whatever the actual connection of his work with the apostle so named.

He begins his prophetic applications with the pregnancy of Jesus's mother, Mary. It was a Christian tenet that she conceived miraculously with no sexual relationship. Jesus was the divine Son of the heavenly Father and had no human father; her husband Joseph was a foster-parent. Matthew detects the miracle in Isaiah 7:14:

> Behold, a virgin shall conceive and bear a son, and his name shall be called Emmanuel.

Which, Matthew explains correctly, means 'God with us'. One might suspect that the Virgin Birth was invented to fit the prophecy, but that is not a tenable view. The criticism that does arise is that Matthew gives the prophecy a doubtful meaning to fit the Virgin Birth. The uncommon Hebrew word *'almah*, used here, denotes simply a young woman. The few individuals called so in Hebrew literature are virgins, but virginity is not inherent in the term. Nevertheless, thanks to Matthew, this verse becomes part of Christian teaching. In the context, Isaiah is speaking of an event due to happen soon, not seven centuries away; he is probably referring to the birth of a royal heir through whom David's line is to be carried on. Granted inspiration, however, a sort of inspired ambiguity is acceptable. The verse can have an inner meaning elucidated by the advent of Christ. And thus it was argued in Christianity.

Shortly afterwards, Matthew quotes a prophecy in Micah 5:2, foretelling that another successor of David, possibly the Messiah, will be born in the same place as David himself:

> And you, O Bethlehem, in the land of Judah, are by no means least among the rulers of Judah; for from you shall come a ruler who will govern my people Israel.

The original adds that 'his origin is from of old, from ancient days'. This ancient origin may refer to divine preordination or to the long line of Davidic descent. Matthew applies the verse to Jesus's own birth at Bethlehem.

Now he takes his readers into deeper waters. When these two texts were written, they clearly referred to the future, but Matthew enlarges on the idea hinted at in his handling of Isaiah, that the Old Testament also contains prophecies that are, in effect, coded. No one would have read them as prophetic at the time, but their complete sense is seen only retrospectively in the light of Christ; therefore, they foreshadowed him.

Matthew tells how, when Jesus was just born, King Herod wanted to find and kill him. Joseph was warned in a dream to take his wife and the child and go away into Egypt for safety. The Holy Family stayed there until Herod was dead and were then recalled. And 'this was to fulfil what the Lord had spoken by the prophet, "Out of Egypt have I called my son".' The verse in question is Hosea 11:1, and it alludes, on the face of it, to the Lord summoning Israel – metaphorically his 'son' – out of Egypt in the days of Moses. But the divine Sonship of Christ gives it a new meaning. A little further on, Matthew tells of Herod massacring male infants in Bethlehem in the hope of killing the infant Messiah and 'then was fulfilled what was spoken by the prophet Jeremiah':

A voice was heard in Ramah,
wailing and loud lamentation,
Rachel weeping for her children;
she refused to be consoled,
because they were no more.

This is from Jeremiah 31:15. But the original is in the present tense, and its apparent theme is the Israelites' grief at their misfortunes.

Matthew continues with reinterpretations in the same style, making passages out to be prophetic, or at least anticipatory, when they may not have been so in the minds of their authors. The most conspicuous case is in chapter 21, where Jesus rides into Jerusalem on the back of an ass, with her colt carrying some of the disciples' garments (or the other way about). Matthew quotes Zechariah 9:9:

Tell the daughter of Zion,
Behold, your king is coming to you,
humble, and mounted on an ass,
and on a colt, the foal of an ass.

This too 'took place to fulfil what was spoken by the prophet'.

The awkward introduction of a second animal occurs in this Gospel only. Matthew wants a precise fulfilment of Zechariah, although he may in fact be misreading the original.

His insistence that things took place to fulfil prophecy might create an impression that fulfilment was consciously contrived, an unhappy notion when applied to the entry into Jerusalem. However, some at least of his fulfilments, such as the payment to Judas of thirty pieces of silver, were not contrived. The other Gospels add a few similar items. John improves on the others in the account of the Crucifixion.

This Old Testament matter is not prophecy invented after the event, but in general it is prophecy *recognized* after the event, not at the time of writing – or so it is made out to be. The same principle is carried further in other Christian exegesis, and many things in the Old Testament are explained as anticipatory symbols or 'types'. The process can be studied in the Letter to the Hebrews attributed to Paul. The most notorious instance is the explanation of the voluptuous love-poems in the Song of Solomon as foreshadowing, even allegorizing, the mutual love of Christ and his Church.

From the perspective of the present it is odd to see how much weight Christians gave to this kind of thinking, and odder to see how much conviction it carried with potential converts. St Augustine, in the fifth century, says that after the Romans destroyed Jerusalem and many Jews were dispersed among the nations, the Church gained ground everywhere because the Jews brought their scriptures and people could see how Christ was prophesied in them. A supplementary claim of the same kind was that Virgil, a pagan living before Christ, foretold him in his Fourth Eclogue. In some medieval churches Virgil was commemorated at Christmas as a 'Prophet of the Gentiles'. Dante translates lines from the Eclogue in his *Purgatorio* (XXII:70–72) and introduces another Roman poet, Statius, as converted by it.

There are only three Old Testament prophecies that point towards Christ at all plainly. One is the text already quoted, about the birth at Bethlehem. It goes on for two more verses, and, as it stands, suggests a Davidic ruler of Israel, but it does look ahead into the future. According to Matthew 2:5 it was recognized at the time of Jesus's birth as a Messianic prophecy indicating the birthplace. There is a sort of confirmation of this in John 7:41–2, where the recognition exists but is used *against* Jesus. Doubters say he is not the Christ, because the Christ has to be born in Bethlehem and Jesus comes from Galilee. A sceptic might argue that the doubters were on the right track because the birth at Bethlehem is fictitious – it was invented to fit the prophecy and refute the objection.

However, two Old Testament allusions cannot be dismissed by charging that their fulfilment was fabricated. Underlying both is Judaism's conception of two-level prophecy. A major factor in its growth, as we saw, was the persecution of Jews by Antiochus Epiphanes. This could be seen as a 'type', foreshadowing troubles yet to come. Such thinking could be generalized. A text might refer to an event already known, or expected within a moderate time; but without prejudice to that meaning, it could still have a second meaning, perhaps a more important one that looked further ahead and gave it additional dimensions. On this basis, Christians could justify their reading of the verse in Isaiah about the young woman bearing a son. Its immediate reference might be to the birth of a royal heir, but that was not necessarily the whole of its content. The emphasis on the mother and the epithet 'Emmanuel' could hint at a profounder allusion going beyond – to Christ, 'God with us', whose birth would perfect the fulfilment.

Now the author of Daniel, chapter 9, has a predictive passage on these lines, which is remarkable, although the New Testament does not take it up. It has a primary meaning, but a second meaning is present, giving an apparent forecast of the date of Christ's death.

In 9:2 Daniel recalls the prophecy of Jeremiah (25:11–12 and 29:10) about the Lord's people going through seventy penitential years in Babylonian captivity. Jeremiah may have picked on seventy simply as a round number, a human lifetime. The captivity did not last quite so long. But the author of Daniel, writing, probably, about 164BC, is all too painfully aware of the tribulations and backslidings in the centuries since it ended. The expiation cannot have been adequate in the Lord's eyes, the final peace of Israel has not dawned. As mentioned, he imagines Gabriel reinterpreting Jeremiah's prophecy. Gabriel reveals that the seventy years allotted for purification must be understood as seventy 'weeks' of years, making 70 × 7, that is, 490. There is a division between the first seven 'weeks' and the subsequent sixty-two, which has been explained variously, but after a total of sixty-nine weeks an 'anointed one' is to be 'cut off', in other words killed. The final week of the seventy is to bring invasion and chaos, with Jerusalem suffering at the hands of 'the prince who is to come'.

On the face of it this is prophecy after the event, composed during Antiochus's onslaught. The 'anointed one' must be the Jewish high priest Onias III, who was murdered in 171BC. The seventieth week is the time of persecution that followed. As the primary reading of the passage, this need not be disputed, yet it leaves the 'weeks' unaccounted for. If this is to be the inner meaning of Jeremiah's time units, the stretch of 490 years ending with Antiochus must start from his prophecy introducing it or from the deportation to Babylon. Either way, the interval is much too short.

We might be content to judge, with a modern commentator, that 'the writer, who no doubt knew little of the chronology of the post-exilic period, would not be disturbed by this discrepancy between his symbolic numbers and the historical facts'. But in verse 25 'Daniel' raises an unexpected issue and is not imprecise at all. He defines a quite different starting-point for his 490 years. This gives the passage its second meaning and makes the 'anointed one' a type of another. The count is said to begin 'from the going forth of the word to restore and build Jerusalem'.

Jeremiah has nothing whatever to correspond. He speaks of the coming downfall of Babylon and the exiles' return, but not of a restoration of the war-ruined city, and indeed there was none when the captivity ended or for decades afterwards. The expression 'word' is a strong one, denoting an order or edict. The only thing that fits is the commission to rebuild Jerusalem given to

Nehemiah by Artaxerxes I, in the twentieth year of the Persian king's reign. His twentieth year was 445BC.

The alternative starting-point opens up an alternative meaning. Until modern times, commentators not only recognized this meaning but made it primary. Pascal did so in his *Pensées*, as did Ronald Knox in his translation of the Bible, published as recently as 1955. If we start counting from 445BC, the 490 years extend into the Christian era. The calculation may have played a part in the growth of Messianic expectancy, since the 'anointed one', on this showing, may be the Anointed of God; the idea of his being killed would have been an obstacle, but there were Jews who could surmount it. Given a slight blurring of the sixty-ninth week, putting his death in the course of it rather than at the end, we arrive at a span of years, AD31 to 38, that overlaps Pilate's governorship of Judaea. The anointed one who is slain can be Jesus Christ.

That is as far as the second meaning goes. Nothing in the years 38 to 45 corresponds to the violent final week. Yet a count beginning from the Persian king's order scores a hit or a very near miss with the execution of Jesus. It makes sense of the 490 years, and nothing else does. Nor is this long-range prediction merely one among many of the same kind, the exception that happens to succeed. It stands alone with no scriptural parallel.

The other impressive prophecy was written earlier, but it deserves climactic treatment because of its fame, its significance and its ramifications. The prophet is the anonymous Second Isaiah, whose share in the book bearing Isaiah's name is an outpouring of joy at the fall of Babylon to Cyrus the Persian, bringing release for the captive Israelites. At this point the disillusionment affecting the Daniel author is still far off, and anticipations are bright.

In four passages, sometimes called the 'Servant of the Lord Oracles' or 'Servant Songs', the prophet introduces a figure who has no exact precedent. Several biblical characters are referred to in passing as God's 'servants', but Second Isaiah seems to have a person in mind whose status as his 'servant' will be more specific. The first of the Oracles is 42:1–4, where the Servant's main

... in the future. The Lord has appointed him,
...g forth justice to the nations'. Next is 49:1–6.
... of the Servant himself is heard, ambiguously. In
...ells us that the Lord has said, 'You are my servant,
... whom I will be glorified' – so the Servant is a
...ication of Israel. But in verses 5–6 the Lord has formed his
Ser...nt 'from the womb' so that Israel may be gathered to him;
the Servant, as gatherer and unifier, will be 'a light to the nations'.
Somehow the Servant both personifies Israel and, in himself,
embodies its mission as the prophet sees this. A third passage,
50:4–9, is usually ranked with these two. The Servant speaks
again, telling how he has endured contempt and hostility but has
stood firm, inspired and sustained by God.

The fourth Oracle, 52:13–53:12, is totally different. The
Servant now has an unparalleled role. He undergoes terrible
suffering, dies, yet lives on and is exalted. According to a Christian
belief dating from early times, the prophet is foreseeing Christ.
Phrases in the passage are familiar through Handel's *Messiah*, and
reinforce the tradition. I recall hearing of a biblical scholar who
quoted it in a lecture to a Jewish audience and was reproached for
quoting a Christian text, so complete has the adoption become.

In the RSV translation that follows, there are divergences from
other versions on a few doubtful points, but the main drift is
undisputed. The passage falls into three unequal parts. At the end
of chapter 52 the Lord speaks:

13. Behold, my servant shall prosper, he shall be exalted and
lifted up, and shall be very high.

14. As many were astonished at him – his appearance was so
marred, beyond human semblance, and his form beyond that
of the sons of men –

15. so shall he startle many nations; kings shall shut their
mouths because of him; for that which has not been told
them they shall see, and that which they have not heard they
shall understand.

In 53:1–11 we hear an unidentified voice telling the story. In verses 2 and 3 translators differ about the tense of the verbs, but in the RSV the passage is consistently narrative except at the end and nearly all of it undoubtedly is. That in itself is extraordinary in a prophecy.

1. Who has believed what we have heard? And to whom has the arm of the Lord been revealed?

2. For he grew up before him like a young plant, and like a root out of dry ground; he had no form or comeliness that we should look at him, and no beauty that we should desire him.

3. He was despised and rejected by men; a man of sorrows, and acquainted with grief; and as one from whom men hide their faces he was despised, and we esteemed him not.

4. Surely he has borne our griefs and carried our sorrows; yet we esteemed him stricken, smitten by God, and afflicted.

5. But he was wounded for our transgressions, he was bruised for our iniquities; upon him was the chastisement that made us whole, and with his stripes we are healed.

6. All we like sheep have gone astray; we have turned every one to his own way: and the Lord has laid on him the iniquity of us all.

7. He was oppressed, and he was afflicted, yet he opened not his mouth; like a lamb that is led to the slaughter, and like a sheep that before its shearers is dumb, so he opened not his mouth.

8. By oppression and judgement he was taken away; and as for his generation, who considered that he was cut off out of the land of the living, stricken for the transgression of my people?

9. And they made his grave with the wicked and with a rich man in his death, although he had done no violence, and there was no deceit in his mouth.

10. Yet it was the will of the Lord to bruise him; he has put him to grief; when he makes himself an offering for sin, he shall see his offspring, he shall prolong his days; the will of the Lord shall prosper in his hand;

11a. he shall see the fruit of the travail of his soul and be satisfied.

In the rest of verse 11, and in verse 12, the Lord speaks again, confirming what has been said.

11b. By his knowledge shall the righteous one, my servant, make many to be accounted righteous; and he shall bear their iniquities.

12. Therefore I will divide him a portion with the great, and he shall divide the spoil with the strong; because he poured out his soul to death, and was numbered with the transgressors; yet he bore the sin of many, and made intercession for the transgressors.

Jewish interpreters of this Oracle treat it as a sequel to the other three. The Servant is Israel personified, undergoing agonies, bearing the weight of the world's evils but vindicated at last. That may be the primary meaning, but in this case there is a second meaning that overshadows it. Something else has taken charge, transforming and superseding. The passage has details, as the other Oracles have not, which the Israel symbolism definitely cannot cover. Furthermore, if the Servant is Israel, there is a problem with the 'we' at the beginning of the main passage. It would have to refer to the Gentile kings in 52:15, making them recall their contempt for the trampled Chosen People, and confess that Israel's endurance and rebirth will bring the Gentiles' salvation. But the prophet has just said that these kings never heard the Servant's history and, even when informed, will be 'shutting their mouths', not launching into a flood of testimony. These objections seem to apply no matter how the character is interpreted.

The Servant is more than a personification. He is a person. And the orthodox account of Christ's sufferings, death and resurrection is here, accidentally or not. The order is loosely narrative, with backtrackings and observations, rather as if the unidentified speaker were preaching a sermon. To put the things applicable to Christ in order, making use of the Gospels, we have:

His rejection by his people (53:3)

His silence before his accusers (53:7)

His trial and condemnation (53:8)

His disfigurement by scourging and other torments (52:14, 53:5)

His crucifixion, perhaps – 'lifted up' (52:13)

His death in the company of criminals (53:8–9, 12)

His atonement, guiltless himself, for others' sins (53:4–6, 9–10, 12)

His burial in the tomb of the wealthy Joseph of Arimathea (53:9)

His triumph over death and after it (52:13, 53:10–11)

His creation of a community of believers, his spiritual offspring (53:10–11)

But here we have to pause for reflection. What exactly is being foreshadowed? Not the career of the 'Historical Jesus', whatever that may mean, but the Christian account of the Passion and Resurrection: the core of the *kerygma*. The distinction is real, as I can witness myself. I was brought up with the assumption that Jesus was simply an ethical teacher, an enlightened moralist. I don't mean that my parents favoured that view of him against others, I mean that it *was so*. Anything else about him was hardly ever mentioned and only as legend or fantasy if it had to be. In effect, he was the preacher of the Sermon on the Mount and not much besides, and the first Christians merely repeated his exhortations. Then, at the age of fourteen or so, I came across a book by an evangelist referring to Isaiah 53 as a prophecy of him. I looked it up and was completely bewildered. What on earth was the evangelist driving at? This had no connection with anything I had ever heard. The ethical teacher wasn't there. Eventually, of course, I found that he was real, but that his teaching, as far back as it could be traced, was linked with the *kerygma*.

It is the latter that we are getting in this Servant Oracle. While most of the ingredients are in the Gospels, it is not plain history. If film had been invented in Jesus's time, no film could have shown the essentials of it, the inwardness. What prophetic experience could have taken hold of it, hundreds of years before, and put it into writing?

A sceptical opinion would be that there is nothing prophetic here at all. The passage is an invention by Second Isaiah, and Christians spun their *kerygma* out of it to explain what they needed to explain. This theory, however, would only create another mystery. It would leave us in the dark as to the person Second Isaiah does intend; and the fact that commentators rejecting the Christian meaning have offered quite a number of contradictory guesses is sufficient proof that no cogent alternative exists. Moreover, the motif of atonement for the sins of humanity is foreign to Israelite thinking in the sixth century BC, as is the notion of an effective life after death. To account for the Oracle we would almost have to postulate divine inspiration anyhow, planting ideas in the prophet's mind that were still far from dawning. The theory would fail at the other end, too. Christians noticed this passage, and in the New Testament we find them quoting from it occasionally, as they quote from other scriptural texts; but only in corroboration of what they are saying, never as its basis.

The vital point is that the passage is unique. Christians obscured its uniqueness by their determination to find prophecies of Christ throughout the Old Testament, making this only one among many. It is not. The others may have a cumulative effect for readers disposed to believe already, and early in the Christian era they did, but they cannot seriously compete. Isaiah 53 is special on any showing. Something has happened in this one case that is not a scriptural norm, does not happen anywhere else. Once again,

---

though, we must be clear about it. The prophet is not anticipating a plain 'Historical Jesus'. He is anticipating Christian belief, or at least an early version of it. Whether that can be explained remains to be seen. It is far from clear how prevision could reveal not visible facts, but interpretations of them. Furthermore, what sort of prevision would this be in any case, when the speaker's apparent standpoint is after the events, not before them?

Did Jesus himself prophesy? Or, if the facts about him are held to be undiscoverable, is he represented as prophesying?

He speaks of himself in the third person as the Son of Man. In conjunction with 'Son of God' the phrase may assert his human nature. However, it is two-edged and can have a future reference. Jewish speculation already included that being known as the Son of Man who was a sort of celestial viceroy and would appear at the end of the present world. Speaking of oneself in the third person can signify status, authority, royalty. Shakespeare's Julius Caesar does it: 'Shall Caesar send a lie?' and 'Caesar doth not wrong.' Jesus is royal in some sense, as he acknowledges when questioned by Pilate, but his kingdom is spiritual, not political. It is 'the kingdom of God' or 'the kingdom of heaven'. Nevertheless, he talks of apocalyptic events to come when he, the Son of Man, will return as a king in truth. He foretells a resurrection of the dead and a Last Judgement; the wicked will be banished; the world as we know it – the present age – will end, and a new world will come into being, with eternal life for the blessed. Much of this scenario adapts Jewish beliefs. For several centuries Christians debated its implications. Some expected a future reign of Christ on earth, others did not. Whether he made the colossal claims he is said to have made, and what he meant if he did, are questions outside our present purview. One remarkable feature of the Gospels is that they manage to present a figure who talks as only a madman would, yet is manifestly not mad: women trust him with their children.

Fortunately, his sayings can be reviewed on a more mundane level. In Matthew 24, where he is talking about the end of the world, he implies that it may be remote. Nation will rise against nation, a prospect presupposing the demise of the Pax Romana, and such catastrophes will be only the birth-pangs. He states a prior condition that will surely be a long time in the making: 'The gospel of the kingdom will be preached throughout the whole world, as a testimony to all nations; and then the end will come.' He warns against speculation about the date: 'Of that day and hour no one knows' . . . except his heavenly Father.

Is he predicting that his kingdom will appear only at the end, when it is proclaimed everywhere? It seems that it will only be fully realized then. Yet in the early days of his ministry he speaks of it as imminent, 'at hand'. To judge from some of his parables it is already in active preparation. From a prophetic point of view, one text is especially worth quoting, in its three versions. Addressing a group of hearers, he says (Mark 9:1):

> Truly, I tell you, there are some standing here who will not taste death before they see the kingdom of God has come with power.

In Luke (9:27):

> I tell you truly, there are some standing here who will not taste death before they see the kingdom of God.

And in Matthew (16:28):

> Truly, I say to you, there are some standing here who will not taste death before they see the Son of Man coming in his kingdom.

If we discount Matthew's apocalyptic touch, we have the same prediction in all three Synoptic Gospels. Albert Schweitzer, seeing no fulfilment in the lifetime of anyone who was present, came to the momentous conclusion that Jesus could be wrong.

Something that can be read in a similar sense is embedded in a confusing episode where he foretells the profanation and destruction of the Temple in the Roman siege. This is in Matthew 24, Mark 13 and Luke 21; the military aspect is clearest in Luke.

While the author of Luke is writing after the event, as, probably, is the author of Matthew, they may well be enlarging on a prediction that Jesus really uttered. That is not the difficulty. The difficulty is that he speaks in the same passage of troubles prior to the end of the world, of the end itself, and of the Son of Man's advent, and declares that 'this generation will not pass away till all these things take place'. Almost certainly those words, if he spoke them, were meant to apply only to Jerusalem's ordeal, but they are so closely entangled with the rest that they seem to apply to everything. As an eminent biblical scholar once remarked, it would have been simpler if the Second Coming had happened in AD70.

Traditions of such sayings doubtless encouraged the belief that he would return soon, or fairly soon. The three Synoptic writers are still clinging to that hope, and this is why they mingle the themes in their passages about the prophecy of Jerusalem's fall, putting everything close together in time and decking the story out with celestial portents and the appearance of the Son of Man in the clouds. John expresses no such hope. But the phrase 'some standing here', or an equivalent, fostered a notion that one of the disciples would live until the Second Coming, whenever it did occur. John 21:21–24 mentions a rumour that this Gospel's putative author was the disciple in question. It quotes Jesus as saying to Peter, 'If it is my will that he remain till I come, what is that to you?' An early apocryphal work declares that at the end of John's life, or what was supposed to be the end, he disappeared and no body was ever found. A sixth-century historian, Gregory of Tours, mentions his asserted survival in more positive terms. According to a further legend he was taken up bodily into heaven: Dante knows this legend and rejects it. As an immortal, John is ancestral to one or two others, such as the Wandering Jew.

Did Jesus ever prophesy in the sense considered in this book? Gospel texts depict him foretelling his Passion and Resurrection, but however compelling they may be, acceptance of them is a matter of faith. A sceptic can always argue that such sayings were invented or 'remembered' later, to prove that his death was part of a divine plan and that this included his return from the dead. As for his sayings about the end of the world, the Last Judgement and so on, modern readers may choose to accept them in whatever way they can; or reinterpret them as symbol or allegory; or dismiss them as fantasies due to apocalypse-minded myth-makers, whether truly spoken by him or interwoven with his story by others. They cannot be discussed as predictions when there is no telling what literal events they predict. The forecast of the Temple's destruction is different. There is no reason to reject it, and the Temple was indeed destroyed. But it need not imply superhuman knowledge or supernatural inspiration. A wise observer might have judged that fanatical nationalism would lead to rebellion and disaster. Jews who opposed the idea of a holy war were already urging that it would be unwinnable.

The question of prophecy by Jesus must turn on what he meant by the kingdom and what he said about it. If it were to be realized only at the end of the world, such assertions of its nearness as the one that perplexed Schweitzer are perplexing indeed. Several passages imply otherwise, however, and the clearest of these is a parable about wheat and weeds ('tares') in the same field (Matthew 13:24–30, 37–43). Here an unspecified time elapses between the sowing of the wheat, which means the founding of the kingdom, and the removal of the weeds, meaning its purification at 'the close of the age', as the RSV has it.

The kingdom, as it exists on earth, is the community of believers who confess Christ as Lord. Early in his ministry, when he says 'the kingdom is at hand', it is not because the world is about to end but because the community is about to start taking shape, the way to salvation is about to open. In the time of the Gospels the community is informal and embryonic, but its founder knows that it must be institutionalized, must become the Church (Matthew 16:18). The parable of the wheat and weeds shows his awareness that the Church in the world will not be an assemblage of saints. It will exist for an indefinite time and be contaminated by evil, containing the bad as well as the good, although it will finally be perfected. In another parable with the same message, the kingdom is a fishing-net gathering good and bad fish. The fishermen catch the fish while at sea, then come ashore to sort them out; the earthly kingdom will endure for an unknown stretch of time, drawing in members of very various quality, and will be purified only at the last, by separate action.

The puzzling words about 'some standing here' can, therefore, refer simply to an early and public manifestation of the kingdom. They are placed in the Gospels just after Peter has acknowledged Jesus as the Christ. He assents but commands his disciples not to make it known. The first intimation of his death follows closely. The kingdom's predicted visibility may be the sequel, when the Church will be publicly in being, will proclaim him openly as the risen Lord, will spread with its Good News.

That dawn's exaltation, at least as Christians liked to recall it, is conveyed in the early chapters of Acts. The risen Christ, before his departure, tells the apostles that they will receive power (here is the 'power' of Mark 9:1) when the Holy Spirit descends upon them. It descends on the day of Pentecost. Peter addresses a crowd in Jerusalem telling them what has happened, and many are convinced and are baptized into the Church. Soon afterwards, the apostles begin to work miracles of healing. The high priest asks by what power (here is the word again) they do these things; Peter invokes the name of Jesus Christ. In 4:33 the apostles give testimony of the Resurrection with 'great power' (again). This interpretation can accommodate even Matthew's reference to the Son of Man by the belief in Christ's presence in his Church, the belief that the community of the people of God is one with him. The time-hallowed phrase is 'the Mystical Body of Christ'.

Any feeling that this is too slight, too local, to count as a fulfilment arises from the notion that the manifested kingdom would have to be spectacular from the start. Not so. Any visible beginning will do. Jesus forestalls the misconception when he compares the kingdom to a grain of mustard seed, a tiny thing, yet one that will grow into a tree. The listeners who were promised that some would live to see the kingdom may have had their homes far from Jerusalem and not witnessed the beginning, but the Church would presently have appeared in their midst, a ramifying reality, spreading its branches beyond its mustard-seed origin.

Consideration of Jesus as a prophet, in the predictive sense, can thus be confined to three topics. His forecast of the destruction of the Temple is on record and correct. However, it implies nothing paranormal or supernatural. No more need be involved than the perceptiveness of an opponent of militancy, convinced of the disaster in preparation. More interesting is the prediction, in the parables of the wheat and the fishes, that the Church will be a mixed body with evil in it alongside good, and with so much evil that at the end of the world, or the 'close of the age', it will need a divine cleansing. Jesus is sounder in his anticipations than optimists who have fancied that a holy utopia can exist here and now. Still, it is doubtful, in this case also, whether a special prevision is indicated. A Jew familiar with Israel's long history would have known that the Chosen People were always like that, with divisions between the faithful and the unfaithful. There was every reason to expect that the Church, a new Israel growing from the old, would be similarly flawed. And so it proved.

The 'some standing here' prophecy remains. A natural conjecture is that it is fictitious and that it was invented or 'remembered' about the middle of the first century and got into a stream of tradition that the Synoptic writers drew upon. Yet it seems too quiet for that. The Christians' thoughts were focused on Christ's return in glory. When would it happen? We can see the kind of assurance they wanted in the passage where this hope intertwines the fall of the Temple with the Second Coming, so that it looks as if both are to be expected in the lifetime of 'this generation'. Christians would have desired more than a general, enigmatic remark about 'the kingdom'; invention would have gone further. The balance is in favour of authenticity.

But as a prophecy, how is this saying to be taken? Traditional orthodoxy can cover the facts. Jesus spoke in the knowledge that he would die and rise from the dead. His disciples would be galvanized by the miracle and the Church's triumphant manifestation would follow. Fair enough. Is there an alternative to orthodoxy? What did he have in mind if not that? Without his death and the Resurrection, or at least the belief in it, nothing particular would have happened. Perhaps he expected something else and was wrong. Yet his words turned out to be right, even if his expectation was not.

Discussion of this prophecy can hardly be taken any further. It must end in plain assertion, on the positive side ('I accept the Christian story, this really happened') or on the negative side ('I don't know what happened, but the Christian story is impossible'). The prophecy is not a mistake; it works, if properly understood; but it cannot be reduced to purely 'rational' terms. A mystery remains.

Chapter Four

Antichrist and Apocalypse

Writing to his Thessalonian converts, St Paul gives the earliest known warning that the Second Coming may not, after all, be imminent. The year is AD 52 or thereabouts. It transpires that some of these neophytes are neglecting their work and the customary business of living, because they have been persuaded, perhaps by a forged letter from Paul himself, that the end is near and ordinary life will cease. He tells the recipients of his message to go on normally and disown the holy drop-outs. 'If anyone will not work, let him not eat.'

Doubts have been expressed about authenticity, but it is reasonable to go on accepting the author as Paul in the absence of proof that he is someone else. In any case, his message is the important thing. As part of the warning, he introduces a new motif. Before Christ's return there must be a prelude presided over by an alarming figure, a sort of 'darkest hour before the dawn'. The passage is in 2 Thessalonians, chapter 2.

> *3.* Let no one deceive you in any way; for that day will not come, unless the rebellion comes first, and the man of lawlessness is revealed, the son of perdition,

> *4.* who opposes and exalts himself against every so-called god or object of worship, so that he takes his seat in the temple of God, proclaiming himself to be God.

> *5.* Do you not remember that when I was still with you I told you this?

6. And you know what is restraining him now so that he may be revealed in his time.

7. For the mystery of lawlessness is already at work; only he who now restrains it will do so until he is out of the way.

8. And then the lawless one will be revealed, and the Lord Jesus will slay him with the breath of his mouth and destroy him by his appearing and his coming.

9. The coming of the lawless one by the activity of Satan will be with all power and with pretended signs and wonders,

10. and with all wicked deception for those who are to perish, because they refused to love the truth and so be saved.

When Paul wrote this, Christians had already been in trouble with hostile authorities, and he expected more problems. Again, there is a reminiscence of the traumatic Antiochus. The Lord's return will be preceded by a 'rebellion', an apostasy. Some Christians will desert, as some Jews deserted under the Syrian king's pressure. A similar foreboding affected Judaism before Christianity, but Paul connects it with a specific deceiver who will be the ultimate diabolic agent, the Man of Sin, Antichrist. Thus the apostle launches another prophecy, destined to endure through the centuries.

He does not use the actual word 'Antichrist'. Other early Christians do, however. Two epistles ascribed to John take up the word, although they give it a more general sense, saying that the fulfilment has already come, not in a single individual, but in heretics who deny the Incarnation. For Paul, however, and for most Christians afterwards, Antichrist is a single arch-enemy who will arise on the eve of the Second Coming. He is careful to give a further safeguard against the notion that something must happen soon. Not only must Antichrist appear before Christ, Antichrist himself has a prerequisite. His advent is held back by something or someone that 'restrains'. Eventually this will stop restraining, and only then will come the disclosure. Paul has discussed the subject with the Thessalonians, but his meaning is withheld from us. It is not clear why he has to be so cryptic. The restrainer is an impersonal agency in verse 6, a man or maybe an angel in verse 7. Some of the Fathers of the Church, commenting on this text, saw an allusion to the Roman Empire. As long as an emperor was enforcing the Pax Romana and curbing religious and political upstarts, the full Satanic lawlessness could not erupt.

Even if Paul had that in mind, the course of events put Rome in a more equivocal light. On 18 July 64 a fire broke out in the city that raged for a week, causing immense damage and countless casualties. The emperor Nero took measures to relieve the distress, but after a promising start he had become unpopular, and his unpopularity told against him. It was rumoured that he had enjoyed watching the flames while he sang a song of his own composition, accompanying himself on a lyre. Next came a far worse accusation – that he had started the fire himself to clear a space for a huge new palace. There were reports of gangs that had set light to buildings, obstructed fire-fighters and shouted that they were acting under orders. Whose orders? The emperor's?

Denial was insufficient. The blame had to be shifted. Nero did not reject the stories of incendiaries, but he claimed that they were Christians. By now the community in Rome was by no means negligible. According to Church historians, Peter and Paul were both in the city. In the words of the Roman author Tacitus:

> All human efforts, all the lavish gifts of the emperor, and the propitiations of the gods, did not banish the sinister belief that the conflagration was the result of an order. Consequently, to get rid of the report, Nero fastened the guilt and inflicted the most exquisite tortures on a class hated for their abominations, called Christians by the populace. Christ, from whom the name had its origin, suffered the extreme penalty during the reign of Tiberius at the hands of one of our procurators, Pontius Pilate. The mischievous superstition, thus checked for the moment, again broke out not only in Judaea, the first source of the evil, but even in Rome, where all things hideous and shameful from every part of the world find their centre and become popular.

Accordingly, an arrest was first made of all who pleaded guilty;

then, upon their information, an immense multitude were convicted, not so much of the crime of firing the city, as of hatred against humanity. Mockery of every sort was added to their deaths. Covered with the skins of beasts, they were torn by dogs and perished, or were nailed to crosses, or were doomed to the flames and burnt, to serve as a nightly illumination, when daylight had expired. Nero offered his gardens for the spectacle, and was exhibiting a show in the circus, while he mingled with the people in the dress of a charioteer.

Peter and Paul are said to have been among the victims. The Christians who 'pleaded guilty' may have been courting martyrdom; the information on which others were convicted may have been extracted by torture; no one knows.

Ever after, this onslaught was regarded as the first real persecution of the Church. Strictly speaking, it was not. The victims were not punished for their Christianity as such; there was no law forbidding it yet. In practice, however, a distinction was hard to draw. Their religion made Nero's actions possible. It had recruited converts chiefly among the lower echelons of society and was, therefore, in the eyes of Roman citizens, a cult for slaves and the riffraff. Its pretensions, based on the alleged divinity of a shamefully executed trouble-maker, were monstrous. As for what Tacitus calls 'hatred against humanity', Christians antagonized people by their denunciation of pagan 'sins', by their contempt for the gods and by their talk of impending doom and judgement.

Yet with all these things working for him, Nero had overreached himself. Romans were sorry for the scapegoats. Tacitus again:

> Even for criminals who deserved extreme and exemplary punishment, there arose a feeling of compassion; for it was not, as it seemed, for the public good, but to glut one man's cruelty, that they were being destroyed.

Christians were left alone for the rest of the reign, but Nero's personality was a major factor in the sequel. His infamous reputation is largely deserved – among many extravagances and crimes, no one could overlook his killing of his mother – yet he was far from being a commonplace and forgettable tyrant. He stood out. He had genuine artistic interests, which, it must be added, contributed to the case against him. He fancied himself as a poet, a singer, a musician and an actor, but although he took great pains, his gifts were less than impressive. Nevertheless, he insisted on giving public recitals and exploited his position to assemble captive audiences and carry off the prizes at festivals. The future emperor Vespasian was one of the few who dared to walk out when he was singing or even go to sleep, and his consequent dismissal from the imperial presence kept him in safe obscurity until the reign was over. On the credit side, Nero granted partial autonomy to Greece as a home of culture, and he began cutting a canal through the isthmus of Corinth. His diplomacy in the east earned him a good reputation there, especially with the Parthians beyond the frontier. He is said to have considered leaving an unappreciative Rome, and making Jerusalem, of all places, his capital.

He could still win cheers from a Roman crowd by a spectacular parade, but it was too late. The rich and respectable detested him, and disasters like Boudicca's revolt in Britain had long since undermined his authority. In 68 he was ousted in a coup headed by Galba, a provincial governor. Deserted by almost everyone, he committed suicide in a house near Rome, lamenting that the world should lose such an artist as himself and quoting Homer with his last breaths. He was only thirty.

Galba became emperor, but not for long. Two more imperial claimants followed within a few months, and the Empire was in danger of coming apart. It was stabilized by Vespasian. His son Titus, having crushed the Jewish revolt and destroyed the Temple, reigned for a couple of years and was succeeded by his brother Domitian, who lasted from 81 until 96, when he succumbed to a conspiracy. Before that, an excusable fear of assassination had caused him to begin lashing out at suspected enemies. A number of Christians were condemned as seditious. This was the second persecution, and, while limited in scope, it showed that the threat remained. Christians regarded Domitian as a second Nero, and so did others, such as the Roman satirist Juvenal (*c.*55–*c.*127). Although Domitian lacked the flamboyance of the original, he went further in what Christians saw as blasphemy, insisting on being referred to as 'our Master and our God'.

The original Nero had not faded into oblivion, and his dreadful yet haunting reign had left an indelible impression. Loathed by some, admired and even liked by others, he could not be exorcized. It was widely supposed that he had not really died but had escaped over the eastern frontier to a friendly Parthia and would return with an army. Two, possibly three, pretenders impersonated him, and the story of his survival found its way into the pseudo-Sibylline verses. There is no telling whether an appreciable number of Christians believed it literally, but many did believe that his spirit lived on and they had reason to fear a *Nero redivivus*, Nero revived, who might be identified with Domitian or some future persecutor.

It was not long before the legend-making set Nero up as one of the earliest of a select group of immortals – King Arthur, Frederick Barbarossa and others – who live on indefinitely and will some day return. He might even be Antichrist, waiting in some hidden retreat until the time came for the emergence foretold by Paul. St Augustine, in the fifth century, mentions versions of his survival still circulating even then (*The City of God*, XX:19).

There are people who suggest that Nero is to rise again and become Antichrist, while others suppose that he was not killed, but withdrawn so that he might be supposed killed and that he is still alive and in concealment in the full vigour of the age he had reached at the time of his supposed death, until 'he will be revealed at the right time for him' and restored to his throne. For myself I am much astonished at the great presumption of those who venture such guesses.

Antichrist had other guises. An early development of the theme was a belief that he would inflict the last and worst persecution. The prophecy inspired medieval speculation and drama. Antichrist's advent was reported several times during the witch-mania of the sixteenth and seventeenth centuries, when all sorts of delusions were rampant about satanic activities. In 1599 he was reported to have been born in Babylon. The following year he was born in the neighbourhood of Paris, his mother being a Jewish woman impregnated by the Devil. On 1 May 1623 he was born for a third time, near Babylon again. These stories proved to be false alarms. In 1900 the Russian philosopher Vladimir Solovyev wrote a modern version of the prophecy, which a biographer of Hitler thought might have influenced the Führer. However, Antichrist has not yet shown himself, unless extreme Protestants have been right all along in identifying him with the pope and explaining his promised destruction as the end of the papacy. One side-show of anti-papalism made him the son of the legendary woman pope, Joan, alleged to have succeeded Leo IV in 855: the boy was spirited away to a secret place, from which he will step forth as Antichrist when the time is ripe.

The Neronian ordeal, with its attendant mystery and its aftershock in the reign of Domitian, is the background of the last book of the New Testament. Its name in English is Revelation. Not, by the way, Revelations. Oscar Wilde must accept some of the blame for the currency of a wrong title when he put it in *A Woman of No Importance*:

> *Lord Illingworth*: The Book of Life begins with a man and a woman in a garden.
> *Mrs Allonby*: It ends with Revelations.

The work in question is a Christian apocalypse carrying on the Jewish tradition. 'Revelation' in fact has the same meaning as 'apocalypse', and in some English Bibles that is what the book is called.

It is the most bewildering of scriptural prophecies. The Protestant Reformer John Calvin, who wrote commentaries on the rest of the New Testament, is reputed to have left this book alone because 'anybody who studies it is either mad when he starts or mad when he's finished'. Nevertheless, it is the source for familiar words and phrases – 'Armageddon' as the name of a final battle, 'the Four Horsemen of the Apocalypse', 'the Number of the Beast'. Verses from it are embedded in Handel's *Messiah*. It has played a crucial role in dozens of predictions of the end of the world, all proclaimed despite Christ's warnings against speculation on the subject, and all abortive. In the light of scriptural scholarship we can dismiss many of the notions wrung from the text by expositors, including such eminent figures as Isaac Newton . . . many of them, but not quite all.

If I may be allowed a personal reminiscence, this was the first book of the Bible that I looked into for myself and not as a lesson. No one had drawn my attention to it, and yet, for some reason, I took it for granted at the age of eleven that it foretold the future. What future? When I was a little older, I made futile attempts to connect it with what was going on in the world. Luckily, I missed someone's calculation that made the Number of the Beast fit Hitler. If I had seen that, there would probably have been no holding me, although, having many other interests, I would not have fallen into the obsession bewailed by Calvin.

The author calls himself John. Early tradition assigns both Revelation itself and the fourth Gospel to the apostle of that name, though he would have had to be living and writing at a very advanced age. Another difficulty is that the books diverge widely in style, in outlook and even in the literacy of the Greek. Yet they have points in common, such as the designation of Christ as the Lamb and the Word, that tell against total separateness. One theory is that the apostle had a circle of pupils or disciples who took notes of his reminiscences, discourses and poetic imaginings and worked them up into books in different ways. It would not have been impossible for the same person to pass from the philosophic and mystical thinking revealed in the Gospel to the fiery image-making of the Apocalypse. For convenience, we may take the author at his word, call him 'John' whoever he was, and leave it at that.

He introduces himself on the island of Patmos in the Aegean, as an exile or fugitive. Irenaeus, a second-century native of Asia Minor who travelled west and became Bishop of Lyons, gives us a date: he puts Revelation at the end of the reign of Domitian – that is, about 96. His testimony carries weight because he takes us closer than anyone else. He was a pupil of Polycarp, the bishop of Smyrna (now Izmir), and Polycarp had known the apostle John himself, of whose authorship Irenaeus has no doubt. A date during Domitian's persecution tallies with indications in the text. The book as we have it may not have been composed on the island; it may give literary form to experiences that happened there.

John addresses the Revelation to fellow Christians in Asia Minor, inviting them to read it aloud together. Most of it consists of a series of visionary scenes, described in vivid detail. These are not mere individual fantasies or hallucinations: Revelation has antecedents in Jewish writings, especially Daniel. It is planned and structured, often by the use of numerical patterns, and some of the images are explained. John says he *saw* all this, but his words need not be taken too literally. He is following prophetic convention. From a Christian standpoint, nothing rules out the view that his book is a flight of imagination induced and controlled by the Holy Spirit.

At the start Christ appears to him, tells him to write what he sees – 'what is and what is to take place hereafter' – and entrusts him with messages for seven Christian communities in Asia Minor. Then a door opens in heaven. John ascends and sees God enthroned, with various beings in the heavenly court. God is emphatically not an old man with a beard. He is suggested more by imagery of light and colour than by anything anthropomorphic. In human fashion, however, he holds a scroll covered with writing and sealed with seven seals. It is a book of destiny, and only Christ is worthy to open it and reveal its contents. John symbolizes Christ by a Lamb 'as though it had been slain'. The Lamb opens four of the seals and four mounted men appear, on horses of different colours. These are the Four Horsemen of the Apocalypse. One is a crowned conqueror, the others are bringers of war, famine and death, and they probably represent the pagan

Revelation or Apocalypse

imperialism that has created the world in which John lives. The triumphs of men such as Alexander and Caesar have exacted a fearful price.

When the Lamb opens the fifth seal, John sees the souls of martyrs who have already died, clamouring to know how long they must wait for the persecutors' downfall. They are told that it is not yet and that more will have to suffer. The visions are now moving into the future. The sixth seal is opened, and an earthquake and other portents herald the visitation of God's wrath on sinful humanity. After a scene in which the faithful are reassured, the Lamb opens the final seal. This action introduces a new set of seven: John sees seven angels with trumpets. They sound them one after another. Six of the blasts inflict divine judgements on the earth – fire, darkness, pollution of water, swarms of monstrous locusts and diabolical cavalry. A large part of the population is killed. The survivors, however, do not repent of their idolatry and wickedness.

While this is happening, Christians are not silent. John represents the Church by two 'witnesses' who defy the pagan world. After a long ministry, they are slain by a 'beast from the bottomless pit' (to be explained later). Then they return to life. Another earthquake follows, and, for the first time, pagans are shaken and give glory to God. The seventh angel sounds his trumpet, and the time of trouble, abruptly, is over. Voices chorus in heaven: 'The kingdom of the world has become the kingdom of our Lord and his Christ, and he shall reign for ever and ever.'

I have summarized this part of Revelation briefly because it seems to me that there are no real predictions in it at all: none that can be pinned down and tested against facts. Enthusiasts have claimed to find fulfilments in history and make out, for instance, that the locusts and cavalry symbolize Arab and Turkish conquests. Such remote happenings, meaningless to John's audience, are most unlikely to be intended. The only good ground for detecting them would be a long-term chronology in the text, and none exists. John's two witnesses denounce paganism for 1260 'days', but this period has no relation to real time. It stands for a confrontation between God's people and the powers of evil, derived from Daniel, and based on the persecution of Jews by the never-forgotten Antiochus. It appears, variously expressed, in other passages.

The story seems to be over. It is not. John has been told (10:11) that he must prophesy again, and he embarks on a new series of visions that lead to the triumph of Christ by another route. Making a fresh start in historical time, from the beginnings of Christianity, he gives glimpses of events in the recent past, in his own day and after that. In this central part of the book, prediction becomes an issue, even though, as with the locusts and cavalry, we have to get rid of some aberrations.

In chapter 12 John describes a 'great portent in heaven' (by which he means the sky, not the abode of God): 'a woman clothed with the sun, with the moon under her feet, and on her head a crown of twelve stars'. The woman is about to give birth. She is twelve-tribed Israel bringing forth the Messiah, and perhaps, in a visionary sense, Mary as Israel's representative. (She is not, by the way, Joanna Southcott, who, in 1792, claimed to be this woman. Having built up a following, Joanna announced that the Messianic birth would take place in 1814. No birth occurred, and she died soon afterwards. Her principal legacy was a box that would transform society when opened in the presence of an assemblage of bishops. The bishops declined to cooperate, and the box was opened in 1927 without them. It contained a lottery ticket and a night-cap. Surviving Southcottians said it was not the real box, and they had the genuine one with sacred writings in it, but few of the public were convinced.)

John follows his first celestial portent with another, 'a great red dragon, with seven heads and ten horns, and seven diadems upon his heads'. He is the Devil, the diadems symbolizing his power over the world. He hopes to swallow up the newly born child, Christ, but is prevented. The next verses in chapter 12 look out of place in the drama that is unfolding.

7. Now war arose in heaven, Michael and his angels fighting against the dragon; and the dragon and his angels fought,

8. but they were defeated and there was no longer any place for them in heaven.

9. And the great dragon was thrown down, that ancient serpent, who is called the Devil and Satan, the deceiver of the whole world – he was thrown down to the earth, and his angels were thrown down with him.

The fall of Satan and his angels belongs to a distant past, about the time of the Creation, either shortly before it (according to Milton) or shortly after it (according to Dante). John may be recalling it here, rather awkwardly, as an image of Satan's new defeat by the advent of Christ. The symbolism shifts, and the woman is God's new Israel here below, the Christian body. The dragon pursues her, but she escapes to a safe retreat: the Church, as such, cannot be destroyed. But he can attack her offspring, the Christians, and for that purpose he forms an earthly institution. In chapter 13 John's imagery grows bizarre, yet he is now close to history and human realities. He exhibits Satan's master-work in the contemporary world.

1. I saw a beast rising out of the sea, with ten horns and seven heads, with ten diadems upon its horns and a blasphemous name upon its heads.

2. And the beast that I saw was like a leopard, its feet were like a bear's, and its mouth was like a lion's mouth. And to it the dragon gave his power and his throne and great authority.

This Beast has been mentioned in passing as the would-be destroyer of Christ's witnesses. Now it is revealed in all its repulsiveness. Some translations call the Beast 'he', but the RSV's 'it' corresponds to the neuter Greek word *therion* and is more appropriate. In chapter 17 an angel gives John a second view of it and explains some of its features. Elucidation requires some skipping backwards and forwards.

The heads and horns show its close link with the similarly equipped dragon, but it is a composite monster, recalling Daniel

7:2–7, where four beasts typify four empires, the Babylonian, Median, Persian and Greek. This one combines features taken from all four. It resembles a leopard (Daniel's third beast) and has a bear's feet (from the second beast), a mouth like a lion's (from the first) and ten horns (from the fourth). It is a super-empire, surpassing its predecessors. The angel in chapter 17 shows it with a companion, an evil woman who rides on it, 'Babylon the great'. In the first century 'Babylon' had become a sobriquet for Rome, and the woman's identity as the city 'which has dominion over the kings of the earth' is clinched by the statement that the Beast's seven heads stand for Rome's proverbial seven hills, on which she is seated.

The Beast, therefore, is the Roman Empire. The reason for its rising out of the sea may be that the Empire began as a Mediterranean domain, although by John's time it had spread beyond. From Nero onwards, it appears, the Devil has empowered it as his great anti-Christian instrument. The capital's seven hills do not exhaust the significance of the heads, however, for they are also seven 'kings', the emperors prior to Domitian: Augustus, Tiberius, Caligula, Claudius, Nero, Vespasian and Titus. Julius Caesar did not have the imperial title, and the three who flitted across the stage after Nero do not count. The 'blasphemous name' on the heads alludes to the emperors' divine titles, although none of the seven blasphemed as far as Domitian did.

John's account of the Beast in chapter 13 resumes:

3. One of its heads seemed to have a mortal wound, but its mortal wound was healed, and the whole earth followed the beast with wonder.

4. Men worshipped the dragon, for he had given his authority to the beast, and they worshipped the beast, saying, 'Who is like the beast, and who can fight against it?'

5. And the beast was given a mouth uttering haughty and blasphemous words, and it was allowed to exercise authority for forty-two months;

6. it opened its mouth to utter blasphemies against God, blaspheming his name and his dwelling, that is, those who dwell in heaven.

7. Also it was allowed to make war on the saints and to conquer them. And authority was given it over every tribe and people and tongue and nation.

The 'wound' is a reference to Nero, who is represented as one of the heads. Officially he stabbed himself, but as we saw, his death was widely denied. He had survived, according to rumour, and would return. Some Christians, evidently including John, did not go as far as that but believed in a survival in spirit and a figurative return in the person of Domitian. Persecution had not ended with the death or alleged death of the prototype-persecutor. The wound to the head had also been a wound to the Beast itself: the battle of pretenders after Nero's departure had threatened the break-up of the Empire, but Vespasian had pulled things together and healed the wound in that respect too. The Empire seemed indestructible. 'Worshipping' the dragon and Beast need be no more than a general expression for pagan religion, and the 'blasphemies' are edicts and proclamations calling the emperors divine, demanding homage to their statues and publicizing libels against the Christians, such as Nero's charge of incendiarism. The period of forty-two months is another version of the '1260 days'.

John's expository angel in chapter 17 echoes the Nero legend further, with a double symbolism. The Beast is anti-Christian, the persecutor Nero embodies it, and the two are fused. The Beast 'was and is not and yet is', and the time-frame in which the angel exhibits it is the imperial recovery under Vespasian after what seemed a mortal crisis (17:10). He adds that the *Nero redivivus* Domitian, called the 'eighth' emperor in succession to the seven, will embody it anew.

In the part of chapter 13 already quoted, John is dealing with recent historical events and employs the past tense. Having set the stage, he proceeds, in verses 11–17, to something more ambiguous, making a fairly consistent shift to the present. But the scene is not the actual present, or, at least, is not confined to it. He is giving a visionary commentary that includes things in another setting.

11. I saw another beast which rose out of the earth; it had two horns like a lamb and it spoke like a dragon.

12. It exercises all the authority of the first beast in its presence, and makes the earth and its inhabitants worship the first beast, whose mortal wound was healed.

13. It works great signs, even making fire come down from heaven to earth in the sight of men;

14. and by the signs which it is allowed to work in the presence of the beast, it deceives those who dwell on earth, bidding them make an image for the beast which was wounded by the sword and yet lived;

15. and it was allowed to give breath to the image of the beast so that the image of the beast should even speak, and to cause those who would not worship the image of the beast to be slain.

16. Also it causes all, both small and great, both rich and poor, both free and slave, to be marked on the right hand or the forehead,

17. so that no one can buy or sell unless he has the mark, that is, the name of the beast or the number of its name.

In later chapters, this Second Beast is called the False Prophet, but again 'it' is an apter pronoun than 'he', at least here. Like the First Beast, the Second is primarily a personification. Whereas the First Beast rose from the sea, the Second rises from the earth, from the land. If John intends a geographical contrast, he may have Asia in mind, the unbounded eastern territory. The Second Beast symbolizes pagan religion acting in support of the Empire, with a priesthood conducting emperor-worship. Its wonder-working alludes to known priestly trickery, sometimes including effects produced by ventriloquism. It inspires persecution.

Yet at first glance, it seems superfluous. John has just spoken of the First Beast being worshipped and 'making war on the saints'. What does the Second add? What is distinctive in the persecution it brings? A hint emerges in verses 15–17. John is talking about something that is emphatically not happening in his own time. To reach this point, the Roman Beast must become far more terrible; and the Second will be a new religious force at work in the change. John pictures a regime that might almost be called totalitarian. All dissent is to be punishable by death. In whatever way the metaphors are taken, the 'mark' stands for official approval, isolating and condemning to ostracism everyone in the Roman world who is not so approved. In this passage, Revelation is becoming predictive.

Is there a clue that would make the prediction more specific and open to verification one way or the other? What about that strange phrase 'the number of its name'? It expresses some aspect of the principal Beast to which its subjects will have to relate themselves. Immediately after comes this verse, the most famous in the whole book:

> Here is wisdom. Let him who has understanding reckon the number of the beast, for it is the number of a man; and its number is six hundred and sixty-six.

Translations vary slightly, but this reading seems to harmonize with everything else and to be the soundest rendering of the Greek.

John's riddle involves a technique known as gematria. Our so-called Arabic numerals did not reach the classical world, and in Hebrew and Greek, numbers were represented by letters of the alphabet. Thus, given a person's name, the numbers matching its letters could be added together to give a sum corresponding to it. 'Jesus', transliterated in Greek as 'Iesous' with a long *e*, adds up to 888 (10 + 8 + 200 + 70 + 400 + 200), which is, therefore, Jesus's

№ 666

number. The Beast, presumably, has a title or manifestation that makes 666, an echo of the Jesus number but inferior, and something about it can be revealed by decoding the number.

The technique is still possible, even though numerals now exist and the attachment of numbers to letters is artificial. This unfortunate fact has spawned all too many would-be solutions. If A = 1, B = 2 and so on, or indeed if letters are assigned any consistent values, gematria can be applied to a name in English or French or any language that has an alphabet. The wilder 'explanations' of 666 have been inspired chiefly by religion or politics. Muhammad can be made to work and so, with a little orthographic cheating, can l'Empereur Napoléon. Brewer's *Dictionary of Phrase and Fable* mentions Charles Bradlaugh, the Victorian freethinker, without telling how the calculation was made. The so-called black magician Aleister Crowley plausibly went back to Greek, and observed that TO MEGA THERION, the Great Beast, gave 666 – not a bad notion, but he spoiled it by adopting the title himself. Another modern person can be made to fit very well: if A = 100, B = 101 and so on, Hitler gives 666 precisely.

It is worth noting such fantasies as a warning, but they can all be dismissed, and not solely because they cancel out each other. John is addressing readers in his own time, inviting them to solve his riddle. There would have been no point in doing so if the answer was a name – Hitler, for instance – that they could not have guessed, the name of someone far off in an irrelevant future. A believer in long-range foresight might argue that John aimed his invitation at readers who would be living in that future. It would still have been absurd and unfair to vex the generations between with an insoluble problem. And while his visions about the Beast range as far ahead as the Empire it stands for, they cannot go beyond: he thinks there is no 'beyond' and history will end with the Beast still in existence. It follows that the 'man' encoded by 666 is associated with the Empire. Latter-day candidates are not.

A solution, at least a primary one, has been known for a long time and is almost certainly correct. There are several considerations in favour of it which have been pointed out by commentators, but I am not sure if anyone hitherto has brought them together and shown how they converge.

We might hope to go directly to the heart of the problem by finding what is said by the author closest to John's time, the aforementioned bishop Irenaeus, who dates the book 'almost in our generation'. In fact, the approach he offers is roundabout, and he does not claim to be sure of the answer. He even says that some copies give the Number as 616; he rejects this reading firmly and rightly, but a few manuscripts that do give 616 attest the uncertainty. He has two solutions, although he does not make it clear whether he has heard them from somebody closer to the source or hit on them himself.

One of his candidates is LATEINOS, Greek for 'the Latin' or 'the Roman', which adds up correctly. 'Those who now reign,' Irenaeus remarks, 'are Latini.' This seems to lack point, since the Roman-ness of the evil power is evident, and 'Lateinos' sheds no further light. It once had some popularity among Protestants because it could extend the Beast's meaning to cover not only the Roman Empire but the Roman Church afterwards, with its enthronement of Latin. As in other cases, it is unlikely that John would have referred to something remote and not linked with his contemporary message. While a warning against the Church going astray would have been possible, he shows no sign of regarding this as a danger. 'Lateinos' can be read as the name of a man, in keeping with John's words, but the man is the mythical Latinus, king of Latium in central Italy long before the Christian era. He is too marginal. Moreover, the correct Greek spelling is 'Latinos'. Irenaeus – or his informant – cheats a little, by changing the spelling to get 666. As we shall see, this solution is relevant, but it is not the whole story and leaves an impression that John could have done better.

Irenaeus thinks so himself. He prefers TEITAN, that is, 'Titan', a name of the Sun. It has an attractive symmetry:

T		E		I
T		A		N

600	+6	+60 = 666

Irenaeus likes this solution. It has a strong pagan flavour – from his point of view, an anti-Christian flavour. 'This name is thought among many to be divine, so that even the Sun is called Titan by those who now prevail . . . it is also ancient, and trustworthy, and a royal, or even rather a tyrannical Name.' Irenaeus is right. 'Titan' is used in Greek to mean the sun-god and, specifically, Apollo, whose association with the sun was added to his other functions. TEITAN has more point than LATEINOS, although here also Irenaeus manipulates the spelling.

The Number, let us recall, is the number of a man, and neither of these solutions leads to a specific and appropriate person. With their contrived spellings, they look like epithets devised to confirm the '666' nature of a man identified otherwise. The blending of the Beast with Nero points to him. At first sight he is disappointing. 'Neron', the Greek form of his name, adds up to 1005. If we make him 'Nero Caesar', 'Neron Kaisar' in Greek, we get 1337, which is a near miss for 666 × 2, but not good enough. Nevertheless, 'Neron Kaisar' is the answer, and Irenaeus misses it because it does not occur to him that John could deviate into another language. 'Neron Kaisar' can be transliterated in Hebrew to give 666 exactly. Moreover, if some copyist left off the final *n* and made it 'Nero' in the plain Roman style, the Hebrew transliteration would have given 616, the irregular version of the Number. So Nero accounts for that too.

By gematria, then, he virtually has to be the 'man', as indeed we would expect. When John's Greek-speaking readers ceased to think of the Hebrew alphabet, the clue was lost. But at a stage when the 'Nero' solution was still known, it looks as if members of some Johannine circle played a sort of game, underpinning it with Greek words that would apply to him and also make 666, if with a little ingenuity. Two results of their game, 'Lateinos' and 'Teitan', drifted through to Irenaeus. While neither of those words would suggest Nero, Nero, once thought of, could have suggested both of them.

He was a Roman, a 'Latin', one of 'those who now reign', as Irenaeus puts it. The 'Titan' application is more interesting. Nero actually was flattered in solar terms. The first step was taken by Seneca, his tutor and adviser, probably soon after his accession and certainly early in his reign. Seneca composed a satire on Nero's deceased predecessor, Claudius, in the course of which Apollo addresses the Fates who are spinning the thread of the young new ruler's destiny:

> Cut no years short from this illustrious life,
> For he whose life you spin, my counterpart,
> Yields not to me either in face or grace
> For beauty, nor for sweetness in his song . . .

Apollo compares Nero to the brightest stars and continues:

> Nay, rather he's the Sun himself, what time
> The blushing Goddess of the Dawn leads in
> The earliest light of day, dispersed the shades –
> The Sun himself with shining countenance
> Who pores upon the world, and from the gates
> Of his dark prison whirls his chariot out.
> A very Sun is NERO and all Rome
> Shall look on NERO with bedazzled eyes.

When Nero became famous for his musicianship, coins were issued depicting Apollo playing a lyre, and the figure was unmistakably the emperor. During his tour of Greece in 67, when he granted the Greeks a measure of self-rule, one of the resolutions of thanks was proposed by a speaker who hailed him as an incarnation of Apollo and a New Sun. He was willing to go along with this. Further coins showed his head encircled by Apollo's sun-ray crown, and a colossal statue of himself in front of his palace was similarly crowned.

Three solutions are thus accommodated, not as rivals but as aspects of one, the natural and logical 'Nero' solution. Is this all? I believe not. Why does John resort to Hebrew, which his readers probably won't know or think of? Why not keep to Greek and say the number is 1005 (Neron) or 1337 (Neron Kaisar)? Surely because 666 is already given, and John finds a way of fitting it to Nero by bringing in Hebrew. To quote Austin Farrer: 'He *wants* Nero to be 666 rather than some number more obviously obtainable from his name for the Greek reader.' And so we come to an explanation of 666 that may be the fundamental one. For this, we take leave of gematria and turn to the numerology of Pythagoras.

In addition to being a pioneer mathematician, Pythagoras (sixth century BC) was a religious teacher, whose influence descended through Plato to later philosophers, and was alive, even reviving, in the first century AD: witness a noted mage of that period, Apollonius of Tyana. Pythagoreans took a deep interest in the properties of numbers. They knew about square numbers, which are familiar enough today, but they also knew about triangular numbers, which are not so familiar. The numbers from 1 to 4 can be represented by dots arranged in a triangle:

Ten dots altogether. Pythagoreans called this diagram the 'tetraktys', from the Greek for 'four', and attached mystical meanings to it. The essential point is that $1 + 2 + 3 + 4 = 10$, so 4 'triangulated' is 10, and 10 is a triangular number. Any number can be triangulated in the same way. You start from 1 and go up to the number in question. Thus, $1 + 2 + 3 + 4 + 5 = 15$, so 5 triangulated is 15, and 15 is a triangular number. The formula for triangulating any number, n, is $n(n + 1)/2$.

In Revelation 17:11 the Beast's new manifestation as Domitian is an eighth added to the series of emperors, and labelled as such:

> As for the beast that was and is not, it is an eighth but it belongs to the seven, and it goes into perdition.

Triangulate 8: $1 + 2 + 3 + \ldots + 8 = 36$. Now take a further step and triangulate 36: $1 + 2 + 3 + \ldots + 36 = 666$. The Number of the Beast is a double-triangular, an unusual number in a class that thins out rapidly the higher you go. It is generated from 8, the ordinal number of Domitian, *Nero redivivus*.

This solution of 666 requires no knowledge of letter values or gematria – triangulation is simple arithmetic. Someone who worked on the fourth Gospel, John or another, seems to have known about it. The number of fishes in the miraculous draught (John 21:11) is 153. It is hardly likely that on such an occasion, in the presence of the risen Lord, Peter would have counted 153 'large fish' one by one; but 153 is 17 triangulated.

There is a limit to legitimate speculation about John's mental processes, but the triangular solution is impeccable. The others are in harmony with it, but they fall short. Perhaps he started from the persecution he was aware of himself, Domitian's, and related it to the tradition and legend of Nero. He could have defined Domitian as number 8 in a series of emperors by piecing together a list of the seven before him. With 8 fixed upon as Domitian's number, he could have developed 666 from it by the double triangulation, noticed its inferior echo of the Jesus number, 888, found that he could fit 666 to the prototype-persecutor, Nero, and gone on from there.

If the facts were at all like this, we have a clue to the 'wisdom' achieved by penetrating the secret. It means, or at any rate it includes, the perception of a link between the two emperors to whom the Number applies, Nero and Domitian. Diabolic power passes from one to the other, so Christians must never think that danger is past, they must always be prepared. There are loose ends: the question of prophetic foresight does finally arise. No decision on that, one way or the other, can affect the validity of the foregoing. (For additional discussion of the Number of the Beast, see Appendix 1, page 308.)

When Irenaeus discusses Titan, the sun-god, as numerically linked with the Beast, he writes in the future tense as of an evil yet to come. The basic application to Nero is sound enough, yet it need not rule out a reference to the future as well, a future in which the Beast's solar quality will come to the fore. We have seen cases of twofold meaning in prophecy. There can be no doubt as to John's ingenuity when he chooses to exert it, and his anticipations in 13:15–17 must be taken seriously, at least in the sense that he means them, whether he is right or not.

He pictures a persecution going far beyond anything imaginable in his own time and associated with a change in the Roman Beast, a totalitarian change. This has, in fact, been hinted at further back, when he has a vision about a 'great tribulation' (7:14). The faithful who are to suffer and triumph in it are a 'great multitude which no man could number, from every nation, from all tribes and peoples and tongues'. John implies that it will be universal, will involve immensely more Christians than there are at the time of writing, and will therefore not happen for a long while.

His perception is correct. The great tribulation came, accompanied by the change in the Beast. Moreover it was a long while coming, and in the form it took it could not have been rationally anticipated. In his own day we can see the seeds being planted, but only hindsight can recognize them for what they were or trace the tendency of the years that followed. Christians were, of course, courting trouble. They boycotted the gods, on whose goodwill much was held to depend, and they refused the loyalty test of homage to the emperor's statue. Among pagans who thought of them at all, the dislike felt in Rome during Nero's reign continued to be intense and could easily deepen into hatred. Christians were seen as subversive and socially contemptible, and their worship of a crucified criminal was regarded as absurd and degrading. Occasionally mob violence broke out. Since Christianity was an unlicensed cult, its practice was technically illegal. The climate of opinion was thus conducive to persecution, and persecutions continued to happen.

Such persecutions remained local and sporadic for many years, however. The Empire was unassailable, and almost everybody did worship the Beast without being coerced into doing so. The martyrs who were burned alive or thrown to the lions in the arena were not numerous. Inconspicuous Christians were allowed to lead normal lives, under however threatening a cloud, and the more articulate were able to write and teach. General persecution did not even become an issue until 212, when the emperor Caracalla extended Roman citizenship to most of his subjects everywhere. Citizenship carried religious obligations, so his edict created a new hazard for provincial Christians who had not previously been citizens. Yet nothing came of it until the 250s, when the emperor Decius tried to impose conformity across the Empire. His attempt petered out. On the one hand, executions of the resolute remained few; on the other, many of the less dedicated bought themselves a spell of immunity by more or less meaningless recantations. The Church recovered from both kinds of misfortune. A period of peace followed in which it gained ground noticeably. Almost two centuries after Revelation was written, a public-affairs commentator in the modern manner would probably have predicted a gradual acceptance and a live-and-let-live future. The commentator would have been wrong. A new factor had entered the imperial scene, which was to vindicate both John's prophecy of the great tribulation and the solar reading of the Number.

The first impulse had come from a remarkable woman, Julia Domna (*c.*167–217). She was a Syrian living in Emesa, the present-day Homs, on the Orontes River. Her father had the rank of a prince and was the hereditary priest of the city's sun-god, whom the Bible would have called a baal. Julia was viviacious, well read, a patron of the arts and sexually liberated. Her portrait shows a rather impressive face, with a firm jaw, a small mouth and a halo of elaborately and tightly curled hair. She became the wife of Septimius Severus, an army leader of African origin, who picked her out by her horoscope.

Severus was emperor from 193 to 211. He harassed Christians, and Julia helped to counteract their influence, if with no very deliberate intent. She sponsored a 'Life' of Apollonius of Tyana, the Pythagorean sage, who came to be revered by some pagans as a retort to Christ. More important was her introduction of Severus to her family god. He was captivated and made the

'Unconquered Sun', Sol Invictus, his patron deity, and identified himself with him. The couple appeared together on coins as Sol and Luna, Sun and Moon. Severus's cosmopolitan and levelling policies weakened traditional loyalties. Old-style paganism was wearing thin, and he felt the need for a fresh glorification of the imperial office. He liked the concept of the emperor illuminating the Empire just as the Sun illuminated the world, and he had himself portrayed with an aureole of solar rays.

When he died – at York, after a campaign in Scotland – his son Caracalla, author of the citizenship edict, succeeded him. Caracalla first ruled jointly with his brother, Geta, then alone. Both kept the new cult alive. A coin depicted Geta as the offspring of the Unconquered Sun, and Caracalla employed a lion emblem to stand for the god as the source of his authority. He was assassinated in 217, and after a short phase of confusion the soldiers stationed at Homs enthroned a young and handsome great-nephew of Julia. He was a priest of the god. Approved in Rome, he became the first emperor of Asian birth. He had assumed the god's local name, Elagabalus, but because of the solar connection this is often given as Heliogabalus, and appears as such, surprisingly, in *The Pirates of Penzance*.

The emperor's proudest title was 'Priest of the Unconquered Sun-god Elagabalus'. He brought a black stone symbolizing the god to Rome and installed it in a new temple on the Palatine Hill. This deity was to be supreme, and the rituals of others, including Christ, were to be transferred to his temple in a subsidiary role. A mature and intelligent ruler might have made this policy a step towards monotheism, but Elagabalus was neither mature nor intelligent, and the policy made little progress. His irresponsibility, extravagance and sexual bizarreries infuriated the Romans, and he was murdered in less than four years. He might have discredited the sun-god for ever. The fact that he did not shows the strength of the need for such a deity.

A long imperial crisis, with many pretenders and various external threats, was brought to an end in 270 by the emperor Aurelian. During an eastern war he won a battle near Homs – Homs again! – and ascribed his victory to its sun-god. He proclaimed Sol Invictus 'Lord of the Roman Empire' and built him a temple in Rome with its own highly privileged college of priests. The Orontes, someone remarked, was flowing into the Tiber. Aurelian's Unconquered Sun was much more than the original Syrian baal. He was a theological composite, with elements of Apollo and also of Mithras, a Persian god popular with the troops. This Supreme Being was to be, in the words of a modern historian, 'the centre of a revived and unified paganism, and the guarantor of loyalty to the Emperor'. The familiar gods and goddesses were not negated – this was a religious age, indeed a superstitious one – but they were subordinated to the godhead presiding over the Roman world. Emperors were now to be his viceroys below, earthly 'suns' more or less identified with him, and associated with him on coins. The civilization centred on him was 'the Eternal Light'.

The new monotheism was part of a broader imperial revival. Its chief architect was Diocletian, a soldier of Balkan origin who rose by way of the army and became emperor in 284. He launched constitutional changes, with a division of power at the summit, and carried out administrative and economic reforms. At a heavy price in authoritarianism and taxation, the Empire was practically refounded, to survive for another century and a half. Diocletian invoked the sun-god at his accession. Personally, he preferred more traditional deities, but he played along with the imperial mystique and enhanced it by surrounding the throne with an elaborate ceremonial that was eastern in origin, like the solar religion.

And now came the clash. If Sol Invictus was the Supreme Being, and the world's welfare depended on him, another Supreme Being could not be tolerated. Christianity had to go. There were more down-to-earth motives for suppression – the Church was a self-governing body, independent of the State, and emperors had always mistrusted such bodies. Trajan had even vetoed a fire-brigade, and the Church was now vastly more formidable than a fire-brigade. It could not be fitted into the new absolutism. Despite the urgings of Galerius, his principal colleague, Diocletian was hesitant about taking action. At last he sent a soothsayer to consult an oracle of Apollo at Miletus. Apollo – not the most impartial of deities, under the circumstances – expressed his enmity for Christians. The pagan priesthood largely concurred, and John's Second Beast was rampant. Diocletian yielded, and in 303 the drive to annihilate the Church began.

During the next few years the Empire was distracted by a fresh wave of contending would-be emperors, some of whom were more anti-Christian than others, but pressure was generally intense. Christians became, so to speak, un-persons. Their assemblies were broken up, their buildings were wrecked, and their sacred books were confiscated. In 304 refusal to sprinkle incense on the imperial altar became a crime punishable by death, and thousands were executed for this refusal. Revelation 13:15 was fulfilled. However, the Church had grown too strong during the respite after Decius. Its members were numerous, widespread and drawn from a broader range of social classes. Moreover, the atmosphere had changed. Public opinion, so far as such a thing existed, was much less hostile, and many pagans had Christian friends whom they respected. Many Christians, especially women, were persons of standing in society, known for their good character. Finding they had an uphill struggle, the persecutors lost interest.

The decisive shift came with Constantine, who took over the Empire piece by piece. A committed monotheist, he put the Unconquered Sun on his coins and allowed himself to be portrayed as a solar emperor, mystically identified with the deity, on a triumphal arch that is still standing. But he gradually came to the conclusion that the One God was not Sol Invictus but the God of the Christians. In 313 he published an edict of toleration. Later, as sole ruler, he favoured the Church and sponsored its first general council. The birthday of the Unconquered Sun, 25 December, became Christmas Day. In John's words, the 'multitude which no man could number' had come through the tribulation. Christ was victorious. A long time was still to elapse before the Empire became officially Christian, and a longer time before heresy, popular in high places, yielded to Catholic orthodoxy. But the corner had been turned.

In the light of these facts, some kind of precognition is a real issue. John foresees a totalitarian change in the Roman Empire: correct. He foresees an Empire-wide and exterminatory persecution: correct. He, or someone developing his thoughts, associates this with an imperial sun-god: correct. In John's time an increased imperial absolutism was perhaps predictable, and some Christians were already expecting a worse persecution than they had experienced so far, because of the notion of Antichrist. But the third of John's previsions is a different matter. A take-over of the Empire by a Syrian solar baal was not on any agenda in the first century nor for long afterwards. Nobody would have dreamed of such a thing. Yet that was how 'Titan', for the moment, triumphed. The Orontes did flow into the Tiber.

One or two details are worth noting. Under the persecuting regime, John says, people will not be able to buy or sell unless they have the mark, 'that is, the name of the Beast or the number of its name'. I don't know what he means by the mark, but the plain, mundane necessity for buying and selling is money. Coins of the solar emperors met John's requirement. On one side they had an imperial inscription, the name of the Beast. On the other they had the Sun, who, as Titan, added up to 666 – the number.

These prophecies did not create their own fulfilment. None of the protagonists did what they did because John said they would. Severus did not elaborate his wife's cult as a move against the Christians suggested by Revelation or by the interpretation in Irenaeus. He is unlikely to have known of either book, and he would never have worked his way through Irenaeus's to the paragraph about Titan, which is near the end.

If there is a case for thinking that John foresaw something in the early fourth century, is there a case for thinking that he foresaw anything beyond? In Revelation he tells of the Church's deliverance and goes on to seven final plagues, the last demonstration of God's anger against the pagan world. The evil powers make some kind of counter-attack. It would be pleasant to relate this to the attempted revival of paganism by the emperor Julian, the Apostate, who wanted to reinstate the sun-god . . . but no, I don't think so, partly because of the result of the counter-attack – the battle of Armageddon. Armageddon is Megiddo in Palestine, the site of several battles, but none that would fit here or have any relevance to Julian.

An unexplained detail does remain in John's description of the Beast. It has seven heads – emperors – and ten horns. The horns are an inheritance from Daniel, where they belong to the fourth beast, one of those from whom John's is constructed. But they are more: they wear diadems, as they do not in Daniel. There is a suggestion of power about them, they should be functional in the total conception. In chapter 17 John sees the opulent evil woman, the 'great harlot' Babylon, who represents the city of Rome. She rides the imperial Beast over a watery wilderness. The passage is leading up to Babylon's fall, in other words the ruin of Rome. The expository angel speaks:

12. 'The ten horns that you saw are ten kings who have not yet received royal power, but they are to receive authority as kings for one hour, together with the beast.

13. These are of one mind and give over their power and authority to the beast;

14. they will make war on the Lamb, and the Lamb will conquer them, for he is Lord of lords and King of kings, and those with him are called and chosen and faithful.'

15. And he said to me, 'The waters that you saw, where the harlot is seated, are peoples and multitudes and nations and tongues.

16. And the ten horns that you saw, they and the beast will hate the harlot; they will make her desolate and naked, and devour her flesh and burn her up with fire.'

Some commentators have argued that John is talking about events expected soon. Nero has survived, he is in Parthia, and he will reappear to wreak vengeance on the city that turned against him; the ten 'kings' are Parthian satraps or regional governors, who will supply him with forces. The theory is open to at least two objections. It implies that the Beast in this passage is specifically and personally Nero, and that John believes in his literal survival and the myth of his return. It also implies that the prediction is totally wrong, since none of this materialized. I think better of John on both counts.

His prophecy is interesting because it is not obvious. An anti-Roman writer might well have fantasized about Rome falling to a foreign invader. That is what we would expect here, in view of the precedent in Isaiah, the downfall of the original Babylon before the Persian attack. John imagines no such thing. He is right, it never happened. The angel indicates a more complex process. The city's ruin is to come from within the Empire and to be partly the work of royal upstarts associated with it.

If anything is being forecast, it belongs to the fifth century, when the Empire was disintegrating in western Europe and Africa, and Rome itself finally met with catastrophe. That scene can still be within John's purview because it concerns the imperial Beast, and the passage does have points of correspondence to it. Barbarians were settling in the Empire and carving out territories under their leaders, at first more or less by agreement and as nominal supporters or allies rather than conquerors. There would be no sense in trying to make a list of ten, because the round number is taken from Daniel, but the development was real. Alaric, king of the Visigoths, was given a provincial governorship by Arcadius, the emperor ruling in the east. In 401 he moved into Italy and allied himself with the western emperor, Honorius. His successors were to occupy part of Gaul, at first by agreement. Gaiseric, king of the Vandals, was invited into North Africa by the governor there. He crossed from Spain in 429 and founded a domain of his own, with a capital at Carthage. The Anglo-Saxons entered Britain from the continent as auxiliary troops, in the service of a regime that was independent but still within the imperial orbit; they were allotted land, and legend names a chief, Hengist, as the first king of Kent.

'Making war on the Lamb' is an extreme expression. Most of the barbarians were Christian, after their fashion. However, the

Visigoths and Vandals were Arian heretics, denying Christ's full divinity, and while Alaric did not persecute the orthodox masses, Gaiseric did. As for the Woden-worshipping Anglo-Saxons, they trampled on British Christianity wherever they went.

These rulers pursued their interests in different ways. Half in and half out of the system, they sometimes propped it up, sometimes followed their own bent. The most important of them turned against the imperial city. Alaric broke with Honorius, besieged and captured Rome in 410, and allowed his troops to pillage it for six days. The unprecedented disaster was an appalling shock, as Augustine testifies in *The City of God*. It was not the last. Gaiseric, who had built up a powerful navy, sailed across from Africa and did likewise in 455. This time the sack of Rome continued for fourteen days, and the Vandal king carried off the empress. Neither the city nor the western Empire recovered. But John's victory of the Lamb is more than rhetoric. Towards the close of the fifth century the Frankish king Clovis was converted to orthodox Christianity and wrested a large part of Gaul from the Arian Visigoths. Soon Roman and Celtic missionaries Christianized the Anglo-Saxons. Heresy and heathenism both faded.

So here again, the case for prevision is arguable. However, this is the last instance. When 'Babylon' has fallen and been mourned by merchants and others who did well out of her, Revelation still has some way to go. After a further conflict in an indefinite future, the Beast and the False Prophet are cast into a lake of fire. Chapter 20 begins with the imprisonment of Satan himself, which, for some reason, has to be temporary. The martyrs, with other faithful Christians, rise from the dead and reign blessedly with Christ for a thousand years. Whether or not John is conscious of it, this is another proof that his visions imply a long lapse of time before the end, long enough for a vast expansion of the Church. Without that, his eventual kingdom of the saints would be impossible – there would be too few. After the thousand years, Satan is released and attempts another assault, but is thrown into the lake of fire where the Beast and False Prophet already are. The rest of the dead are raised and the Last Judgement ensues. John concludes with a world-renewal, centred on a resplendent New Jerusalem.

While much of this last part is eloquent, it has no predictions of the sort that can be checked. A school of thought in the early Church took the thousand-year reign of Christ literally, as a kind of utopia that will flourish in the last days. They had some support from Jewish speculation about the Messiah and his kingdom. This 'Millenarian' reading did not meet with the Church's approval and delayed the admission of Revelation to the canon of scripture. When it was finally included, as the last book of the New Testament, the millennium had to be explained differently. Augustine gives an explanation in *The City of God*, XX:7–9. I don't understand it; others may. The Millenarian reading of this passage seems the natural one. The word 'millennium' is allowed this sense in the *Concise Oxford Dictionary*.

Revelation is an extraordinary work, by an extraordinary author. He says he is writing of 'what is and what is to take place hereafter'. The acceptance of his book as inspired scripture has been responsible for the many attempts to find predictions in it. Since some of his imagery makes sense in terms of his own time, 'what is', it is tempting to look for fulfilments in 'what is to take place hereafter'. Most such efforts fail to match historical realities to his words, not because his predictions are wrong, but because, most of the time, he is not really trying to predict. He is weaving myths of the future rather than narratives of it. But in chapters 13 and 17, about the Empire and city of Rome, he does predict and with success ... or so it appears. The multiple aptitude of his famous Number is fascinating on any showing. In these exceptional chapters, a future that can be verified does seem to break in on him. The parallel with another biblical exception, the fourth Servant Oracle in Isaiah, should not be overlooked.

Chapter Five

Merlin

After John's Apocalypse, further Christian prophecy might have seemed anticlimactic. It happened all the same, in a none too creditable way, through a fresh rehandling of the Sibylline texts. Jews had already circulated their pseudo-Sibylline matter, purporting to show that pagans had acknowledged the true God, confirmed the Old Testament and foretold the Messiah. That process was still going on during the first century of the Christian era and, to a slight extent, later, but after the failed uprising of 132, the rabbis refused to countenance it and it dwindled away.

Christians, however, began to revise the Jewish Sibylline matter itself, adding and changing in the interests of their own beliefs and inserting references to Nero and Antichrist. Several Fathers of the Church imagined the results to be authentic and ancient, and claimed the Erythraean Sibyl as an inspired prophetess, even an honorary Christian. That is why she is cited as predicting doomsday in the medieval hymn *Dies Irae*, familiar from Verdi's *Requiem*, and why Michelangelo portrays her in the Sistine Chapel. St Augustine, whose works were to guide Christian thinking for a long time, was more cautious. In *The City of God*, completed in 427, he approves a prophecy of Christ ascribed to the Sibyl and gives a Latin translation. Otherwise he is rather negative, merely observing that the Sibyl has things to say elsewhere against paganism and is therefore on the side of truth.

Christians produced two original works in the Sibylline manner. Both were speculations about the end of the world, but they gave it a new prelude. The first was called the *Tiburtina*, after one of the more obscure classical Sibyls. The other, attributed to a fourth-century bishop named Methodius, was actually written much later and in response to the rise of Islam. Both, at least in their final form, introduce a new character. Unwilling to picture humanity petering out, the authors foretell a Last Emperor who will wind up history in a sunset glory. 'Methodius' imagines him coming back from apparent death – possibly a first hint towards motifs such as the return of King Arthur. The Last Emperor will reign in peace and prosperity, uniting the civilized world, and during his time Christianity will triumph and many heathens and Jews will be converted. His Empire will survive barbarian irruptions, but when he judges that his work is complete, he will abdicate in Jerusalem. Then Antichrist will be manifested, bringing tribulation and persecution. All will end with the Second Coming of Christ.

These effusions were taken seriously during the early crusades. More than one crusading leader was cast briefly as the Last Emperor. A very minor one, Emico of Leningen, cast himself in that role. Apart from the imperial daydream, there was nothing very novel here, and the orientation was wholly towards the world's end. It is often stated that expectation of that event caused excitement in the year 1000. However, there is no evidence that there was a major scare.

Prophecy in general was discouraged by an obstacle that Augustine had put in the way, and in *The City of God* he reveals his dislike of it. He stresses the divine inspiration of scripture and quotes the Old Testament texts believed to foreshadow Christ. In other areas he is more than doubtful, not because he denies that precognition is possible, but because he mistrusts its source. While strongly and rationally opposed to astrology, he admits that astrologers' forecasts are sometimes right, but he explains this fact by a pronouncement calculated to deter prophets. Devils, he says, can have some knowledge of things to come, and they can impart this knowledge to astrologers, so that astrology seems to work and the credulous are led astray. The same condemnation applies to any predictions that are not from God.

Nevertheless, in the twelfth century, prophecy exploded. The explosion accompanied the birth of one of the great themes of European literature, and this happened when it did because of a distinctive milieu. The phenomenon had its roots among the Welsh, a Celtic people close to the edges of Christendom. Their ancestors had shared in the early Christianity of the British Isles, and the young Celtic Church was different – not heretical, not split off from the main body, but different.

It was formed around communities rather than bishoprics, and it was less hierarchical and less authoritarian. The Irish, the most learned nation of western Europe, had books that were suppressed on the continent. There was a clear divergence of attitude. In most of the Roman Empire Christians had been persecuted by pagan authorities urged on by pagan priesthoods, so that the gods and goddesses of the old order were seen as demons, with a mythology that was a mass of lies. But in Britain Christians were few and martyrdoms were rare, while Ireland was outside the Empire and was not involved. Celtic Christians were less disposed to turn their backs on the pagan past and were less conscious of evil powers. Gods and goddesses had to be demoted, but they could survive disguised as kings and queens and enchanters and fairy-folk, in a mythology that was not afraid to acknowledge them. They could be portrayed speaking reverently of Christ, even being baptized, without any outright transformation. The pagan Celts had had their druids, a shamanic order of priests and magicians and healers, with cosmic lore, teachings about the afterlife and the otherworld, rituals and ceremonies. Although the druids faded out, the Welsh bards and their Irish equivalents were, to some extent, the druids' heirs. By the twelfth century religious conformity had taken hold, yet something of the old attitudes and something of the mythology survived. There was still a difference.

Merlin is usually pictured as King Arthur's court wizard. However, he makes his literary début as a prophet, and he is still a prophet in Arthurian romance, although he has other functions. He appears first with his familiar name in the Latin writings of Geoffrey of Monmouth, a cleric from Wales who was teaching at Oxford from 1129 to 1151. Geoffrey's best-known work is *The*

History of the Kings of Britain, in which we meet Arthur as well as Merlin; of this, more in a moment. An earlier publication of his concerns Merlin only and purports to give his prophecies.

This work draws on Welsh traditions. The Welsh told of two seers in ancestral times. The earlier, named Ambrosius, lived in the fifth century AD, and as a boy, according to legend, he astonished a British king by a display of paranormal powers. The other – with slightly more historical solidity – was named Lailoken and lived towards the end of the sixth century in Cumbria. Driven out of his mind by a vision, he wandered in southern Scotland as an inspired madman, gifted or afflicted with second-sight. Welsh poets gave Lailoken the alternative style 'Myrddin' and attributed prophecies to him. 'Merlin' is Geoffrey's adaptation of 'Myrddin'. In his writings, he blends the two seers into one, putting Merlin in the fifth century and crediting him with Ambrosius's feats, describing him, in fact, as 'Merlin also called Ambrosius'. Yet the gap of time between the two is so wide that they cannot actually have been the same person.

There is evident confusion here, but there are also clues pointing to an explanation. A Welsh text says that before Britain was populated, its name was Myrddin's Precinct. If the island had no human inhabitants, this original Myrddin must have been a mythic being, a god. One conjecture is that he was a god of inspiration with an oracle in southwest Wales, where Merlin is supposed to have come from; 'Myrddin' is connected etymologically with 'Carmarthen'. Any human under the god's influence would have been an inspired person, a Myrddin-man or -woman, or simply a Myrddin. Tradition could have told of several, with the northerner Lailoken counted as one. Geoffrey, not understanding, may have thought that the inspired Ambrosius in the fifth century, another Myrddin, was the same, and combined the two into a single character.

Geoffrey shows some awareness that a Myrddin-Ambrosius in the fifth century, an 'original' Merlin, would have been a transitional figure. C.S. Lewis made the point. He would have been a druid after his fashion yet also a Christian after his fashion, in a Celtic world where distinctions were not as clear-cut as they became later. When Geoffrey introduces his character he is vaguely conscious of a background divinity or sub-divinity. Merlin speaks of a spirit that teaches him and must not be invoked frivolously.

Before Geoffrey the most famous Welsh prophecy was about a national revival or rather *revanche*. The Welsh were a remnant of the British Celts who had once occupied England as well, but had been overrun and absorbed, sometimes dispossessed, by the Anglo-Saxon settlers. The fifth-century Ambrosius is quoted as foretelling the Britons' collapse but also a triumphant counter-attack. A poem called the *Armes Prydein* ('Omen of Britain'), composed about 930, predicts a broad-based Celtic resurgence that will drive out the conquerors. Myrddin, whoever is meant in this context, is quoted in support of this. The hope was soon proved to be illusory. The English king Athelstan (*c*.895–939) took on the Welsh and their allies and defeated them all.

In 1134 or 1135 Geoffrey produced a long series of Prophecies that he claimed were Merlin's, using his own Latinization of 'Myrddin'. He gave them to the public as translated from Welsh, but he did not stop there. Wanting to give his prophet historical substance, he wove him together with his Prophecies into his larger work, *The History of the Kings of Britain*. He had started this before publishing the Prophecies and finished it in the later 1130s; it was destined to be one of the most important books of the Middle Ages. It purported to be an account of the Britons, ancestors of the Welsh, and their past glories under a long series of monarchs before the Anglo-Saxons, ancestors of the English, moved in from overseas and gradually dominated what is now England.

Geoffrey begins his *History* somewhere about 1100BC, by expanding a Welsh legend of a Trojan prince named Brutus, who brought a party of Trojan followers to this island, then called Albion. It was renamed 'Britain' after Brutus, and he became its first king, his successors reigning until the coming of the Romans. Most of the monarchs in Geoffrey's narrative are fictitious, although a few are based on history in a loose way. The Roman phase is reduced to an ill-defined protectorate, with the line of kings going on.

Geoffrey's build-up to Merlin and Arthur, whose reign is the climax of the book, follows Britain's separation from Rome about AD410. He relates that a noble, Vortigern, seized power and drove the two rightful princes into exile. One of them was Aurelius, the other was Uther, who was to be the father of Arthur. Vortigern allowed heathen Saxons to settle in the country, at first as auxiliary troops. Many more came in after the first wave, and they got out of hand and ravaged large parts of Britain. Vortigern fled to Snowdonia in northwest Wales and tried to build himself a stronghold, but it kept collapsing. His soothsayers told him that he must find a boy without a father, kill him and sprinkle his blood on the foundations. The young Merlin was discovered at Carmarthen, and it transpired that his mother had been impregnated by a spiritual being, so that he had no father humanly speaking. Brought to the building site, he said the foundations were undermined by a subterranean pool with two dragons in it. The pool was uncovered, Vortigern had it drained, and the dragons emerged from hiding. One was red, one white. They began to fight. The king asked for an explanation, and Merlin summoned up his prophetic spirit and began to speak.

The red dragon, he announced, stood for the Britons, the white one stood for the Saxons. He then went on to utter his Prophecies, and this is where Geoffrey fits them into the story, with some additions. Afterwards Vortigern asked about his own fate, and Merlin told him that the two princes were returning and would probably kill him. They did return and the usurper was slain. Aurelius became king, and during his reign, Merlin grew up rapidly and performed further feats. A Saxon poisoned the king, and Uther succeeded him. Between them the brothers managed to contain the Saxons, although not to subdue them completely or decisively.

Among the guests at a royal banquet in London was Gorlois, the Duke of Cornwall, with his beautiful wife Ygerna. Uther was seized with desire for her, and Gorlois withdrew from the court and shut Ygerna away in his fortress at Tintagel on the Cornish coast. Merlin, however, used magic to make Uther an exact replica of her husband, so that he had no difficulty in gaining access to her. Her real husband, Gorlois, had just died in battle, so Uther was able to return to his true likeness and make Ygerna his queen. The son who resulted from this exploit was Arthur.

The *History* goes on to establish the main pattern of Arthur's reign. After Uther's early death, says Geoffrey, the young king routed and dispersed the Saxons, married Guinevere, ruled with great popularity and prosperity, and founded a famous order of knighthood. He conquered various countries. After about twenty-five years his nephew Modred attempted to overthrow him. In a final battle Arthur was grievously wounded. Geoffrey makes it 'mortally', but is silent about his dying and indeed about what happened to him. He later wrote a narrative poem, *The Life of Merlin*, tracing the prophet's career further, and in this he reverted to Arthur's passing, but still left room for uncertainty.

This story of post-Roman Britain made Arthur a quasi-historical sovereign with a magnificent entourage and a triumphant reign. It supplied a frame, not only for Merlin, but for the whole cycle of romance that followed. Historically, it was not quite baseless. The Anglo-Saxons did settle in Britain during the fifth century. When they grew in numbers and expanded their holdings, the Britons, or some of them, resisted, although the extent and effectiveness of their struggle are matters of debate. A few of Geoffrey's characters have a hazy reality. Arthur himself is a hero of early poetry and storytelling in the more Celtic parts of the country, especially Wales. He is glimpsed in various contexts as a war-leader against the Saxons, as an ill-defined 'king' and as the lord of a fabulous domain that is sometimes close to being sheer fairyland. The legends probably derive from a real person in the fifth century, maybe more than one. But on any showing, Geoffrey's creation of a mighty ruler out of scanty materials was a brilliant achievement, and so was his creation of Merlin.

We must now take a step back to the encounter with Vortigern at the pool, and consider the seer's actual message. Merlin submits to his controlling spirit and pours out the Prophecies compiled or concocted by Geoffrey. A few of them echo genuine Welsh matter, but they seem to be mainly his own invention. Merlin goes on and on, for fourteen pages in a standard translation. Lamenting the Saxon invasion, he promises that 'the Boar of Cornwall' will bring relief. Here is the first announcement of Arthur, who, at this point in the *History*, is to appear fairly soon but not quite yet. Merlin foretells his victories and lasting fame, and says his end will be shrouded in mystery. This is prophecy-after-the-event, because, from Geoffrey's standpoint, Arthur is long past. As we read on, we realize that that description applies further, but not throughout.

The Prophecies fall into two parts. In the first portion, Geoffrey is making Merlin give riddling predictions of events that have already happened, or, to be precise, he is making Merlin spin riddles that are usually obscure but sometimes fit actual events, so that these predictions have been 'fulfilled'. A reader who supposed the Prophecies to be genuine fifth-century work would conclude that Merlin did have knowledge of the future, and many readers were naïve enough to think so. The latest of the pseudo-predictions concern 'the Lion of Justice'. This was a sobriquet of King Henry I, and when Merlin says the Lion's cubs 'shall be transformed into salt water fishes', he refers to a shipwreck in 1120 when the king's son and many of his companions were drowned. Reaching the true time of composition, we enter the second part of the Prophecies, although with nothing in the text to show it. Henceforth Geoffrey is making Merlin foreshadow events that are future for himself and therefore unknown to him. We might expect some caution, but not at all – the series continues for much longer, getting more and more remote from any credible reality.

The only prediction that scores in plain terms is adapted from the prophecies of Celtic recovery.

The mountains of Armorica shall erupt and Armorica itself shall be crowned with Brutus' diadem. Kambria shall be filled with joy and the Cornish oaks shall flourish. The island shall be called by the name of Brutus and the title given to it by the foreigners shall be done away with.

Armorica is the ancient name for the northwest corner of France, which was colonized by Britons in the post-Roman period and became Little Britain or Brittany, as it still is. Merlin is foretelling a combined resurgence of Celtic lands in the west. The prophecy had a partial fulfilment in 1603, when James Stuart became king of England as well as Scotland and the term 'Britain' came back into use for the whole island. However, the term 'England', Angle-land, was not done away with.

That is about the best Geoffrey can do. The Brutus item is embedded in fantasies. A few of the Prophecies are topographic – the Thames will surround London on all sides, and the English Channel will become so narrow that people will converse across it – but between these two predictions, which are at least explicit, if their fulfilment is difficult to picture, is the following:

> The Hedgehog will hide its apples inside Winchester and will construct hidden passages under the earth.

This Hedgehog will also build a palace, and wall it round with six hundred towers.

As Merlin continues he introduces more symbolic animals – a heron, another boar, a fox, a wolf, a bear, a lion, an ox, an adder. . . . Here is a prediction with several of the animals gathered together:

> The Fox will come down from the mountains and will metamorphose itself into a Wolf. Under the pretence of holding a conference with the Boar, it will approach that animal craftily and eat it up. Then the Fox will change itself into a Boar and stand waiting for its brothers, pretending that it, too, has lost some of its members. As soon as they come it will kill them with its tusk without a moment's delay and then have itself crowned with a Lion's head.

There are more dragons, and a giant or two. Here is one of the latter:

A Giant, snow-white in colour and gleaming bright, will beget a people which is radiant.

And more about a lion:

A man shall come with a drum and a lute and he will soothe the Lion's savageness. The various people in the kingdom will be pacified as a result, and they will encourage the Lion to take the saucer of medicine.

The actions and interactions of these characters drift into a future that is undefined. Some of the prognostications look as if they might make sense, rather as a political cartoon makes sense, and perhaps in Geoffrey's mind they do, but the reader seldom gets a key. Last comes an upheaval in the sky, with planets and constellations in chaos. Floods and storms ensue, and the Prophecies abruptly end. Merlin has been saying all this to Vortigern and his retinue. When the king enquires about his own destiny, he gives the ominous answer already mentioned, with another reference to Arthur as the Boar of Cornwall.

What is Geoffrey doing in these fourteen pages? There are, of course, unknown factors. More material than is now apparent, such as lost manuscripts and oral bardic traditions, may have been present in the background, and certainly no criticism of Geoffrey can annihilate Merlin. What we actually have, however, is a literary *tour de force* based on him. It may seem odd that Geoffrey should have gone to such prodigious trouble. Why compose this farrago, and, what is more, why force it in as a digression? The poet Wace, who popularized the *History* in a French version, left out the Prophecies because they baffled him. But whatever Geoffrey's original purpose was in writing them, he puts them into the book to build up Merlin for the role he is to play later as a kind of magical sponsor of Arthur. The prophecies-after-the-event in the first part gave him credentials. If he foretold Henry I, for instance, he must have been a true and inspired seer. That being so, the rest must command respect.

So far as can be made out, most of the Prophecies are not

prophecies at all. They are inventions by Geoffrey, and this complex exercise is a mystification. He reckons that by producing something very novel and very long, with a few valid 'predictions' to look good and a mass of inscrutable ones to be argued over, he can make Merlin into a unique figure, a great and eloquent British mage. There is nothing like the Prophecies in secular literature before him; nothing on such a scale or with such a wealth of fancy. He was more spectacularly right in his calculation than he had any reason to expect. The irony is that this author, who was not a prophet himself and never pretended to be, had as powerful an impact on prophecy as any individual after the passing of the biblical era.

With Geoffrey's framework in place and an influx of traditions from other sources, Arthur became the centre of a vast body of romance. Camelot and the Round Table knighthood; the love stories of Lancelot and Guinevere, Tristan and Isolde; the Quest for the Grail – these themes and many more took shape in most of the languages of Europe. Merlin himself proved too fascinating to leave alone. Geoffrey had credited him with such feats as transferring Stonehenge from an original location in Ireland. In the *History*, his stratagem for Arthur's conception is the reader's last glimpse of him, yet he has already given the reign a magical aura. Arthurian romancers brought him into the reign itself, establishing the kingdom, setting up the Round Table, obtaining Excalibur and warning Arthur against potential trouble, ineffectually in the case of Guinevere. Thanks largely to Merlin's expanded role, the Arthurian Britain of medieval romance became a chivalric utopia, and for a while the reign was imagined as a golden age, in intention if not always in practice.

Merlin continued to have a distinctive fame of his own, based on Geoffrey's account of him, which was generally believed. His Prophecies often looked as if they meant something – they were so curiously specific – and they attracted readers and interpreters. A question arose. Could Christians study them with a clear conscience? Merlin was plainly not inspired by God, and if Augustine was right, he might have been sinister, a sorcerer, and the spirit that spoke through him could have been a devil. An answer came from the learned Gerald of Wales, often called Giraldus Cambrensis (*c.*1147–1223). Whatever the case might be with other nations, the Welsh were special. They had a prophetic tradition that was neither divine nor diabolic. It flourished in its own right and was wholly legitimate. Fair enough, in view of the background in Celtic Christianity, with its less black-and-white attitudes. Gerald pressed his point further with an ingenious argument. Many people in Wales possessed the gift – he believed, very plausibly, that there were two Merlins – and they were perfectly innocent, the reason being that the Welsh were descended from the Trojans, as Geoffrey made plain. Troy had its seers who were not diabolic in the least and who were vindicated by events. Cassandra, for instance, correctly foretold the city's fall.

Justifications such as Gerald's and the sheer impetus of Geoffrey's work had two momentous effects. First, prophecy by non-divine inspiration began to be acceptable. Augustine's anathema ceased to hold the field undisputed. It was destined to revive, with bitter results, but it was in abeyance for the moment. Some authors remained dubious about Merlin and made out that his mysterious father was a devil, but they allowed that his inherited supernatural gifts were sanitized by his mother's virtue. Second – and this was still more important – Geoffrey, through Merlin, extended prophecy's range and subject matter. Hitherto, Christians such as Pseudo-Methodius had confined themselves to religious topics and a limited area of speculation, the prelude to the end of the world. They concerned themselves with the Last Emperor, Antichrist, the final persecution and the Second Coming. Geoffrey's Merlin keeps clear of these mysteries. He is talking (so far as his images can be deciphered) about prominent people, conflicts, public events and natural disasters. He has no time-scale and at the end he simply breaks off. With this famous precedent it became possible to do likewise: to predict anything at any time, either by 'interpreting' Merlin or independently, without worrying about the end of the world.

Within less than a decade, Abbot Suger of St Denis (1081–1151) revealed his faith in the British seer by praising him for his accuracy about Henry I. It seems not to have occurred to him that this could be prophecy-after-the-event, as of course it was. When Geoffrey was dead and could no longer be consulted, the Prophecies were copied and passed round, sometimes with notes by other hands. This might never have happened if the Arthurian legend as a whole had not become popular, but it had, and it helped to carry them. Readers tried to apply them to actual events and persons. A commentary was ascribed to a leading scholar of the day, Alanus de Insulis. It was not by him, but it was a work such as he might have written. The Prophecies were translated from Geoffrey's Latin, not only into Welsh but also into French, Dutch and other languages. In Italy, Merlin was put on a level with the Sibyl and even Isaiah. French and Spanish writers produced prophecies of their own under his name.

His exponents seem to have assumed that if they could not make much sense of him, it was their own fault rather than his. François Rabelais was less respectful. In *Gargantua* (1534) work-men who are digging foundations for a building unearth a bronze plate with a long rigmarole in verse engraved on it. This darkly foretells a conflict, violence done to 'the globe' and eventual peace. One character reads it and detects a religious message. Another character dissents.

> The style is like Merlin the Prophet. You can read all the allegorical and serious meanings into it that you like, and dream on about it, you and all the world, as much as ever you will . . .

His own explanation is that the verses give a riddling account of a game of tennis, the globe being the much-battered ball.

People had been 'dreaming' thus for a long time, and even in the Renaissance some continued to dream, or encouraged it in others. Edmund Spenser's allegorical poem *The Faerie Queene* (1590–96) brought Merlin into its narrative and gave him a new vogue in England. More prophecies were fathered on him, some of them in rhymed English verse, ostensibly translated. Shakespeare invented one in *King Lear* (1604–5) as a joke. Another concerned a rock off the Cornish coast at Mousehole, named after the prophet.

There shall land on the rock of Merlin
Those who shall burn Paul, Penzance and Newlyn.

A version in Cornish is at least closer to the language Merlin would have spoken. The prophecy was 'fulfilled' in 1595 when Spanish raiders came ashore at Mousehole and set fire to several villages. But while the verse is on record soon after the raid, it cannot be proved to have been current before then. The new interest was kept alive well into the seventeenth century by two dramatists, William Rowley and Thomas Heywood. I have seen some of their fictions reprinted, in all seriousness, in a book published in 1969. An astrologer, William Lilly (1602–81), thought the mantle worth donning and wrote under the pseudonym Merlinus Anglicus Junior.

These fantasies and fabrications cease to be interesting. Geoffrey's achievement, memorable as it was, did much to open the way for characters such as Lilly, and for the endless procession of soothsayers, cranks and professional psychics in later times. But if we go back to the twelfth century and look in a different direction, we find something very interesting indeed.

Chapter Six

The Calabrian Abbot

Since Geoffrey of Monmouth's *History* was widely thought to be factual, at least in substance, and the Prophecies of Merlin were taken to be a seer's inspired utterances, he put prophecy on the map, so to speak, and enabled it, for the first time in Christendom, to range freely over future events. Meanwhile, prophecy resurfaced within the Church. Although a cleric himself, Geoffrey was seldom much concerned in his writings with ecclesiastical or theological matters. The new prophets were deeply concerned, however. Like Geoffrey, they shifted the focus to happenings nearer than the Last Days. The Merlin phenomenon was not directly responsible, but it helped to form a receptive public, with far-reaching results. Soon it was involved itself.

The ground-breaking prophetic author was a contemporary of Geoffrey's, St Hildegard of Bingen (1098–1179). Brilliant and versatile, she accomplished much in art and music, in science and administration. She also had visions rather like William Blake's. In 1141, she recorded, a shaft of light pierced her mind and heart: 'and suddenly I knew and understood the explanation of the Psalms, the Gospels, and the other Catholic books of the Old and New Testaments, but not the interpretation of the text of the words nor the division of the syllables nor the cases and tenses'. The flash of celestial comprehension taught her what scripture was *about*, without detailed scholarship. Her prophecies, rooted in visions, were chiefly warnings of disaster to which the corruptions of the Church would lead, as they eventually did in the Great Schism and the Protestant breakaway. The respect that Hildegard inspired was due to much more than her revelations, but they were not forgotten.

The genius who followed soon after, and whose influence is still with us, was Joachim of Fiore, sometimes given incorrectly as 'Flora' or 'Floris'. He was born in southern Italy about 1135, and, in his youth, made a pilgrimage to the Holy Land. Entering the Cistercian order, he became abbot of Curazzo in Calabria. Very little is known of him until 1184 when he met Pope Lucius III, who wanted to hear what he had to say about the Sibylline texts. Clearly he had a reputation, and the pope commissioned him to write a book on the relation between the Old Testament and the New.

Joachim was about fifty years old at the time. Ideas began to rush to him in a flood, and when the government of the monastery interfered, he left to stay at another as the guest of its head. For a time he went away to live by himself, but disciples gathered. The pope – Rome was always friendly to Joachim – allowed him to form a congregation of his own, San Giovanni in Fiore, which went on after his death *c*.1202.

During his later years Joachim was busy with further books, predicting a hitherto unimagined future. He had bursts of illumination like Hildegard's. His fame spread. Richard Coeur de Lion, in Sicily on his way to the Third Crusade, invited him over from Calabria. Joachim told the king that he would be victorious, that his arch-enemy, Saladin, would be killed and that Christians would be free to go to the Holy Land. He expounded a passage in Revelation, and they discussed Antichrist, both expecting him soon. As a prognosticator in the short term, Joachim was not outstanding. His achievement was different. In essence, he was a biblical scholar who found hidden meanings by what was thought to be more-than-mortal insight. By developing these he created a prophetic system that has been described as 'the most influential known to Europe until the appearance of Marxism'.

When he interpreted Revelation, it was not in the style of would-be expositors who interpret it out of context. He knew the Bible thoroughly, and he also knew his theology, including, of course, the doctrine of the Trinity – Father, Son and Holy Spirit, three equal Persons in one God. His revolutionary idea was to relate the Trinity to the movement of time. He said that each Person presided over a phase of history, by which he meant chiefly the history of the people to whom God was known – the biblical patriarchs, the Israelites, the Jews and the Christians, up to the Christendom of the twelfth century, with its Catholic Church centred on Rome. In Joachim's world this was the history that mattered, and everything else was related to it, although, to be fair, not much was known beyond the Christian horizon.

Joachim is often said to have divided history into three ages. Strictly speaking 'phases' is a better term, because they overlap with no sharp transitions. 'Age' is a proper word so long as we think of dominant characteristics at one stage or another, rather than rigidly defined periods. According to Joachim there was an Age of the Father, a time of law and fear and obedience, more or less corresponding to the Old Testament. Next came the Age of the Son, a time of grace and faith and the Gospel, which was still going on. Christians in general went no further, but Joachim did. There would be a spell of apostasy and tribulation, after which a Third Age would dawn, the Age of the Holy Spirit.

He was inventive. He made his points with number-symbolism and diagrams. He drew parallels between characters in different parts of the Bible, so that they shed light on each other and on his whole system. Original as all this was and radical in its implications, he was not mounting a direct challenge to the Church. Christ, the Son, had founded it and its claims were valid but, in their present form, only until the end of the present age. It would go on, but transformed. The popes were the successors of Peter as they said, but the Third Age would be more expressive of John, the John of the Gospel and Epistles. New religious orders, free from the taint of power and wealth, would lead the way into it. Hierarchies would vanish and be replaced by communities. It would be a time of contemplative wisdom, of love and peace and enlightenment for all.

The abbot was controversial and became more so. Opponents called him a heretic and insinuated that he split up the Trinity into three gods. On the other hand, there was talk of his canonization.

Dante puts him in Paradise among the wisest, calling him 'Joachim, spirit-fired, and prophet true' (*Paradiso* XII:141), and probably derives imagery from his diagrams. After Joachim's death, however, admirers began pushing his teaching to extremes. They took a hostile line on the papacy, which he had definitely pictured as continuing in the Third Age, in however changed a form. They invented prophecies which they pretended were his, some of which became better known than the genuine ones. Unfortunately, he had given them an excuse for extremism. His belief that major events were imminent, as shown in his assertion to Richard that Antichrist was on the doorstep, had led him to predict the end of the present age in 1260. The date created an atmosphere of urgency and immediacy.

Meanwhile, the Franciscans were involved. St Francis founded his order in 1210, and people soon began to see it as foreshadowing the fulfilment of Joachim's prophecies. Francis's simplicity, humility, dedication to poverty and love towards all creatures seemed to be pointing the way. He may have been influenced indirectly by remnants of Celtic Christianity, transmitted from Irish monks who had spread through Germany and Switzerland. Indeed, Joachim's Third Age itself recalls Celtic ways in some respects, although he can hardly have known. The early Franciscans could easily be seen as one of the companies of devoted men who were to inaugurate the change.

After Francis's death in 1226, his successor as head of the order, Brother Elias, virtually abandoned the founder's ideals. A dissentient party, the Spiritual Franciscans, insisted on poverty and put Francis on a level with Christ as the initiator of the Age of the Spirit. In 1254 a Franciscan named Gerard of Borgo San Donnino produced a book called the 'Eternal Evangel' or 'Everlasting Gospel' (the reference is to Revelation 14:6), which he said was to supersede the Bible and be the scripture of the Third Age now dawning. No complete copy exists, but it appears that he combined three of Joachim's treatises and added an introduction of his own to put them in a proper light. The book was condemned, partly on the grounds that it made outrageous claims for the Franciscans, and it is described as diabolical in a classic of

French literature, the *Roman de la Rose*. Joachim had never so much as hinted at the Bible becoming obsolete. In time to come, however, the extreme views in the 'Eternal Evangel' were frequently assumed to be his.

The crucial year 1260 went by, and nothing, apparently, had happened. A few, however, believed that the initiator of the Third Age was present and active in an unexpected form. Guglielma of Milan was revered in her circle as the Holy Spirit incarnate. As the Son had become a man to establish the Second Age, so the Holy Spirit had become a woman to establish the Third. Guglielma went far beyond Gerard. The male papacy was finished, and one of her female disciples would be pope with women cardinals and heal all religious divisions, even winning over the Jews and Saracens. New Gospels would be written. Guglielma was no obscure eccentric, and some of her followers were educated and wealthy, with a stake in society. She died in 1282, and the group survived for a while, with gatherings around her tomb. In 1300 it fell under a ban, and Inquisitors burned her bones to extinguish any hopes of a resurrection.

All was not over. Despite the scandal of the Eternal Evangel and the inadmissibility of the Milanese avatar, mainstream Joachimism did not expire, and it grew more like an ideology, able to surmount the absence of instant change. It was developed by theorists who may be called Joachites. The approach to the Third Age became more complicated, a semi-political prelude. It introduced two new prophetic figures, the Angelic Pope and the Second Charlemagne.

The Angelic Pope is puzzling. He appears first in an independent prophecy that was current in the middle years of the thirteenth century. This is mentioned in 1267 by the Franciscan polymath Roger Bacon (*c.*1220–92), renowned as a pioneer of experimental science and credited (wrongly) with inventing gunpowder. The Angelic Pope was to purge the Church of corruption and internal disputes, and he would win over those outside by his goodness, truth and justice. The schismatic Greeks would return to the Roman fold, the Jews would acknowledge Christ, most of the Tartars would be converted, and the Saracens would fade out. The world would rejoice in a renewal. Bacon speaks of a revelation, not to himself, that this is to happen in his own time.

The Joachites annexed the Angelic papacy to their programme, claiming it would be part of the prelude to the Third Age. In 1294 it suddenly seemed to have been realized. An aged and saintly Neapolitan hermit, Pietro di Morrone, was elected pope virtually by acclamation. He was reluctant in the extreme, but he consented at last, taking the name Celestine V. He rode humbly on an ass, attended by the kings of Naples and Hungary, who were on foot. Public enthusiasm was boundless. It soon turned out that Celestine was totally unequal to the tasks of administration, and that he knew no canon law and not much Latin. After five months of chaos he resigned, and was succeeded by Boniface VIII, who, as a cardinal, had done most to get rid of him. Celestine was not free for long: Boniface put him in prison, where he died in 1296. Dante calls Celestine's abdication 'the great refusal' and places him in a depressing ante-chamber of Hell, not only for deserting his post but for letting in a pontiff whom the poet abhorred.

In spite of the disappointment, his 'brief shining moment' fixed the image of the Angelic Pope in Joachite thinking. Celestine remained the prototype, while Boniface typified the evil forces that opposed his manifestation. When he did come, he would purify the Church and inaugurate the Age of the Holy Spirit. There might even be a whole succession of good pontiffs. Understandably, as time passed, few ventured to salute any actual pope as the Angelic one, although the Renaissance brought some half-hearted guesses. Supporters of Marcellus II, elected in 1555, probably had hopes of him, but he died within weeks and was never proved to be either Angelic or otherwise. After Marcellus, the atmosphere of the Catholic Church was, to put it mildly, unfavourable.

The Second Charlemagne was the Angelic Pope's political counterpart. He, too, had his origins outside Joachimism and further back. The two late Sibylline prophecies, the *Tiburtina* and the one ascribed to Methodius, foretold the Last Emperor, whose reign would be glorious, but he was, precisely, a *Last* Emperor. He would not launch a new era, his regime would come to an end, and Antichrist and the Second Coming would follow. Closer to reality, and more relevant to Joachite hope, was Charlemagne, who united much of Europe and refounded the western Roman Empire on a Christian basis in the year 800. His domain broke up, but a partial Holy Roman Empire flourished throughout the Middle Ages, mainly in Germany and Italy. Its ruler during much of the thirteenth century was the brilliant Frederick II (r.1220–50), the 'wonder of the world', seen by some as a Messiah, by others as Antichrist. After his death he was rumoured to be still alive, sleeping in the Kyffhäuser mountain in central Germany. The folklore image of the sleeper soon grew hazy, and he was more and more identified with the earlier emperor Frederick I, Barbarossa (r.1152–90), a hero in his own right and less controversial. In the end, he was definitely Barbarossa, and there was a prophecy of his return.

Joachites had no great interest in the posthumous Frederick, but his career with its cryptic sequel had caused stirrings and speculations. The idea that the Empire ought to comprise all Christendom was a living doctrine. Dante maintained it strongly. Charlemagne was recalled with nostalgia, and in the fourteenth century Joachites began to talk of a future emperor. There had been a folk-belief in Charlemagne's literal return, anticipating Frederick's, but they did not mean that. They meant a Second Charlemagne, to be crowned by the Angelic Pope. He would be an emperor of comparable but greater achievement, who would unite Christendom, dispel the horrors of the expected time of trouble and usher in the Third Age. The Joachite hope of an earthly 'good time coming', however conceived, appealed to popular imagination and helped to inspire movements of protest and revolt, a very significant development. Prophecies from other sources, including Merlin's, were interwoven with Joachim's. Unwisely, some Joachites tried to cast actual rulers in the imperial role. Arnold of Villanova picked out Frederick of Trinacria, king of Sicily (r.1296–1337), a descendant of Frederick. He urged him to fulfil the prophecy, without success. Since Charlemagne's empire had embraced both Germany and France, it was possible to look for the Second Charlemagne in either country. On the whole it was France that gained ground, and the French king Philip IV (r.1285–1314) was a candidate.

Prophecy had its most public impact in Florence, when the famous Dominican preacher Girolamo Savonarola (1452–98) was thundering at the Florentines' morals. Opinions differ as to whether he should be counted as a Joachite, but he was certainly aware of the Joachite tradition. Claiming to be divinely inspired, he predicted that Charles VIII of France would invade Italy to chastise the peninsula for its sins. Florence already had a special prominence in the Second Charlemagne mythos, and when Charles arrived with an army in August 1494, on his way to conquer the kingdom of Naples, people did not regard him as Savonarola did. He was an unimpressive figure, and the report that he had six toes on each foot was a distraction, but at least his name was Charles. Several French poets exhorted him to fulfil the Joachite programme, and one of them, Guilloche of Bordeaux, said his features agreed with imaginary descriptions of the Second Charlemagne and foretold that he would subjugate Italy, capture Rome, become king of Greece and conquer the Turks.

Savonarola changed his mind and began to regard the French king as a renewer rather than a scourge. This view seemed to be confirmed when Charles departed peacefully in November. There was, alas, no Angelic Pope to give him an imperial crown. Ironically, the pope at this time was Alexander VI, the exceedingly un-angelic Borgia. Savonarola, however, began to talk about the Angelic one and even suggested that he would reign in Florence as a new Rome.

Charles's campaign in Italy was abortive, and he returned to France. Savonarola, still imbued with prophetic fervour, had tried to set up a theocracy in Florence, frowning on art and almost every kind of amusement, but his insistence on his own gift of prophecy led to his excommunication and eventually to his death as a heretic. During the ensuing decades, prophecy of this kind was not silent, but it became less coherent and less interesting. Attempts to enlist the emperor Charles V (r.1516–56) led to

nothing. No one expressly claimed to be the Second Charlemagne until Napoleon did at his coronation, and he was laying
claim to the heritage, not looking to the future.

In this partial politicization, the larger vision of the Age of
the Spirit was not lost. Botticelli's *Nativity*, painted in 1500, has
been called 'one of the greatest documents of Joachimist thought'.
A note by the artist shows that he believed he was living in
the predicted tribulation, and it would give way to joy with the
chaining of the Devil, 'trodden down as in this picture'. The
angels whom he paints in the sky are not appearing to shepherds –
that has already happened – but dancing ecstatically. At the
bottom of the picture is a strange separate landscape, which ought
to be closer than the stable but is farther off, in no spatial relation
to Bethlehem. A small vanquished Devil slinks off, an image that,
as Botticelli's note makes clear, locates this landscape in the future.
Angels embrace humans in a union of Heaven and Earth that is
not yet but is prefigured.

Some turned away from Europe and saw the Third Age in the
opening-up of the world through voyages of discovery and
the consequent spread of the Christian faith – the conversion of
the 'Gentiles'. Columbus collected prophecies, including some
of Joachim's, and believed he was preparing the way for
missionaries who would go all over the globe. It has been inferred
that he saw himself as a sort of Joachite Messiah. Nor was it
forgotten that the abbot laid stress on the role of new religious
orders. His description of one such order was an apt foreshadowing of the Jesuits, in the Society's heroic sixteenth-century youth.
If the opening-up of the world was, indeed, the unfolding of the
Third Age, the worldwide Jesuit missions could be seen, by those
who held this opinion, as fitting in.

Protestants disagreed, although a few were sufficiently interested to make out that the Reformation had ushered in the Age of
the Spirit – a view adapted long afterwards by the philosopher
Hegel.

There is more to be said about the Angelic Pope. He was to be
the last representative of the existing papacy and usher in the new

world, doubtless in concert with the Second Charlemagne. In practice, disillusionment tended to blur the picture. The existing papacy might indeed end soon; on the other hand, it might last for centuries. Prophetic inspiration could still be invoked but not to give positive notice of transition. It could become long term, or, at least, provisionally long term; it could range far enough ahead to avoid discredit through immediate failure.

A new kind of quasi-prophetic exercise was to chart the papacy's future course. Joachim had never practised such anticipation in detail – after all, he had expected the transition soon and not suffered the disillusionments – but medieval artists produced a series of symbolic pictures of future popes, falsely attributed to the abbot himself and entitled *Vaticinia de Summis Pontificibus* ('Prophecies of the Supreme Pontiffs'). The French essayist Montaigne mentions it. A first version consisted of fifteen pictures and was optimistic, leading up to the Angelic one. A second set of fifteen was more gloomy. Finally, a combined edition of thirty was put together with the gloomy set first, so that the series had a happy ending.

The last years of the sixteenth century, when the Age of the Holy Spirit seemed very distant, saw a crop of derivatives. These mostly pretended to be much earlier. Their authors started, rather in the manner of Geoffrey's Merlin, with pseudo-prophecies about popes who had already reigned. The accuracy of these gave a bogus credibility to more obscure matter that really did look ahead and, normally, built up to an Angelic climax.

One such contrivance – at least, that is what it appears to be – remains interesting, and it has stirred up debate at papal elections right into modern times. The *Prophecies of St Malachy* are alleged to be the work of a medieval Irishman, the first to receive a papal canonization. Born in Armagh in 1094, he was baptized Mael Maedoc, which was converted into 'Malachy', the name of a biblical prophet. In 1123 he was elected abbot of Bangor in County Down, and in 1134, after a lengthy dispute, he became archbishop of Armagh. He was a friend of St Bernard of Clairvaux and died there in 1148. Malachy was believed to have a gift of prevision or second-sight. Bernard, who wrote a memoir of him, glances at this but says nothing about the *Prophecies* that circulated under his name more than four centuries later.

It is, in fact, misleading to call them prophecies – a better word, if it were more familiar, might be 'adumbrations' – for the text (there are no pictures) consists of 111 concise Latin phrases or mottoes. These apply to each pope in succession, beginning with Celestine II in 1143, together with a few schismatic antipopes. Each phrase is meant to fit its pope in one way or another, by alluding to his name or place of origin or to his family coat of arms or to some feature of his life or reign. The series extends into the sixteenth century and beyond. It ends with the only piece of connected prose, a brief epilogue about the Last Judgement.

There is no known mention of the *Prophecies* before 1595, when Arnold Wion, a Benedictine historian, referred to them in a survey of Joachite literature. He believed them to be authentic. A few decades after Wion, a Jesuit named Menestrier attacked them on the grounds that they had been faked in 1590 to promote a candidate in a papal election. Cardinal Simoncelli was bishop of Orvieto, his birthplace. The papal motto at that point in the series is *Ex antiquitate urbis*, translatable as 'from the old city', and 'Orvieto', in Latin *Urbevetanum*, means 'old city'. Menestrier claimed that the entire series was composed, with *Ex antiquitate urbis* in the right place, to make it appear that Simoncelli was the prophesied pope. (He was not elected.)

Menestrier offered no solid evidence, and another story has had its advocates: that Malachy wrote the *Prophecies* in Rome in 1140 and gave the manuscript to Innocent II. It vanished into the archives, and nobody took it out until the late sixteenth century. While such things do happen, positive proof would be needed to support this view, and none exists. Menestrier's opinion has prevailed.

One reason is simple. A dating in 1590 fits the Malachy document squarely into the context of the other pseudo-prophecies current about that time. And yet there are queries. The author needs seventy-five mottoes for the seventy-five popes and antipopes up to 1590. Why, having gone to so much trouble to make a slot for Orvieto, should he have bothered to invent a further thirty-six with no relevance to the matter in hand? As camouflage? Perhaps. It is true that the other pseudo-prophets also continue. But their usual purpose is different: to build up to the Angelic Pope at the end, in an indefinite future. Pseudo-Malachy does include him, but indicates nothing special and passes on to five more afterwards. His *Pastor Angelicus* is only one in the series, not its climax and conclusion.

Some of the phrases in the earlier portion fit the pontiffs so well, often so ingeniously, that they would be amazing if Malachy wrote them. His precognition would be unique. The advocates of a 1590 authorship retort that they work because they are hindsight, prophecy-after-the-event. Moreover, we have a tell-tale contrast. The phrases after 1590, which are future-oriented on any showing, don't work nearly as well. For the investigator of prophecy it is these that count and it hardly matters who wrote them. The author was certainly someone with an imagination and an interest in more than a single papal conclave. But if they don't work at all, the *Prophecies of St Malachy* are not prophetic. The first seventy-five can be fully explained as prophecy-after-the-event, the last thirty-six are merely guesses.

Let us see. To get the feel of these things, let us look at some of the earlier batch. The phrase that corresponds to the English pope Adrian IV (r.1154–9) is *De rure albo*, 'from a white country' or 'of the Alban country'. This is apt three times over. He was a native of Albion, to give Britain its ancient name; he was born near St Albans; and he became Cardinal Bishop of Albano. Celestine V (r.1294) has *Ex eremo celsus*, 'elevated from the desert' or 'the lofty one from the desert'. This was the pope who lived austerely as a hermit or eremite in wild country and was thrust into the papal chair with the hopes of the Third Age riding upon him. Benedict XI (r.1303–4) has *Concinionator Patareus*, 'a preacher from Patara'. He was born in Patara and joined the Dominicans, the order of preachers.

Many of the pre-1590 mottoes are equally good. After 1590 the impressive cases are certainly fewer; the mottoes tend to be indeterminate and their application, if any, may be far fetched. But the contrast is not as sharp as critics have claimed. What is especially curious is that after a long stretch with nothing very convincing, the mottoes begin to have at least some aptitude. The really interesting contrast is not so much between pre-1590 and post-1590 as between pre-1800 and post-1800, after which year, in fourteen pontificates, nine of the mottoes may be said to work. Thus:

Aquila rapax – rapacious eagle
Pius VII (r.1800–23): not that Pius was rapacious himself, but much of his reign was overshadowed by a struggle with the French 'Eagle', Napoleon.

De balneis Etruriae – from the baths of Etruria
Gregory XVI (r.1831–46): this pope started his religious career in the Camaldolese order, which was founded at a place called in Latin *Balneum*, in Etruria.

Crux de cruce – a cross from a cross
Pius IX (r.1846–78): the first cross can be construed as symbolic of suffering, the second, as the emblem of the House of Savoy, which struck heavy blows at papal power in the course of uniting Italy.

Lumen in caelo – a light in the sky
Leo XIII (r.1878–1903): his coat of arms showed a comet.

Ignis ardens – burning fire
Pius X (r.1903–14): this pope was canonized, and the phrase could refer to the 'heroic virtue' required in a saint.

Religio depopulata – religion laid waste
Benedict XV (r.1914–22): his reign covered the devastations of the First World War and the Russian Revolution, setting up an anti-religious regime in one-sixth of the world. No such phrase is associated with any other pope. Benedict XV and *Religio depopulata* go together, unequivocally.

Fides intrepida – unshaken faith
Pius XI (r.1922–39): this pope was noted for his courage in denouncing totalitarian systems.

Pastor et nauta – pastor and mariner
John XXIII (r.1958–63): before he was pope he was patriarch of Venice, a city of boats and travel by water.

Flos florum – flower of flowers
Paul VI (r.1963–78): the motto is sufficiently fulfilled by a design of three fleurs-de-lis in his coat of arms.

Most of the phrases are admittedly vague, yet they fit their popes as far as they go, and they could not be switched around. The Angelic Pope, *Pastor Angelicus*, appears in the list at a place between *Fides intrepida* and *Pastor et nauta*, corresponding to Pius XII (r.1939–58). Opinions differ as to his character and policies. The interesting point is that his phrase comes in here, not at the end, and with no Joachite implication of his bringing in a new era. The author may have given up on the papal hope; he simply goes on. The next motto after *Flos florum* is *De medietate lunae*, 'of the half moon', which corresponds to John Paul I (r.1978) and looks as if it ought to refer to his short pontificate, although he survived for a full month. John Paul II (from 1978) has *De labore solis*, 'from the toil of the sun' or perhaps 'of the eclipse of the sun' – unexplained, either way. Next, and last, is *Gloria olivae*, which suggests peace-making, or it might apply to a pope from a branch of the Benedictines called Olivetans.

Then comes the epilogue.

In the final persecution of the Holy Roman Church there will reign Peter the Roman, who will feed his flock among many tribulations; after which the seven-hilled city will be destroyed and the dreadful judge will judge the people.

This paragraph, with its uniquely spelled-out name and apocalypse, is quite unlike the rest. It is not certain that Peter the Roman comes straight after the previous pontiff. He may, he may not. The continuous sequence ends with *Gloria olivae*. This is consistent with the end of the papacy in its present form, and a transition to the Third Age, with an unspecified gap between *Gloria olivae* and Peter the Roman.

'Malachy', whoever he was, is not without interest. It is remarkable that his series stops round about the portentous year 2000, since, on the face of it, he had no way of judging how far it would extend. A result of this chronological feat is that he seems to concur with the American psychic Jeane Dixon, who expected the end of the papacy at about the same time. To envisage total abolition would be to go beyond Joachim. Some, however, might like to think that Guglielma of Milan was on the right track in predicting a transfer from men to women: right in principle, that is, even though her own claims for herself and her followers were misguided, and her extraordinary movement succumbed to persecution.

Having considered these offshoots of Joachim's ideas, we may turn back to recapitulate what he actually said. He foresaw a time of trouble followed by the Third Age, the Age of the Holy Spirit, typified by John rather than Peter and initiated by new religious orders. It would be an age of community rather than hierarchy, and peace, liberty, love and illumination would be universal. Joachim believed that the Church would continue, headed by someone who could still be known as the pope; but it would be changed, changed utterly. His theology drew criticism, yet his main teaching was never declared heretical, although the excesses of some of his followers were. During the Spiritual Franciscan excitement, a Church council in Arles pronounced against Joachimism, but the action was local. It hardly matters that the Joachites' predictions were wrong, and there is no telling whether the prophet himself would have agreed with them. Very probably not.

Despite all aberrations, he achieved one tremendous thing: he gave a place in Christendom for optimism about the earthly future. Previously, Christians had reckoned that while there were obviously good times and bad, this was a fallen world and could never be fundamentally better. Sooner or later God would end it. The righteous would enter into a blissful eternity, which would be quite distinct from this present life. The damned would have no hope at all. Joachim made room for a real change in the existing world. It would be too much to claim that he pioneered the conception of progress. That was not thought of until 600 years later, by the Marquis de Condorcet, whom we shall meet again in a surprising context. What Joachim did was to apply Christian doctrine in a new way to a very old idea: that the world goes through stages. He may not have known the mythological background — some of it he certainly did not know — but, even unconsciously, he gave the old idea a new direction.

The earliest European author to state it is the Greek poet Hesiod, in the eighth century BC, who divided time into five epochs, each characterized by its own human species. First came a golden age with a metaphorically golden race — people who lived good and carefree lives, feeding on the bounty of nature, without sickness or decrepitude. Death held no terrors for them. They are long since gone, but their spirits wander unseen, befriending mortals. Next came a silver race, which was matriarchal. The silver people vanished too. Then Zeus created a bronze race, which fed on meat, used bronze weapons and enjoyed violence. After this he made a better bronze race, which temporarily arrested the downward trend. Its men included the heroes who fought at Troy. Last came the time of the iron race, our own, the basest and most benighted. Hesiod is sorry he has to live in it. The point is that, apart from the one limited reversal, implied by the glories of Homeric legend, these ages and races get successively worse. The iron race itself will deteriorate, and the only good to be hoped for is that Zeus will destroy it. The poet gives no hint of a happier era that might come afterwards.

Hinduism has the same motif: a running-down of the universe is preordained. At the beginning of the cosmic cycle is a golden age known as the Krita Yuga, a very long time ago. All beings were wise, righteous, prosperous and happy, and they fulfilled the laws of their nature and status. The Krita Yuga gave way to the shorter and inferior Treta Yuga, and that to the even shorter and more inferior Dvapara Yuga, and that to the Kali Yuga in which we live (it has nothing to do with the goddess Kali). The Kali Yuga is the shortest and worst. In the epic *Mahabharata* a seer expounds this. He assures his listeners that the Kali Yuga will go on getting more evil and lawless.

The gloom is qualified. Virgil, in his Fourth Eclogue, does what Hesiod does not: he portrays the iron age ending and the golden age coming back, through the advent of the wonderful child. The Hindu seer says that at last a planetary conjunction will create the conditions for the work of a Messiah, Kalki, the final avatar of the god Vishnu; he will close the cycle and, so to speak, wind up the world again, restoring the pristine goodness and peace. In both cases, however, the historical process itself is downward, and it takes a divine intervention, after a series of changes for the worse, to make a difference. No Yuga has a better Yuga following it.

In envisaging a history that not only went in stages but moved forwards and upwards, Joachim echoed the mythologies, yet at the same time he altered them. Given the doctrine of the Trinity, his position was logical. God the Father was expressed in the Old Testament and ancient Israel. God the Son was expressed in the New Testament and the Church. The co-equal Third Person should, therefore, be expressed in a future phase, and since the New Testament was a step forward from the Old, the age of the Holy Spirit could only be another step forward.

Joachim's way of thinking survived, although not chiefly in Christianity. Rome never condemned it and Catholics were free to concur, but Rome never encouraged it either. The popular movements inspired by it petered out. Protestants who saw the Third Age in the Reformation were few. So were the Quakers, who came as near as any group to trying to realize it on their own initiative, in reaction against what Protestantism itself had become.

It was in other settings that Joachim's influence persisted, seldom explicit, yet not unacknowledged. As the grip of organized religion relaxed, new ideologies began to foreshadow a quantum leap to a transformed society and, in various ways, to interpret history as a process in stages leading up to it. The ancient Hesiodic schema revived, but Joachim had reversed it and it stayed reversed. The process was now a hopeful one. In 1972

Professor Roger Garaudy, discussing 'Faith and Revolution', referred to 'the first great revolutionary movements of Europe' as 'all more or less imbued with the ideas of Joachim of Fiore' and spoke of the tradition beginning with him and persisting into the twentieth century in which 'the Kingdom of God is not conceived as another world in space and time, but as a different world, a changed world, a world changed by our own efforts'. That is a bold claim, and it could hardly be sustained by assembling quotations. Nevertheless, Joachim's presence is undoubtedly felt.

The German author Gotthold Lessing (1729–81), a powerful voice of the eighteenth-century Enlightenment, discovered the Joachite extremists and their 'Eternal Evangel'. The extremists, of course, misused Joachim's writings in support of notions, such as the Bible's obsolescence, that went beyond his. Lessing, however, was impressed and picked up the idea of a 'new eternal Gospel'. In an essay *On the Education of the Human Race*, published in 1780, he wrote:

> Perhaps even some of the enthusiasts of the thirteenth and fourteenth centuries had caught a glimpse of a beam of this new eternal Gospel, and only erred in that they predicted its outburst as so near their own time. Perhaps their 'Three Ages of the World' were not so empty a speculation after all, and assuredly they had no contemptible views when they taught that the New Covenant must become as antiquated as the old had been ... Only they were premature. Only they believed that they could make their contemporaries, who had scarcely outgrown their childhood, without enlightenment, without preparation, men worthy of their Third Age.

From Lessing's essay a thread runs to two major movements. One is the pioneer Socialism of Claude Saint-Simon, who was propagating his theories between 1817 and 1825. A disciple, Eugene Rodrigues, wrote a book entitled *Nouveau Christianisme*, which followed on from Saint-Simon and argued that Christianity was evolving and could bring a world-renewal. Rodrigues translated Lessing's essay and appended it to his own work, in which he defines three historical phases, resembling Joachim's. There is a movement from the Law of Fear, to the Law of Grace, to the Law of Love. The time has come, he proclaims, for the Law of Love and the Age of the Holy Spirit. When Lessing drew attention to the Joachites, the public was not ready for such a message; now, says Rodrigues, it is; let us unite to demand a new Christianity.

Saint-Simon had a secretary (though not for long) who founded a movement of his own. This was Auguste Comte (1798–1857), regarded as the founder of sociology, a term he coined. He, too, has three stages of history or, more properly, of human thinking, reflected in society. Admittedly, they are not Joachim's. Humanity is said to have passed from a theological phase to a metaphysical phase, and to be moving into a 'positive' phase when science will reign. Hence the name 'Positivism' for Comte's system. It replaces God with Humanity, the Great Being, as the object of worship. Comte, like Lessing, was aware of the medieval Joachites and praised the abbot as 'the pious Utopist whom Dante installed in his Paradise as endowed with the prophetic spirit'. Like Lessing also, he knew of Joachim's teaching in its distorted 'Eternal Evangel' form.

Comte influenced knowledgeable people in Britain, and made a partial convert of one of the foremost novelists of the day, George Eliot. Her novel *Romola* (1863) does not show any clear trace of Positivism, but it does refer to Joachim and the hopes stemming from him. Set in Florence in the time of Savonarola, it links his campaign of reform with the prophetic tradition – an acute insight on the novelist's part, far ahead of the professional historians. One of her characters says:

The warning is ringing in the ears of all men; and it's no new story; for the Abbot Joachim prophesied of the coming time three hundred years ago, and now Fra Girolamo [Savonarola] has got the message afresh. He has seen it in a vision, even as the prophets of old; he has seen the sword hanging from the sky.

Further on in the story, Charles VIII enters Florence with his army and is hailed as the Second Charlemagne. More interesting still, perhaps, is George Eliot's reference to the Angelic Pope. This is in the Proem at the beginning of the novel, where she imagines a Florentine who 'heard simple folk talk of a Pope Angelico, who was to come by-and-by and bring in a new order of things, to purify the Church from simony, and the lives of the clergy from scandal'. At the end of the Proem she speaks in her own person:

> The sunlight and shadows bring their old beauty . . . and men still yearn for the reign of peace and righteousness. . . . The Pope Angelico is not come yet.

Germany had further contributions to make. The philosopher F.W. Schelling (1775–1854), lecturing in Berlin, talked of an approaching Third Age, an Age of the Spirit, with so much ardour that many of his audience felt as if they were witnessing the birth of a new religion. He expounded the relationship of the Trinity with history, and instanced biblical figures as symbolizing aspects of the three stages. The irony was that he had thought of all this himself, and he was astonished when he found that Joachim had worked it out first. Another philosopher with a glancing relevance is Georg Hegel (1770–1831). In his reflections on the history of Germany, he not only divides it into three stages but also employs Joachim's terminology, although, by dating the Age of the Holy Spirit from the Reformation, he shows plainly that he has something else in mind.

Karl Marx (1818–83) went the same way, but with more extensive results. In building up his own form of Socialism he adapted Hegel's ideas. His stages of history (history in general, not German alone) were distinguished by changing relationships between 'haves' and 'have-nots'. To oversimplify somewhat: in antiquity, patricians and slave-owners oppressed plebeians and slaves; in feudal Europe, lords and guild-masters dominated, while serfs and journeymen were underneath; and then came 'bourgeois' revolutions, which created industrial society, with a small number of capitalists exploiting millions of wage earners. Marx predicted a quantum leap that would change everything. The workers would rise. 'Proletarian' revolutions would dispossess the capitalists and open the way to a classless society, which would be different and permanent because it would have no ruling minority and hence no destabilizing conflicts. Marx, like Comte, acquired an English literary disciple of high standing, although William Morris was more fully committed to Socialism than George Eliot was to Positivism. Morris's fantasy *News from Nowhere* (1890) portrays the happy society after the revolution, and his future might be described as the Age of the Holy Spirit without the Holy Spirit.

The purpose of recalling these cases is not only to note how they resemble each other, but to note how they vary. Repeatedly, someone defines stages of history that lead to a quantum leap into a better one. To that extent Joachim is echoed. However, the scenario changes. The stages are not the same and the leap is not the same. The stages may be spiritual phases or intellectual phases or phases of social polarization. The leap may be to the Age of the Holy Spirit as with Joachim; it may be to something totally other, to a scientific era or a socialist era. What persists is the pattern – Joachim's prophetic mould, not its contents.

The pattern turns up in curious places, as in Ibsen's drama *Emperor and Galilean* (1873), in which Julian the Apostate aspires to found a new world order, a 'third empire'. Paganism had its day; Christianity superseded it; now, in Julian's opinion, the 'new truth' is itself outworn and he wants to supersede that. A more recent instance hardly deserves the respect due to the ideologies, yet it shows the pattern's persistence. I have no idea who first thought of the Age of Aquarius. The notion is astrological. Because of the Earth's oscillation, causing the precession of the equinoxes, the stars are slowly changing position. One result is that in the course of thousands of years the Sun moves into a different sign of the zodiac in spring. Earth is under the influence of whatever sign it is in. The successive astrological stages, each lasting about 2160 years, have long since carried us into the Age of Pisces, the Fishes. That accounts for Christianity, since the Fish is an ancient Christian symbol. The Age of Pisces is just about finished and so is Christianity, which will pass away amid the plaudits of those who accept this view. We are supposed to be moving . . . or to have moved . . . or to be on the verge of moving . . . into the Age of Aquarius, when the Sun will be in that sign in spring. As it happens, it will be something like the Third Age of Joachim, a time of 'increasing harmony, understanding and spiritual growth', according to Eileen Campbell and J.H. Brennan, the authors of *The Aquarian Guide to the New Age*. I mention this theory, not to endorse it, but to show the recurrence of a pattern of thinking or, in the Aquarian case, daydreaming.

With Joachim, prophecy has a new dimension. The seer still offers a vision of the future, but the vision embodies a conception of history and the human condition. This has psychological cogency and appears in various guises, with or without direct influence. It may, therefore, be a genuine insight and correspond to a fruitful way of looking at things. The prophecy may have validity *as* an insight, whether or not it is fulfilled literally, whether or not literal fulfilment is even possible. There is another prophecy of which the same can be said . . .

Chapter Seven

The Return of Arthur

In 1113 nine French canons from Laon travelled through Devon and Cornwall. Their cathedral had burned down, and they were raising money to rebuild it. They brought holy relics and invited the sick to make donations and pray for healing. On the way from Exeter, they were told that they were in the *terra Arturi*, King Arthur's country. In Bodmin the people gathered round, and a man with a withered arm approached. He assured one of the party, who had doubtless been speaking of the journey, that Arthur was alive. The Frenchmen were amused, but bystanders took his side and a fight broke out. For whatever reason, the arm failed to improve. Hermann of Tournai, who records this fracas, remarks that the French have the same problem with Bretons, who also insist that King Arthur has never died. The Bretons were akin to the Cornish and had their own Arthurian traditions.

This incident dates from before Geoffrey of Monmouth's *History*. Hermann is giving us folklore, not literary invention. Geoffrey himself is enigmatic about the king's fate and makes Merlin predict a mysterious end. Wounded in his last battle, Arthur is 'carried off to the Isle of Avalon for his wounds to be attended to'. No more is said. Geoffrey knows of a belief in his survival but never mentions it in plain terms.

If Arthur was real, it is easy to see how the fancy might have started. There are well-known cases of unwillingness to accept that a public figure is dead. So far as I know, the public figure is always male. He is not necessarily either good or bad. He may be evil, with such a baleful impact that it is hard to adjust to a world without him, or shed the horror he inspired. Nero is an ancient instance, Hitler a modern one. More often he is a popular hero: he meets a tragic end and the shock of the loss is insupportable. Lord Kitchener, the chief architect of the British effort in the First World War, went down in a ship that struck a mine. Wishful thinking decreed that the report was a cover story and he was on a secret mission to Russia. The Mexican peasant leader Emiliano Zapata was shot by government troops in 1919, but his followers were convinced for many years afterwards that the victim was someone else and Zapata still lived. Even President Kennedy survived his assassination, according to some. Well into the 1970s it was rumoured that the bullet had caused disabling brain damage but was not actually fatal, and he was being kept on a life-support machine. As for Elvis Presley . . .

Usually a notion like this will fade out, if only because a time must come when the central character could not still be alive. This, however, is not always so. The young Portuguese king Sebastian was killed fighting the Moors in 1578, and Spain took advantage of his absence to annex Portugal. It was soon a widespread belief that Sebastian was alive and would return as a liberator. Several pretenders impersonated him, and when Portugal recovered its independence, the new king agreed to assume the crown provided that Sebastian did not come back. He was still hoped for in 1807 during a Napoleonic invasion. 'Sebastianism' crossed the Atlantic with Portuguese colonists, and indigenous tribes in northeast Brazil have a demigod called Sebastian who will come from the sea to save them from poverty and oppression.

A real Arthur, leader of resistance against the Anglo-Saxons, might have become a Sebastian for the Britons' Welsh and Cornish descendants. However that may be, the immortal Arthur of legend, as he emerges into daylight, shows himself in two principal ways. He is in the enchanted island of Avalon (this is the version that Geoffrey evidently heard) or he is asleep in a cave. Both motifs appear to derive from a Celtic myth about a departed god who is sleeping in a cave on a western island.

The Avalon version is the more literary one. Geoffrey produces it again in his narrative poem *The Life of Merlin*, which was written some years after the *History*. His Avalon is a Fortunate Isle over western waters, the home of nine enchantresses, headed by Morgen. She is the woman who appears in later romance as Morgan le Fay and is made rather sinister, but at her début in Geoffrey's poem she is entirely benign. She welcomes the wounded Arthur and undertakes to cure him if he will stay on the island. Again, nothing is said about his ultimate fate. A fourteenth-century Majorcan romancer shifts Avalon and its lady to the Mediterranean. Arthur is still there after an indefinite lapse of time, looking young. He has healed his wounds by bathing in water that flows from the Earthly Paradise, and his youth is restored annually by visits of the Holy Grail.

As for the cave legend, it has fifteen locales, in western and northern England, Wales and the Scottish Border country. It is first on record at Cadbury Castle, an ancient Somerset hill-fort, which was refortified in the 'Arthur' period and is commonly thought to be the original of Camelot – so far as anything is. Other important locations are Craig-y-Dinas in Glamorgan, Alderley Edge in Cheshire and the Eildon Hills near Melrose. The legend varies. Sometimes only the sleeping king is present, sometimes he has a company of knights with him, also asleep. There may be a royal treasure. The story may tell of knights only or treasure only, Arthur himself being somewhere else. The cave is not a real one that can be found and visited in the normal way. It is concealed, generally in a hillside, but it may open at certain times to give a glimpse of the interior, or an outsider may more or less blunder into it. Or a mysterious stranger, possibly Merlin himself, may let someone in for purposes of his own. John Masefield's poem 'Midsummer Night' is based on the Cadbury tradition.

It is an odd testimony to the power of the legend that President Kennedy, who became in retrospect a sort of American Arthur, not only 'survived' but survived in two ways corresponding to the king's. According to one rumour, he was on a sealed-off floor of a hospital in Dallas, an equivalent for the cave. According to another, he was on a Greek island provided by Aristotle Onassis, an equivalent for Avalon.

The prophecy of Arthur's return from his retreat can be documented before Geoffrey, as can his survival itself, although there is no way of telling how it originated and no prophet can be named. In 1125 the historian William of Malmesbury says: 'The tomb of Arthur is nowhere seen, whence ancient ditties fable that he is yet to come.' Wace, who paraphrased Geoffrey in French verse, mentions the Bretons' hope for his reappearance. As we saw, there were similar beliefs about Charlemagne and the emperor Frederick. The belief about Arthur may have hovered as a tradition in the Celtic west, certainly before the one about Frederick, perhaps before the one about Charlemagne. It is implied and sometimes explicit in the cave legends. The whole point of the hero being asleep is that he will eventually wake, to restore justice and peace. The returning Arthur very likely began as a Welsh Messiah, coming back to lead the *revanche* against the English. It has been conjectured that the reputed finding of Arthur's grave at Glastonbury, Somerset, was an English trick to prove that he was dead and discourage the Welsh. However, his adoption by romancers and chroniclers as king of all England, an illustrious forebear whom the Plantagenets took seriously, made his return more of a national affair. He would come back to lead his people, perhaps in an hour of special need, and his ancient glory would revive.

Sir Thomas Malory, near the end of his famous version of the Arthurian legend, mentions the prophecy without actually endorsing it.

> Some men say in many parts of England that King Arthur is not dead, but had by the will of Our Lord Jesu into another place; and men say that he shall come again . . . Many men say that there is written upon his tomb this verse: HIC IACET ARTHURUS, REX QUONDAM REXQUE FUTURUS.

The Latin line, 'Here lies Arthur, king that was and king that shall be,' suggested the title of T.H. White's four-part novel *The Once and Future King*. Since Malory asserts that it is written, or allegedly written, on a tomb, presumably the one in Glastonbury Abbey, it is not clear in what sense Arthur can be future, for medieval Christian doctrine would have ruled out reincarnation. If the tomb was a cenotaph, without a body in it, the 'hic iacet' would be a deception.

At any rate, Caxton's publication of Malory's book in 1485 was extremely well timed. A few weeks later Henry Tudor defeated Richard III at Bosworth and became Henry VII. Tudor propagandists turned the Arthur prophecy into an English counterpart of the Joachites' Second Charlemagne prophecy. Henry was part-Welsh, claiming descent from the Welsh kings Maelgwn and Cadwaladr, a pedigree taking his ancestry far back towards Arthur. He marched from Wales flying a Red Dragon standard. He had his first-born son baptized at Winchester, which Malory said was Camelot, and named him Arthur with the apparent intention that he should reign as Arthur II. The key idea in the evolving Tudor myth, as it has been called, was that Henry had restored the true 'British' monarchy and brought back harmony after many years of usurpation and civil war. Symbolically, he had fulfilled the prophecy of Arthur's return. Unfortunately, Prince Arthur died young, and his brother became king as Henry VIII. Henry flaunted suitable emblems at an ostentatious conference with the king of France and had the design painted on the Round Table in the Castle Hall at Winchester, with himself in Arthur's chair. John Leland, the court antiquary, hailed him in verse as 'Arturius Redivivus'.

With Elizabeth I the Tudor myth rose to a new height. In *The Faerie Queene* Edmund Spenser made out that Elizabethan England was, in effect, Arthurian Britain resurrected. He imagined Merlin delivering a long prophecy about Britain's future, building up to a climax with the Tudors. The prophecy introduces them with an allusion to their ancestral island of Mona – that is, Anglesey. Elizabeth is to rescue the Low Countries from Spain and defeat Philip II, represented by a castle, part of his royal arms as king of Castile.

Tho when the terme is full accomplishid,
There shall a sparke of fire, which hath long-while

Bene in his ashes raked vp, and hid,
Be freshly kindled in the fruitful Ile
Of Mona, where it lurked in exile;
Which shall breake forth into bright burning flame,
And reach into the house, that bears the stile
Of royall maiesty and soueraigne name;
So shall the Briton bloud their crowne againe reclame.

Thenceforth eternall vnion shall be made
Betweene the nations different afore,
And sacred Peace shall louingly perswade
The warlike minds, to learne her goodly lore,
And ciuile armes to exercise no more:
Then shall a royall virgin raine, which shall
Stretch her white rod ouer the Belgicke shore,
And the great Castle smite so sore with all,
That it shall make him shake, and shortly learne to fall.
(III.iii.48–49)

But Elizabeth could not live for ever. When the Stuarts came in, flatterers of James I, who was descended from Henry VII in a different line, tried to keep the myth alive. The poet Michael Drayton saluted him as carrying on the Arthurian revival, but James's troubles with Parliament and growing scepticism about Arthur called a halt.

What is noteworthy in this Tudor mystique is that it was already symbolic. No one talked of an actual return of Arthur, any more than Joachites talked of an actual reappearance of Charlemagne. No Arthurian fundamentalist complained that Henry VII was masquerading. The Tudor myth moved towards a realization that has become possible since. Just as Joachim's scenario, with its advance in stages towards a quantum leap, is a kind of archetype manifested in various ways, so also is the Return of Arthur. It, too, expresses a recurrent pattern; it, too, is a kind of archetype manifested in various ways. As we can find Joachim's scenario, or analogues to it, in other ideologies, so we can find Arthur's return, although in this case with no question of influence. The hope of a new dawn is similar, the imagined approach to it is different.

Here again is prophecy with another dimension. As with the cases noted in Chapter 6, the vision embodies a certain view of history and the human condition, possessing psychological cogency. The prophecy has validity as an insight, even though, in this case, fulfilment is not an issue: Arthur is not going to return literally. It draws attention to a recurrent mode of thought and behaviour.

People may have longings for a better society, they may take action to bring it into being, yet often they see the movement towards it not as a simple forward step but as a revival. They evoke a long-lost glory or promise and regard it as not utterly lost. It can be reinstated for a fresh start, with intervening evils abolished. The Athurian legend expresses – we might say, mythifies – this way of looking at things. Arthur's reign is a long-ago golden age. Evil powers closed in on him and he is ostensibly dead, but he is really living, he is still 'there' (so to speak) and will come back, his glory will be reinstated. This syndrome, this way of looking at things, has been dubbed 'apocalyptic nostalgia'. It is a striking historical phenomenon, which a few examples will illustrate.

One belongs to the sixteenth century, when Christian reformers, both Catholic and Protestant, agreed that the Church had become corrupted and that remedial action was required. Neither party urged what a liberal theologian would urge now – namely, reform through development and progress, through advancing on to new ground and discarding a superseded past. Instead, they appealed to the past itself. In the golden age of the apostles and early saints, Christianity was pure. The reformers' task was to sweep away abuses, restore the true Gospel and recapture the original purity, so that the pristine Church could be reborn. This would lead to radical change, but the stress was on the recovery of the true Faith as bringing it about, not on anything novel or without precedent.

Two centuries later, Jean-Jacques Rousseau (1712–78) became an arch-inspirer of the French Revolution, but not by preaching anything remotely like progress. On the contrary, he taught that humanity had once been free, equal and virtuous in a 'natural' state. Civilization and civilized institutions had ushered in tyranny and misery. Kings, nobles, priests and others had subverted natural law and now maintained the evils. The proper aim was to eliminate or nullify all such elements and set up an order enabling natural goodness to reassert itself. Here was a quantum leap indeed, but with the rebirth of a golden age as its theoretical basis. In a revealing throwaway line, Rousseau admitted that his golden age might be fictitious. The natural condition, he said, is one that 'exists no longer, perhaps never existed, probably never will exist, and of which none the less it is necessary to have just ideas, in order to judge well of our present state'. The compulsion to impose such a fiction is deeply significant. Rousseau's numerous disciples embraced it as fact and acted on it, believing in the ancient felicity and trying to wipe out obstacles to its restoration. It was hardly his fault that the most powerful of them, and the most resolute wiper-out, was Robespierre.

Marxism is an even more remarkable case. It came into the last chapter as an instance of a Joachim-type ideology. In the *Communist Manifesto* (1848) and later works, Marx and his collaborator, Friedrich Engels, traced a series of historical stages – slave society, feudal society, capitalist society – with the final leap to socialist society, evolving without further upheavals into a classless order. But the same compulsion took hold, even here.

Marx and Engels discovered the American anthropologist Lewis H. Morgan (1818–81). Basing his findings mainly on the alleged customs of the seventeenth-century Iroquois, Morgan reinvented the Noble Savage, whom Rousseau had made a popular myth. The Iroquois and similar peoples were wise and free and equal, with communal property and no government. Engels wrote a book of his own agreeing that this was a mirror of the past. There had once been a happy time like Rousseau's, a time of 'simple moral grandeur', before 'the meanest impulses – vulgar covetousness, brutal lust, sordid avarice, selfish robbery of the common wealth' – set economic progress in motion and

produced inequality and oppression. Henceforth, a largely falla-
cious age of 'primitive communism' was *tacked on* at the beginning
of the Marxist story, with the various bad times following. After
the Revolution and a tough transitional phase, it was to be reborn
on a higher plane. The succession of class tyrannies would be
finished for ever. So Marxism ended up as a combination of both
scenarios. But whereas the first version had been founded more or
less on real history, the final, expanded one incorporated a golden
age and its reinstatement, on very dubious grounds. The Return-
of-Arthur syndrome had overcome objectivity.

It is not confined to Europe. The rise of Indian nationalism
under British rule showed it at work. Westernized nationalists
aimed at industrial progress, parliamentary government and so
forth. Such ideals were incomprehensible to the masses and failed
to rouse them. The leader who did rouse them was Gandhi.
Influenced both by Hinduism and by dissident Westerners such as
Ruskin and Tolstoy, he denounced European-style civilization as
an imported blight and appealed to a past Indian golden age of
saints and sages and village communes and cottage industry, which
Muslim and British conquerors had ruined. The right way for
India was to resurrect this. Political independence was a prerequisite rather than a goal in itself. His revival of hand-spinning and
hand-weaving was a step towards the resurrection. Like Rousseau, he admitted that his past golden age might be a fiction; but,
also like Rousseau, he justified talking about it and in much the
same way.

In tracing the syndrome it is easy to lose sight, not only of
Arthur as an individual character, but of other heroes who are also
to return. Some of these also carry symbolic weight. Frederick
Barbarossa, who is to wake up in his mountain cave and come
outside, was given a new meaning by German nationalists. Hitler
called the invasion of Russia, which was meant to put Germany in
a position of impregnable strength, Operation Barbarossa. There
is, however, another case in which something close to the literal
Return had political force. Like Gandhi's movement, it shows
that the syndrome is not purely European.

Buddhists in Tibet and Mongolia speak of a holy place called

Shambhala. It is a hidden fastness among the mountains of north-central Asia, and may have a sort of subterranean extension. It may, indeed, not be 'there' in quite the ordinary physical sense. The belief was studied by Nicholas Roerich (1874–1947), the Russian artist and anthropologist who collaborated with Stravinsky on *The Rite of Spring*. Lamas talked of a Messianic figure destined to emerge from this place and of a future War of Shambhala between good and evil forces. During the early 1920s Russian counter-revolutionaries in Siberia tried to exploit the mystique. They took up stories about a concealed 'king of the world' who influenced events outside by telepathy and through a network of agents. He was biding his time and prophesying a new era.

In Mongolia this mythology was assuming a more specific form and becoming a motive power for nationalism. It was focused on Gesar Khan. Gesar is the hero of a saga existing in several versions, from Tibet through Mongolia to the Altai Mountains and the area around Lake Baikal. If he existed, he lived about the eighth century AD. The principal epic makes him a wonder-working champion of true religion and righteousness. He disappears, like Arthur, and it is understood that he will return, like Arthur. For a while, Gesar's return became a potent hope. He was made out to have been a Mongol, and his secret retreat was the legendary Shambhala. He might not have been there all the time, but, in whatever way, he would be manifested there. When he stepped forth, he would be a warrior for justice, enlisting other peoples for the revival of Asia and the ousting of the white races. The anthropologist Alexandra David-Neel, who translated the Gesar epic, met a Tibetan woman who took her to a lamasery that housed a statue of him. She said she prayed to him for a son who could serve in his approaching campaign. Mme David-Neel was told in several places that Gesar had been reborn and would show himself to the world within fifteen years. Roerich, travelling through Central Asia, heard similar reports.

Mongolia (then called Outer Mongolia) came under Communist domination and the Gesar hope faded out. It has been asserted, however, that Japanese expansionists tried to make use of the mystique of Shambhala. It has even been asserted that German expansionists did likewise. In view of the bizarre ideas of such prominent Nazis as Heinrich Himmler, it is not totally beyond belief. There is a slight indication that some of Hitler's crazier actions could have been affected by a prophecy attributed to the 'king of the world'. (For further discussion of the Arthur myth, see Appendix 2, page 311.)

Another prophecy is a companion to Arthur's, less familiar, but with a fulfilment.

On the approaches to Glastonbury in Somerset, signboards inform the visitor (or used to) that it is the ancient Isle of Avalon. This is not Geoffrey of Monmouth's unlocated Avalon, but, in the early Christian era, an isle or nearly so. The cluster of hills cradling the present town was almost surrounded by water and could be reached by sea-going craft from the Bristol Channel. The highest of the hills is the Tor, a whaleback formation that now has a tower on top. Close by is the smoother dome of Chalice Hill. Wearyall Hill is a ridge pointing seawards. Windmill Hill, on the side towards Wells, is covered with houses.

Why Avalon? Why an isle of enchantment? 'Avalon' means 'apple-place' and this is apple-growing country. There is more to it than that, however. The Tor is thought to have been a pre-Christian sanctuary, perhaps once a goddess sanctuary, and an otherworldly aura clung to it. In Christian legend it was hollow, with the court of the king of the fairy-folk inside. Arthur's connection with Glastonbury, like his survival and destined return, can be documented before Geoffrey. A 'Life' of the Dark Age author Gildas, written about 1130, tells how a local kinglet named Melwas carried off Guinevere and kept her at Glastonbury. Arthur arrived with an army, and, after logistic difficulties because of the water, recovered her by negotiation. The actual name 'Avalon', however strongly suggested mythologically, is first on record here in 1191. Then the monks of the abbey, acting, it is said, on a hint from a Welsh bard, dug down in their burial plot and exhumed Arthur's bones, together with Guinevere's, and a lead cross with an inscription naming the king and including the words *Insula Avalonia*. So he was mortal after all, and died like anybody else; Glastonbury was simply his last earthly destination and the only true Avalon.

The topic is controversial and this is not the place to pursue it; it has been pursued elsewhere at considerable length. Historians who mention the exhumation, with some distinguished exceptions, claim that it was a monastic fraud concocted to confound the Welsh by proving that Arthur would not come back, or to enhance the abbey's prestige and attract funds. This is stated as a fact, but while fraud may be plausible, it is a theory only; there is no evidence for it and some against it. Excavation has shown that the monks did dig where they said and did find a very early burial. Scepticism is proper here, not only about the claims of monks but about the dogmatism of scholars.

Arthur's presence helped to make Glastonbury a national shrine. Yet even with romantic additions about the Grail, he is not the sole cause of its fascination. The strange, haunting landscape is a part of that, but still only a part. Glastonbury is rooted in Celtic antiquity. On the eve of the Christian era, its neighbourhood included lake-villages built on islands, with widespread trade and a respectable level of craftsmanship. If Christianity, when it came, did take over a former holy place, the break may not have been long. Glastonbury is said to have been the home of the first Christian settlers in Britain. Here was the 'holiest earth of England'. The belief took shape – no one knows when or exactly how – around a tangible fact: a very old church within what became the abbey precinct, so old that its origin was forgotten. Legend declared that it had been planted on its site by the hand of God or, more realistically, that it had been built by disciples of Christ. Their leader was identified in the Middle Ages as Joseph of Arimathea, the rich convert who obtained Christ's body after the Crucifixion and laid it in the tomb.

While many believe in this apostolic origin and it cannot be disproved, there is no real support for it. Carbon-dating and other techniques take Christian Glastonbury back to the sixth century, perhaps the fifth, and traces of Roman activity may point to something earlier. Even a date around 500 remains deeply significant. It means that this was a British community with the Celtic Christian tradition behind it. When the advancing Saxons arrived in the mid-seventh century, they were Christian themselves and absorbed the community respectfully and peaceably. This continuity with the 'Arthurian' past has no real parallel anywhere else in England. Glastonbury in this phase has been called a temple of reconciliation, symbolically the birthplace of the United Kingdom. As a Benedictine community it became the scene of another beginning after the Norse devastations, when its abbot, St Dunstan, made it the fountainhead of the restoration of learning in parts of the country that had suffered.

In the Middle Ages Glastonbury's association with Arthur helped to form the corpus of Arthurian literature, and Joseph of Arimathea was involved in romance with the mystique of the Grail. The abbey was now the greatest in England, or an equal first with Westminster, and its church, the ruins of which still stand, was the largest except for St Paul's Cathedral in London. Its domain extended far: its monks and tenants had drained the land round about for farming, embanked the River Brue to prevent floods and built sea-walls to hold back the Bristol Channel. The abbey maintained a school and one of the finest libraries in England. But in 1539, as part of his programme of dissolving all monasteries, Henry VIII swooped on Glastonbury. The abbey and its estates were seized, and the last abbot was hanged and dismembered. After an interim the buildings were taken over by private owners, who had no use for them except as a quarry for marketable stone, and a long process of dismantling began.

Now we encounter Glastonbury's prophet. He is called Austin Ringwode, and he is said to have been the last of the monks. He lived nearby in a cottage until 1587 and made a deathbed pronouncement:

> The abbey will one day be repaired and rebuilt for the like worship which has ceased; and then peace and plenty will for a long time abound.

While there is no early documentation, the fact of such a story being preserved, in a staunchly Protestant county, favours its authenticity as a tradition. It used to be objected that Austin Ringwode could not be found in the abbey's records, but a memoir written in 1586 and printed in modern times has shed light on the matter. Its author, William Weston, has a good deal to say about a very old man living not far from Glastonbury, who kept up Catholic devotional practices and made private pilgrimages to the Tor. He had been employed at the abbey in a lay capacity, as a servant or clerical worker. Weston does not name him – his religious sympathies could have got him into trouble – but in all probability this was Austin Ringwode. His post at the abbey disposes of the objection that no known monk can be identified with him. With the passage of years and the disappearance of all religious houses, a man attached to the community in any way would have been spoken of loosely as a 'monk'.

This prophecy was not a rational forecast. The year of the Armada was imminent, but I do not think that Ringwode expected a Roman restoration by the forces of King Philip II. That is not what he was talking about. His prophecy was local, with no hint of a national change. Under the circumstances it was absurd. The abbey's destruction had already begun, and more than 300 years of desolation followed, with more and more of the fabric migrating into walls, houses and road-beds. A few poets and antiquaries made nostalgic comments but no one talked of a resurrection, and in a Protestant England it was unthinkable.

The point of interest is that in the twentieth century a resurrection has happened, against all expectation. In the 1950s and even later I remember people saying 'Glastonbury is dead', 'Glastonbury will never come back'. The abbey ruins are certainly too far gone for rebuilding, but to prevent further dilapidation they have been repaired as Ringwode foretold. Nor has this been done simply to preserve a historic monument. Services are held and large-scale pilgrimage has revived, Catholic as well as Anglican. All of this was under way before Ringwode's prophecy could have contributed to its own fulfilment. It was virtually forgotten until well past the mid-century, and only one of the many books on Glastonbury so much as mentioned it.

The rebirth has included major arts festivals and a latter-day growth as an 'alternative' spiritual centre, attracting many kinds of mystic and seeker and building an international reputation. The story has been well told by Patrick Benham in his book *The Avalonians*. Austin Ringwode, of course, would have meant a Catholic and monastic rebirth, if only because he could not have pictured a rebirth of Glastonbury in any other way. No other image of the future could have presented itself, at least consciously. He could never have foreseen the modern neo-pagan activities, and he would have disapproved if they had somehow been shown to him. Yet it is odd that he used a circumlocution about 'the like worship which has ceased'. A neo-pagan could take it as applying not only to Christian worship but to whatever went before, to pre-Christian religion such as this ancient place very possibly witnessed and some today believe they are rediscovering.

Chapter Eight

Nostradamus: The Miscellany

Joachim's ideological heirs expected not only the Angelic Pope but their other world-unifier, the Second Charlemagne. Of all who cherished the hope, the best remembered today, although not for this particular interest, is a French prophet in the sixteenth century, Nostradamus.

Few authors in any genre can have been harmed so much by their admirers. They have produced books and films that credit him with foretelling aerial warfare, the Kennedy assassinations and other comparatively modern events. They support their claims with 'interpretations' of his writings that would make any prophet look ridiculous. Actually, he is very interesting, but only if he is studied patiently and impartially, with no preconceived wish either for high scores or for total demolition. Some of his predictions – not many, but enough to deserve attention – have a combined impact that is seldom fully appreciated, even by his devotees.

'Nostradamus' is a Latinization. Michel de Nostredame was born in 1503 in a Provençal Jewish family that converted to Catholicism. He was educated privately, chiefly by an erudite grandfather, and went to Montpellier in 1522 to study medicine. After he received his degree, his life was spent professionally as a doctor. His care of the sick during an outbreak of plague in southern France earned him a glowing reputation. His methods were unorthodox by the standards of the day – for instance, he was reluctant to bleed his patients – and he invented remedies of his own, which he later published. In his spare time he read books on magic and astrology, which were then respectable subjects.

In 1534 an eminent scholar, Jules César Scaliger, heard of Nostradamus and was interested, and invited him to stay at his home in Agen on the Garonne, northwest of Toulouse. He settled in the neighbourhood. His practice flourished, and he married. Then another outbreak of plague carried off his wife and their two children. Scaliger grew unfriendly, and he left the area. For six years he led a wandering life, at one point visiting Italy, where he conferred with scholars, astrologers and alchemists. It may have been in this phase that he began to get a reputation for precognition. According to one anecdote, when he was walking along an Italian street he happened to meet a young Franciscan, Felice Peretti, and addressed him as 'Your Holiness'. Long afterwards Peretti became Pope Sixtus V.

In 1547, after a spell of medical work in Marseilles, Nostradamus came to the small town of Salon in his native Provence and made it his home. A second marriage produced several children. His practice, like Dr Watson's, was not very active, and he gave more time to study and writing. His biographer Jean de Chavigny describes him as a little under middle height, but stalwart and energetic, although in his last years he suffered from gout. His eyes were grey, his beard was long and thick. He needed only four or five hours of sleep. He was quiet rather than talkative, but, on the whole, good company. In 1550 he began publishing astrological almanacs with his predictions for the coming year. These were not very successful, in any sense. Five years later, however, he launched the much greater project that immortalized him.

He started composing long-term prophecies in the form of rhymed quatrains, and grouped them in sets of a hundred, which soon came to be called Centuries. The word has nothing to do with periods of time, and the prophecies were not arranged by the dates of their prospective fulfilments nor, indeed, in any order at all. Nostradamus is believed to have jumbled them as a matter of policy. They apparently went through three stages of composition. Each prophecy originated as rough notes. Then Nostradamus versified it in Latin. Then he paraphrased the Latin in the

French version that survives. Whatever the nature of the message, it emerged by way of a literary process, as at Delphi. The prophecies as we have them are not spontaneous outpourings – the metre and rhyme would be enough to prove that.

They were given to the world in instalments. The first edition (1555) contained three Centuries and fifty-three quatrains of a fourth. The second edition (1557) contained seven. The first three were as before; the fourth was now complete, and so were the fifth and sixth. The seventh was unfinished, as it remains to this day. Nostradamus was adding to the Centuries for the rest of his life. A final edition contained the first six, forty-two quatrains of the never-completed seventh, and three more, making ten in all. It came out posthumously in 1568. Nostradamus had died in 1566, although there was a local legend that he was still alive in a cave, not asleep like Arthur, but continuing to write.

The Centuries are best read in Edgar Leoni's learned and balanced edition, *Nostradamus and his Prophecies*. He adds translations, commentaries and a wealth of background material. Besides the 942 recognized quatrains, he gives 27 more in 'duplicate and fragmentary' Centuries, which are dubious and may be omitted. Throughout the following discussion I use Leoni's text, with his generally modernized spelling. In a few places the old spelling seems to me to be required and I go back to it. The sense is always what matters, and Nostradamus should be allowed to speak to us plainly . . . or as plainly as possible. Mostly, an air of archaism might interfere. Erika Cheetham, author of *The Prophecies of Nostradamus*, gives a mainly non-modernized text, but still makes changes.

I also use Leoni's translations, with a little more freedom, preferring another word here and there or improving the punctuation. In my notes and comments I have, as a rule, gone along with his interpretations, which are often based on earlier ones that have become traditional. Erika Cheetham's commentary, although much more fanciful in the would-be detection of fulfilments, is helpful occasionally. I have invented few interpretations myself, but hope I have managed to add some enhancements of my own.

The first series of Centuries attracted attention quickly and impressed Queen Catherine de' Medici and others at the French court. Nostradamus began to enjoy royal favour. Ronsard, the most famous poet of the day, praised him as an inspired prophet, probably on the basis of a wish to believe rather than anything he had actually prophesied. One of his predictions made a powerful impact when it seemed to be fulfilled, and convinced many courtiers of his gifts. In the summer of 1559, to celebrate two royal weddings, a three-day tournament was held. On 1 July Catherine's husband Henry II rode against a younger opponent, Gabriel de Lorges, Comte de Montgomery, Captain of the Scottish Guard. When they clashed, Montgomery lowered his lance an instant too late; the wooden tip splintered, penetrating Henry's visor – which was not securely fastened – and entered his head beside an eye. He was lowered from his horse, his face covered with blood, and died in agony on 10 July.

It was widely asserted that Nostradamus had foretold the catastrophe. Parisians burned him in effigy and even wanted to burn him in person. The belief was due to the thirty-fifth quatrain of his first Century, which could undoubtedly bear a relevant meaning.

> Le lion jeune le vieux surmontera
> En champ bellique par singulier duelle:
> Dans cage d'or les yeux lui crevera:
> Deux classes une, puis mourir, mort cruelle.

In English:

> The young lion will overcome the old one
> On the field of battle in single combat:
> He will put out his eyes in a cage of gold:
> Two wounds one, then to die a cruel death.

In the fourth line, the word *classes* is tricky. It should be from the Latin *classis*, a fleet. In the absence of any fleets, it has to be assumed that Nostradamus derived it from the Greek *klasis*, a fracture. That is only one of several shortcomings. The epithet 'lion' has no special fitness for either of the antagonists, beyond its connotation of courage and nobility. It is not at all certain that the visor was gold or gilded, and to say that 'the eyes' were put out is inaccurate. On the other hand, the cryptic phrase 'two wounds one' is remarkable. The mortal blow of the splintered lance did cause a double wound: besides the destruction of the king's eye by the larger splinter, the smaller one pierced his throat. The quatrain is an example of what may be called Nostradamus's 'arguable' prophecies — interesting when an event can be construed as bearing them out, often endorsed by commentators but open to criticism. As we shall see, he can do much better. But this fulfilment was close enough for the shaken French court.

Nostradamus shared the Joachite hope for the Second Charlemagne, the ruler who would bring universal peace. However, he held this hope in a modified form only, not picturing the glorious reign as final, a prelude to the Third Age or the end of the world. It might happen, but many further vicissitudes would follow. For a while, to judge from some coded clues in the Centuries, he focused on Henry II, despite his supposed preview of the king's fatal wounding. After that tragedy, his hope went into abeyance in the absence of a candidate, but in 1564, during a royal visit to Salon, he singled out an eleven-year-old prince who was in the party and predicted that he would be king of Navarre and of all France. The same prediction is in one of the later Centuries.

He was right. This prince was to become the renowned Henry of Navarre, eventually king of France as Henry IV. According to Chavigny, the seer was the first to suspect that *this* Henry might bring the great fulfilment. When he acceded to the throne, Messianic hopes began to fasten on him. In 1592 a pamphlet hailed him as *Carolus Magnus redivivus*, and soon afterwards the scientist and philosopher Bruno took up the theme, as did Chavigny himself. All this was long after Nostradamus's death.

He never really explained his methods. The Centuries include a preface in the form of a letter to his son César; it is not very enlightening. Evidently he practised astrology, but it could not have supplied the detailed material in the Centuries. Two introductory quatrains sketch a kind of invocation described in the fourth century by the mystic Iamblichus (*c*.250–330). Performed in solitude at night, it involves a tripod as at Delphi, some water, seemingly in a bowl on the tripod, and a 'slight flame' of inspiration, probably in a trance. A divine being then communicates with the seer. Nostradamus claims that his inspiration comes ultimately from God, but this may be meant chiefly as a safeguard. In an age of witch-hunts, he could have been accused of dealings with Satan.

The end product, after the literary handling, is like nothing before it. Some of the 942 quatrains don't even pretend to be predictive – they are medleys of occult jargon or refer to things already past – but the vast majority do look ahead, and many make more than one prediction. The French is curt, cryptic and often grammatically odd. Latin words and syntax survive from the earlier Latin versions. Other languages put in an appearance – Spanish, Greek, Provençal – and there are anagrams, near-anagrams and outright riddles. Here is an instance of the kind of quatrains that really baffle (IX.48):

> La grande cité d'Océan maritime,
> Environée de marais en cristal:
> Dans le solstice hyemal et la prime,
> Sera tentée de vent espouvantal.

As Leoni translates:

> The great city of the maritime Ocean,
> Surrounded by a crystalline swamp;
> In the winter solstice and the spring,
> It will be tried by frightful wind.

One commentator mysteriously applied this to Central Park in New York; another to Tokyo.

Owing to superficial reading, the quatrains are often given a blanket dismissal as being so nebulous, obscure or ambiguous that we can never tie down their meaning or determine whether they have or have not been fulfilled. That is much too sweeping. It is true for some, not for all. Nostradamus frequently has names of places in plain terms and alludes to individuals in phrases that define them precisely. Quite a number of quatrains are explicit enough to be deciphered and tested. Dozens, maybe hundreds of others, have a sort of semi-intelligibility. These are obscure without being entirely off-putting; they have an air of meaning something if the reader can unravel them. Nostradamus's vogue in his own lifetime was due more to this than to any tangible successes, and it still accounts for much of his fascination.

It is worthwhile comparing the Centuries with the Prophecies of Merlin. Geoffrey of Monmouth makes Merlin score with a few prophecies-after-the-event, but when he plunges into the real future he produces eleven pages of increasingly weird fantasy. The only prediction that makes any clear sense is the one that mentions the name 'Britain' coming back into use, and that is taken from Welsh tradition and was only partially fulfilled. Nostradamus, by contrast, has plenty of prophecies that make at least some sense and a number that have been fulfilled. Merlin's Prophecies are a mystification. A severe critic might say they are an imposture. No one could pin such an accusation on the Centuries.

They remained popular after the prophet's death. New editions kept appearing, and so did commentaries and attempts to apply them to real history. A peculiarity of treating them thus was that the possibilities grew with the passage of time: there was more and more history to apply them to. As a matter of fact, it is surprising that Nostradamus's reputation survived in the hundred years or so after his death, when not much happened that his prophecies fitted. He looks better now than he did then.

It was only to be expected that the twentieth century would surpass previous ones in the production of Nostradamus literature. His devotees have not only claimed that he foretold many things that he didn't foretell, they have tried to use him to foretell the future themselves, only to be confounded when events turned out otherwise. Probably no one has ever made a correct prediction based on Nostradamus. The excess of zeal is a pity, because the fanciful readings and rash forecasts are so easily discredited. There have been so many, with such flagrant disagreement, that attention is diverted from the prophecies that are genuinely worth studying. And there are such prophecies. Responsible Nostradamians (a few exist) have reached a certain consensus, picking out a small but significant number that actually do seem to have been fulfilled, that actually do fit unambiguous realities.

Part of the trouble has been that commentators have wanted to cover too much and supply a complete key to Nostradamus. They have done whatever they could with the whole 942 quatrains or a large proportion of them, so their researches have been spread too widely and too thinly. Few individual quatrains have had enough attention or been subjected to a close enough scrutiny. The right procedure, if conclusions are to be reached, is to set aside the vast majority as opaque or nonsensical or simply wrong and to focus on the select few that do, *prima facie*, fit events that were in the future for Nostradamus. Once these are identified, they can be thoroughly scrutinized in the light of history.

With nearly all these 'good' quatrains, the future realities that they fit, or appear to fit, can be dated, sometimes within a day or so, sometimes within a year or so, but always within a time-range that is not so huge as to be meaningless. When they have been picked out, they don't have to be left in the original Nostradamian jumble but can be arranged chronologically by their dates of fulfilment. That is what I have done in the listing that follows, and I believe that something further emerges about Nostradamus's interests and predictive validity.

A word about criteria: I call the 'good' quatrains Class A. To qualify as a Class A, a quatrain must make at least one prediction that is open to only a single interpretation, juxtaposed with a reality that, for Nostradamus, lay in the future. There must be no ambiguities. Thus, the prediction 'a queen will be beheaded' would not count unless there were some detail to define it more closely; the victim might be Mary, Queen of Scots or Marie Antoinette. The fulfilment must not be attributable to guesswork or ordinary foresight.

Different lines in a quatrain, applying to different future events, should still be clear and preferably related, by the events being close together in time if in no other way. In general, the whole of a quatrain should be accounted for and correct, with no loose ends, no obscure phrases, no downright errors. It won't do to pick out the bits that work and ignore the bits that don't. However, an outstanding bull's-eye in one part of a quatrain may support weak or uncertain material in the rest of it, and allow it to count as a Class A although not all of it measures up fully to the standard. Meanings need not be obvious – research and reflection may be necessary to find them – but they must be plainly there and meet the requirements when they are found.

There are marginal cases: quatrains with possible fulfilments that are open to dispute, like the one about the French tournament. I would call these 'arguable' because commentators have claimed tham as valid without getting too far-fetched. They should not be left out entirely, and may form a subsidiary Class B.

So, how many quatrains are we going to be talking about? An assessment of the Centuries must depend to some extent on personal judgement. My own selection, as I have said, is based mainly on Leoni's readings, which are fully explained and not biased by wishful thinking. On the negative side, dismissal of most of the 942 is amply justified, but a stubborn positive nucleus remains. By my count, Nostradamus has twenty-six Class A quatrains and twenty-four Class B. That makes a total of fifty that are seriously worth attention, which means that a little over 5 per cent of his total can be said to work in some degree. It is easy to say: 'Oh, if you make hundreds of predictions, five per cent of them are likely to be correct just by chance.' But the case is not so plain. Since each of the fifty quatrains includes more than one predictive line, the total of predictions is much higher; and internal links make some of the quatrains fairly complex. Furthermore, it is not true that in a random swarm of predictions, even simple ones, a significant number will just happen to be right. The records of some prominent 'psychics', who make forecasts in the media, have been examined and are abysmal. Compared with them, Nostradamus does well.

Class A falls into two halves. Thirteen of the quatrains can be reckoned as miscellaneous, in the sense that they have no subject matter in common and only loose connections. The other thirteen are more close-knit and, to my mind, extraordinary. First, I shall survey Class A's 'miscellaneous' set, leaving the rest of Class A, the other thirteen, for separate analysis. Class B and general observations will follow.

The miscellaneous Class A quatrains are scattered throughout the Centuries. As proposed, I have arranged them chronologically by the dates of their apparent fulfilment. This arrangement has no relation whatever to their scrambled order in Nostradamus's work as published. The numbers of the quatrains are given solely for reference.

The first fully successful prophecy, by date of fulfilment, is a trifle disconcerting. It abuses a man Nostradamus knew about and evidently detested. His violence of language is untypical.

III.41

Bossu sera élu par le conseil,
Plus hideux monstre en terre n'aperçu,
Le coup voulant crevera l'oeil,
Le traître au Roi pour fidèle reçu.

Hunchback will be elected to the council,
A more hideous monster not seen on earth,
The deliberate shot will put out his eye,
The traitor to the King received as faithful.

This diatribe applies unambiguously to Prince Louis of Condé (1530–69). Although young, he was already a public figure when Nostradamus wrote it. However, the events began to happen only after the quatrain was in print. Condé, a hunchback, was elected to head the council of French Huguenot nobles. Charged with sedition, he swore loyalty to the king in 1560, again in 1562, and was entrusted with the governorship of Picardy. But his plotting continued, and he shares responsibility for the Wars of Religion that afflicted France. Taken prisoner at the battle of Jarnac in

1569, he was shot through the head in cold blood by one of his captors.

To proceed.

VIII.50

La pestilence l'entour Capadille,
Une autre faim près de Sagont s'apprête:
Le chevalier bâtard de bon sénile
Au grand de Thunes fera trancher la tête.

The pestilence around Capellades,
Another famine approaches Sagunto:
The knight bastard of the good old man
Will cause the great one of Tunis to lose his head.

The main event here is in the second half. Tunis, an overseas possession of the House of Habsburg, was captured in 1570 by Algerian corsairs, who installed a ruler of their own. In 1573 an expedition to retake it for King Philip of Spain was led by Philip's half-brother, Don John of Austria (1547–78), the gallant illegitimate son of the emperor Charles V, who retired to a monastery and could be described as 'the good old man'. Tunis was recovered, its ruler being thus decapitated figuratively, maybe literally. In Nostradamus's lifetime Don John was not old enough for a major command. His future exploits, not only this one but a famous victory over the Turks at Lepanto, were unforeseeable. So indeed was the situation in which Tunis needed to be recaptured at all.

The first half of the quatrain synchronizes well enough. Capellades and Sagunto are in Spain. There were outbreaks of plague in that country between 1570 and 1574. Famine, not documented, may be linked with plague in a conventional image of misfortune.

X.18

Le rang Lorrain fera place à Vendôme,
Le haut mis bas, et le bas mis en haut:
Le fils d'Hamon sera élu dans Rome,
Et les deux grands seront mis en defaut.

The House of Lorraine will make way for Vendôme,
The high put low, and the low put high:
The son of Hamon will be the chosen one in Rome,
And the two great ones will be put at a loss.

Henry of Navarre, Duke of Vendôme, ousted the House of Lorraine and became king of France in 1589. Hitherto he had been ridiculed as *le petit Béarnais*, now he was rising to the top, although he still had to fight against opponents who disputed his title. He had been the Protestant leader, and other quatrains make it clear that 'Hamon' or 'Amon', in Nostradamus's jargon, is a coded allusion to the Huguenot heresy. In 1593, however, Henry was reconciled to the Catholic Church, and the capital accepted him. Rome acknowledged him as Henry IV, the opposition dwindled, and the two rival claimants, the Dukes of Guise and Mayenne, were excluded from power.

IX.18

Le lis Dauffois portera dans Nansi,
Jusqu'en Flandres Électeur de l'Empire:
Neuve obturée au grand Montmorency,
Hors lieux prouvés délivré à clere peyne.

The lily of the Dauphin will reach into Nancy;
As far as Flanders an Elector of the Empire:
New confinement for the great Montmorency,
Outside customary places delivered to celebrated punishment.

This quatrain is more complicated, and has an oddity at the end. It matches three events, occurring close together in date, but in a different order. First, during the decades after Nostradamus's death, the only prince to have the title of Dauphin and to bear the French lilies in that capacity was the one who became Louis XIII (r.1610–43). In September 1633 he entered Nancy with an army, in the course of a campaign not relevant here. Second, in March 1635 the Elector of Trier, in the Holy Roman Empire of

Germany, was arrested by the Spanish and taken to Flanders, at Tervuren near Brussels. The pope interceded on his behalf and he was allowed to go to Vienna. Third, in 1632 the Duc de Montmorency, one of the greatest French nobles, was involved in a rebellion by the king's brother. Cardinal Richelieu, the chief minister, wanted to teach the fractious aristocrats a lesson, and that October, amid much publicity and widespread protests, he had Montmorency put in a new prison at Toulouse and beheaded. Out of respect for his rank the execution took place in a courtyard, not on the normal scaffold. This prediction is unambiguous. It would not fit anyone else – not even another person called Montmorency.

These three fulfilments come together in a fairly brief stretch of time, and the quatrain includes a personal name. That would be enough to put it in Class A, but the final words give it a peculiar interest. *Délivré à clere peyne* does mean 'delivered to celebrated punishment'. But Etienne Jaubert, a commentator, asserted in 1656 that the executioner's name was Clerepeyne, in which case we have a play on words that seems beyond coincidence. Jaubert, who was none too responsible, may have made it up, and Leoni found that there was no record of an executioner so named. But that was inconclusive, because the executioner was not a regular one but a soldier chosen by lot, and this man might have been called Clerepeyne. Bear in mind, anyhow, that the fourth line doesn't rhyme with the second. That will be a point to come back to.

VIII.37

La forteresse auprès de la Tamise
Cherra par lors le Roi dedans serré:
Auprès du pont sera vu en chemise
Un devant mort, puis dans le fort barré.

The fortress near the Thames
Will fall when the King is locked up therein:
Near the bridge in his shirt will be seen
One confronting death, then barred in the fort.

This, the first of two quatrains that go together, is a little elusive. It has a clear reference but does not entirely work. The Thames gives the general location. The imprisoned king has to be Charles I. In December 1648, after losing the Civil War, he was confined by his opponents in different places, one of them being Windsor Castle, near the river. Actually it had long since fallen to them, so we would have to take *cherra* as a future perfect – 'will have fallen' – or as meaning something like 'will be in enemy hands'.

In January 1649 Charles was taken to Westminster to stand trial and was held in custody again, a prisoner of the army. A white shirt is mentioned in accounts of his last days. On 30 January he was led out into what is now Whitehall and beheaded, wearing the shirt. Before that, he may have been permitted to stroll outside and then locked up again. Westminster Bridge is close, but there is a difficulty, because in 1649 it was not yet built, and Charles was a long way from London Bridge. Even with a prophet, I don't think 'the future site of the bridge' will do. However, this will be another point to come back to.

IX.49

Gand et Bruceles marcheront contre Anuers;
Sénat de Londres mettront à mort leur Roi:
Le sel et vin lui seront à l'envers,
Pour eux avoir le regne en désarroi.

Ghent and Brussels will march against Antwerp;
The Senate of London will put to death their King:
Salt and wine will overthrow him,
Because of them to have the realm in confusion.

The second line, fulfilled by Charles I's parliamentary execution, is one of Nostradamus's best-known successes. Ordinary foresight is out of the question. In the mid-sixteenth century such an act would have been unthinkable to a French believer in monarchy – or indeed to almost anyone. 'Salt and wine' probably symbolize taxation, which was a major cause of Charles's troubles with Parliament.

The unconnected first line is correctly placed, shortly before the execution. The Spanish, in occupation of Ghent and Brussels, had been fighting the Dutch for many years. In 1648, as part of the settlement at the end of the Thirty Years' War, they made concessions to buy them off. One was to close the Scheldt for the commercial benefit of Amsterdam, even though this was a heavy blow to Antwerp, another of their own cities. Not exactly a march, but an action by the rulers of the first two cities to the disadvantage of the third. The line is an overdramatic military metaphor.

X.100

Le grand empire sera par Angleterre,
Le pempotam des ans plus de trois cents;
Grandes copies passer par mer et terre,
Les Lusitains n'en seront pas contents.

The great empire will be for England,
The all-powerful for more than three hundred years;
Great forces to pass by sea and land,
The Portuguese will not be happy with this.

In the arrangement of the Centuries, X.100 is the last quatrain. Here, as with the one quoted previously, intelligent anticipation is not on the cards. No one in Nostradamus's time could have foreseen the British Empire at all, let alone its duration. The term was coined afterwards by the Elizabethan polymath John Dee, and while Elizabeth's reign made England respected, it was not as an imperial power. The first permanent overseas settlement was Jamestown in Virginia, founded in 1607, and the first conquest was Jamaica, captured from Spain in 1655.

As for the Portuguese, it may look odd to single them out, but in the sixteenth century their importance made it natural. They had opened up the sea route to India and established colonies there. With the rise of the new empire they would be replaced; one might say, supplanted. The allusion shows that the precognition, if any, is of the British Empire's beginnings, when Portuguese resentment could still be an issue. Portugal was subject to Spain from 1580 to 1640. It broke free, but its prominence in

Asia lasted only a short time longer. Rivalry with Britain ended in 1661 with a treaty of alliance. Charles II married Catherine of Braganza and promised to defend Portugal's independence. The Portuguese handed over Bombay, which became the centre of British power in India, and turned their attention to Brazil, their American dependency.

The strangest feature of this quatrain is, of course, the glimpse of the British Empire's duration. It hardly matters what you choose as the starting-point or what Nostradamus may have chosen. 'More than three hundred years' takes you into the twentieth century and the Empire's closing phase. 'Great forces' can apply to naval and military action around the globe during the imperial epoch. Nostradamus mentions the sea first, and the strength of the Empire was based mainly on that element; if British armies were seldom 'great' in size, British fleets certainly were.

> VI.22
> Dedans la terre du grand temple célique,
> Neveu à Londres par paix feinte meurtri:
> La barque alors deviendra schismatique,
> Liberté feinte sera au corn' et cri.

> Within the land of the great heavenly temple,
> Nephew murdered at London through a false peace:
> The bark will then become schismatic,
> Sham liberty will be proclaimed everywhere.

A disjointed quatrain. The principal story is defined by the second line. In 1685, Charles II died. The Duke of Monmouth claimed to be his son by a secret marriage and therefore the true heir to the crown. He was certainly Charles's son, but he failed to prove his legitimacy, and Charles's brother James, Monmouth's uncle, became king as James II. Monmouth launched a rebellion in the West Country, which was quickly crushed, and King James had his nephew brought to London and executed. In the eyes of the opposition, this act was a judicial murder. The 'peace' or pacification was false. James's agent in repression, Judge Jeffreys, aroused intense bitterness that helped to dethrone the king only three years later.

For Leoni the first line is perplexing: 'From the context, the land of the great heavenly temple would appear to be England. The reason is best known to Nostradamus.' The temple seems to tie in somehow with the Monmouth affair, and, if explained, might confirm the interpretation of the second line. I believe an explanation exists and does confirm it, but the issues that it raises belong, like some others, further on.

The 'bark' is the ship of Peter, the papacy, and in the 1680s it was in the throes of a crisis that helps to establish that this is the decade we are looking at. There was no actual split, but the pope, Innocent XI (r.1678–89), was in conflict with Louis XIV of France over Louis's claims to authority over the Church in his kingdom. 'Gallicanism' threatened an outright break, and Louis seized Avignon, which was papal territory. The fourth line of the quatrain could refer to such assertions of freedom or to the slogan of Liberty in the English revolution that deposed James. Or to both. Nostradamus would probably have viewed the liberty as spurious in either case.

IV.89

Trente de Londres secret conjureront
Contre leur Roi, sur le pont l'enterprise:
Lui, satellites la mort dégoûteront,
Un Roi élu blond, natif de Frize.

Thirty of London will conspire secretly
Against their King, the enterprise on the sea:
He and his satellites will have a distaste for death,
A fair King elected, native of Frisia.

This one touches again on the 'Glorious Revolution' and the ousting of James II. His arbitrary rule and attempted revival of Catholicism made him unpopular, and a powerful group plotted to remove him, or at any rate curb him. His daughter Mary was married to the Dutchman William of Orange. It was resolved to invite William to come to England and restore constitutional government. Thirty is a plausible figure for the conspiratorial ring. The invitation was signed by only seven, but the disaffected Princess Anne, James's other daughter, headed a linked group of plotters, the 'Cockpit circle'. Its known membership, added to the seven signatories, comes close to Nostradamus's figure. Anne attended services in the Chapel Royal at Whitehall, where the preacher denounced Catholicism and therefore, by implication, James. An observer counted thirty prominent people as joining her in one of these demonstrations.

In the second line, *pont* with its usual meaning 'bridge' would be nonsensical, unless Nostradamus is thinking of communication between England and Holland. More likely he is adapting the Latin *pontus* meaning 'sea'. After various comings and goings across the water, William sailed with a fleet and troops and landed at Torbay in November 1688. Most of the royal officers deserted. James and his remaining supporters had no wish to be killed in a hopeless resistance, and he escaped to France. A new Parliament declared the throne vacant and offered the crown to William and Mary jointly, with constitutional safeguards. For the first time in England, the succession was elective.

William III was born in The Hague, not in the province of Frisia or Friesland, but the ancient name could stand for Holland in general. Portraits do not show fair hair. Despite that detail, this prediction has the same kind of interest as the one about Charles's execution. In Nostradamus's time the notion of a Dutchman being elected as king of England, after a conspiracy to banish the legitimate sovereign, would have been most unlikely to occur to anyone in the normal course of political reflection.

IV.2

Par mort la France prendra voyage à faire,
Classe par mer, marcher monts Pyrenées,
Espaigne en trouble, marcher gent militaire,
Des plus grandes Dames en France emmenées.

Because of death France will be taking a journey,
Fleet by sea, marching over the Pyrenees mountains,

Spain in trouble, military people marching,
Greatest ladies brought into France.

French armies have crossed the Pyrenees more than once, but a
'death' as the cause of it allows only a single possibility. The
quatrain fits the War of the Spanish Succession. In 1700 the
Spanish king, Charles II, Carlos the Bewitched, died childless,
leaving his dominions (with reasonable hereditary correctness) to
the Bourbon prince Philip of Anjou, a grandson of Louis XIV
who was still reigning. Alarmed at the prospect of Philip
succeeding to the French throne as well and thus uniting the
kingdoms, Britain, Austria and other countries formed a coalition
to keep him out and impose an Austrian archduke on the Spanish.
The resulting war began in 1701. French forces supported Philip,
and Spain was fought over, to its profound distress, incidentally
losing Gibraltar.

The fourth line might have been better placed at the beginning.
It is a somewhat cryptic retrospect accounting for Philip's claim
that caused the war. The Spanish royal line was linked with the
French through the marriage of two Spanish princesses to two
French kings, Louis XIII and Louis XIV himself.

III.15
Coeur, vigeur, gloire le regne changera,
De tous points contre ayant son adversaire:
Lors France enfance par mort subjuguera,
Un grand Régent sera lors plus contraire.

The realm will change in heart, vigour and glory,
At all points having its adversary opposed:
Then France through death will be made subject to infancy,
A great Regent will then be most contrary.

This quatrain can be seen as a sequel to the preceding. After ten
years of war France was disillusioned, exhausted and impoverished, with the coalition's armies on every side. A partial recovery
led to the Treaty of Utrecht in 1713, allowing Philip to rule in
Spain after all. But the vaunted 'glory' of Louis XIV was at a low

ebb. He died in 1715. His only son was already dead, and so was the grandson to whom the succession would have gone. The new king was his great-grandson, the five-year-old Louis XV, making a regency necessary. Previous French regents had been women, but this one, uniquely, was a man, Philippe, Duc d'Orléans. The masculine *un* in the fourth line is decisive: Philippe is the only French regent whom the line fits. Hence there is no other reading of the rest. He was very 'contrary' indeed, 'contrary' with the stress on the first syllable meaning 'opposite', not 'contrary' with the stress on the second syllable meaning 'perverse' or 'wilful'. Philippe was a living reaction against the late king with his grandeur, morality and power politics. He was interested in art and chemistry; he caused financial havoc by backing the Mississippi Scheme, France's equivalent of the South Sea Bubble; he disowned the Stuart Pretender whom Louis had supported; he was irreligious; and he was sexually uninhibited. Also unlike Louis towards the end, he was popular.

V.38

Ce grand monarque qu'au mort succédera
Donnera vie illicite et lubrique:
Par nonchalance à tous concédera,
Qu'à la parfin faudra la loi Salique.

He who will succeed that great monarch on his death
Will lead an illicit and debauched life:
Through nonchalance he will give way to all,
So that in the end the Salic Law will fail.

Louis XIV at his height was called the *Grand Monarque*, and here is that unique sobriquet intact. The successor is therefore Louis XV, whom III.15 left as a child. After the regency ended, he had a long reign. This quatrain notes some of his less attractive features, saying much in deceptively few words. His 'illicit and debauched life' is notorious. *Nonchalance*, not caring, if more reproachful than 'nonchalance' in English. It is reflected in the remark *Après nous le déluge* attributed to his best-known mistress, Mme de Pompadour. The 'giving way' is illustrated in state affairs. In 1748, after the

War of the Austrian Succession, he conducted peace negotiations, and although France had done well in the war, he was persuaded to renounce most of what he could have gained.

The Salic Law debarred women from ruling in France, except as regents acting in the name of child-kings who would assume power as soon as possible. However, Louis's weakness and irresponsibility – not any liberalism of outlook – did enable women to rule. When Mme de Pompadour gave her mind to it, she practically became the government. The later mistress, Mme du Barry, a far less gifted person, could still force the dismissal of Choiseul, Louis's most capable minister.

IX.77

Le regne pris le Roi conjurera,
La dame prise à mort jurés a sort:
La vie à Reine fils on déniera,
Et la pellix au fort de la consort.

The realm taken, the King will conspire,
The lady taken to death [by those] sworn by lot:
They will refuse life to the Queen's son
And the mistress, at the fort of the wife.

(The highly compressed sense is helped by improved punctuation.) In view of the picture of royalty in distress, the obvious application is to the French Revolution. The first line corresponds to a phase in 1791–2 when the revolutionaries had taken control and Louis XVI was concocting plans of escape and intriguing with foreign powers for intervention – the actions that led to his being convicted of treason, of conspiring against Liberty, in fact. Nostradamus's verb is interesting. Kings might be accused of all kinds of villainy, but they were seldom thought of as conspiring. Louis was. He was guillotined in January 1793.

With Louis XVI identified, the lady in the second line has to be his wife Marie Antoinette, officially deposed, put on trial as the Widow Capet and executed. It is said that the jurors who sent her to her death were chosen by lot, and this was a novelty. I am not sure of the literal fact, but their names and occupations are on record, and they look like a mixed group of revolutionaries, a grab-bag. The phrase 'by lot' could be a gibe. I recall someone ridiculing the composition of a research team, who said the organizer had 'drawn names from a hat'.

Marie Antoinette was guillotined in October 1793. *Reine fils* in the third line could mean 'the queen's son' or 'the queen and her son'. Since her own death has just been noted, it is better to take this line as referring to her son alone, correctly designated, because she *was* queen when he was born. The young Dauphin, nominally Louis XVII, was kept in custody. His fate is doubtful, but he never reappeared. He is thought to have been killed; he was certainly 'refused life'.

After the foregoing, the natural reading of the last line is that the 'mistress' is Mme du Barry, who was arrested in November 1793. The *pellix/consort* antithesis rather suggests that she was the mistress of Louis XVI, whereas she was actually the mistress of his predecessor. Still, there could be a touch of irony in Nostradamus's saying what he does and, indeed, in his mentioning her at all, since she was not one of the Terror's major victims. When Marie Antoinette was first at court, she loathed Mme du Barry and persistently snubbed her. Yet now they were brought together in misfortune. If Nostradamus had this in mind, he would doubtless have wanted the mistress to be in the same prison as the wife. In reality she was not lodged in the Conciergerie, where the queen had been, but in the prison of Sainte-Pelagie. However, she was condemned and executed – 'refused life' – for 'wasting the treasure of the state' by her past extravagance.

These, then, are the thirteen Class A quatrains that may be called the miscellaneous set. Arranged in order of date as here, they cover about 230 years and end in November 1793. In view of the claims made by Nostradamian zealots, a question may be asked at once. Don't they go any further? They do not. The other thirteen are, as we shall see, different. Meanwhile, we can summarize the good predictions thus far. The number must depend to some extent on individual judgement, but I make it 45, as follows:

III.41
Condé's election as head of the Huguenot council
His treachery to the king
The shot through his head

VIII.50
Don John's capture of Tunis
Plague in Spain at about the same time

X.18
Henry of Navarre's accession to the French throne
His recognition by Rome
The exclusion of the other two claimants

IX.18
Louis XIII's march into Nancy
The arrest of the Elector and his transfer to Flanders
The execution of Montmorency in unusual circumstances
(Clerepeyne possibly, but too uncertain to include)

VIII.37
Charles I's imprisonment near the Thames
His condemnation to death
His shirt

IX.49
Action against Antwerp
Charles I's execution by Parliament

X.100
The British Empire
Its 300-year duration
Supersession of Portuguese in Asia

VI.22
Execution of Monmouth by his uncle James II
Divisions in the Catholic Church

IV.89
Conspiracy in London against King James
Maritime activity
Flight of James

Election of William III
His Dutch origin

IV.2
French involvement in Spain through a royal death
Consequent warfare by land and sea
Misfortune for Spain
Origin of the trouble in dynastic marriages

III.15
French exhaustion in the War of the Spanish Succession
Encircling by the enemy coalition
A child becoming king through the ruler's death
Reign of the only male regent in French history
His difference in character

V.38
Death of the Grand Monarque, Louis XIV
Licentious habits of his successor, Louis XV
Louis's weakness and irresponsibility
Unprecedented power of women in France

IX.77
Take-over of the State by French revolutionaries
Louis XVI's 'conspiring' with royalists and foreign powers
Marie Antoinette's condemnation to death
Selection of jurors by lot?
Death of the Dauphin
Death of the former royal mistress, Madame du Barry

These predictions are not dispersed singly over some vast expanse
of text. They are all in the thirteen quatrains, with appropriate
linkages.

Chapter Nine

Nostradamus: The Sequence

The last of the Class A quatrains listed as 'miscellaneous' in Chapter 8 is the one about the French Revolution, IX.77, which goes as far as November 1793. Beginning directly after that, within a matter of weeks, comes a period of eighty years in which the record is quite different. The remaining thirteen Class A quatrains all find their places in this period and are far from miscellaneous. Their single apparent theme is the Bonaparte phenomenon. Ten of them fit the original Napoleon, and three fit his nephew Napoleon III. In that whole stretch of eighty years, there are no non-Napoleonic events to which any of Nostradamus's quatrains can be matched with assurance. The Bonapartes monopolize the fulfilments.

The ten quatrains fitting the first Napoleon are the more important. One man predominates from 1793 to 1815, as he does in the history of the time. It is as if Nostradamus, cherishing the dream of a Second Charlemagne, focused on a future ruler of France who claimed to inherit Charlemagne's status. A residual but disenchanted interest carries over to his nephew.

Five of the major ten are in Century IV, but I doubt if that is enough of a concentration to be significant. The others are scattered. All ten apply to Napoleon with no credible application to anyone else. After a prefatory quatrain giving an overview, the rest can be arranged chronologically by the dates of the events they fit. Assembled in this way they form a sequence linking them in mutual support. They stretch from end to end of Napoleon's public career, with a cumulative effect.

As with the miscellaneous series, most of the interpretations that follow have been published before, some of them in the emperor's lifetime. I continue to rely on Leoni, although dissenting when he raises needless uncertainties by overlooking important points. While not inventing much myself, I have added details that have gone unnoticed hitherto, partly because better information has become available.

To begin with the prefatory quatrain, the overview:

I.60
Un Empereur naîtra près d'Italie,
Qui à l'Empire sera vendu bien cher;
Diront avec quels gens il se rallie
Qu'on trouvera moins prince que boucher.

An Emperor will be born near Italy,
Who will cost the Empire very dear;
They will say that from the sort of people who surround him
He is to be found less prince than butcher.

Napoleon Bonaparte was born in Corsica, close to Italy, and made himself Emperor of the French in 1804. The second line says '*the* Empire', not '*his* Empire'. A sixteenth-century author using those words would be much more likely to refer to the ancient Holy Roman Empire of Germany than to a realm as yet non-existent. Napoleon, the upstart with a rival imperial title, did cost the Holy Roman Empire dear. He abolished it in 1806. He dominated most of Europe through army chiefs and his own relatives, to whom he gave royal status but who, like himself, were decidedly un-royal. The loss of life in the wars his system produced was enormous. Metternich, Austria's foreign minister and a spokes-man of the old order, quoted him as saying that as a soldier he had different values: he would sacrifice a million men if necessary, and their deaths wouldn't mean much to him. Whether or not the remark is authentic, Metternich reported it, and people thought it credible and repeated it. That is, 'they will say', as Nostradamus foresees.

Is there an alternative reading? The first two lines might apply

to a Holy Roman Emperor born near Italy who did the Empire
grave harm. Ferdinand II, who was born in Graz – reasonably
near Italy – and reigned from 1619 to 1637, has been named as a
candidate. He launched the Thirty Years' War by an attempt to
subdue dissident parts of his dominions and employed some
ruthless commanders. This identification would still be predictive.
But Ferdinand was a legitimate sovereign, not thought of in the
way indicated in the third and fourth lines. Much of the
devastation of Germany was due to foreign intervention rather
than his own actions. It has to be Napoleon.

The story begins:

VII.13

De la cité marine et tributaire
La tête rasé prendra la satrapie:
Chasser sordide qui puis sera contraire,
Par quatorze ans tiendra la tyrannie.

From the marine and tributary city
The shaven head will take the satrapy:
To chase the sordid one that will then be against him,
For fourteen years he will hold the tyranny.

The fourth line shows that this quatrain is about someone who
will wield autocratic power, probably without royal legitimacy,
for fourteen years. That eliminates nearly every recorded ruler
whom the rest might be made to fit. Napoleon remains. What we
can detect here is a sketch of his rise to the supremacy he did hold
for fourteen years. The meaning of the phrase 'shaven head',
applied to him, emerges from the interpretation.

In 1793 the Mediterranean port of Toulon was a base for
French royalists, under the protection of a British force commanded by Admiral Hood. The British war aim, in concert with
continental allies, was to suppress the French Revolution and
restore the monarchy. But Hood raised his own national flag over
the city, and his conduct could be construed as intended to create
another Gibraltar. Toulon was 'marine' as being a seaport and
'tributary' as being under foreign control. Thanks mainly to the

brilliant young officer Bonaparte, the French Republic recaptured it in December. He became well known, a popular hero, and his promotion ensued. In 1796 the five-man Directory that governed France sent him to take charge of an army facing the Austrians in Italy. He won decisively and dictated terms of peace himself.

Here Nostradamus's word 'satrapy' comes in. 'Satrap', meaning a provincial governor in ancient Persia, was used in France to mean an over-mighty subject who made the government uneasy. That was what Napoleon now was, owing, ultimately, to his success at Toulon. Resentful of the corrupt Directory – a sordid institution, rather than a sordid person – he declared in the spring of 1798 that it 'must be overthrown'. He could not take any action at once because he was occupied with an expedition to Egypt, his own idea. Nostradamus's 'satrapy' may have a second aptitude: Egypt was formerly a satrapy of Persia. Presently the Directors were wondering if they could leave him in Egypt with his army, cut off by the British fleet, or otherwise keep him away from Paris. When he got back in October 1799, they had notions of putting him on trial for insubordination or even shooting him. They did neither.

He now approached two of the Directors, Barras and Sieyès, who were thinking of constitutional change. He conspired with Sieyès, and in a coup launched on 9 November (18 Brumaire in the French revolutionary calendar) he ousted the entrenched politicians who wanted him outlawed and dissolved the Directory. With his co-conspirator he set up a Consulate of three, but he himself, as First Consul, had the real authority.

Now, the 'shaven head'. This is an image corresponding to his accession to power. Through most of the 1790s many men still wore wigs, as the kings of France had done for a long time. Napoleon did not. He kept his hair long in the revolutionary fashion. In 1799, however, he arrived at his momentous meeting with Barras and Sieyès with it cut much shorter. The haircut was a political statement marking a crucial shift to the right. This had a limit: he never went to the length of wearing a wig, although when he became First Consul, his two colleagues did. In the ensuing years his hairline receded. The 'shaven head' is slightly anachronistic where it occurs, but the point is made.

The sting of this quatrain is in the tail. Nostradamus surprises the reader with a sudden exactitude, refuting any attempt to dismiss the rest as too vague. Napoleon's personal rule – his tyranny, in the eyes of a believer in legitimate royalty – was inaugurated by the coup of Brumaire. It lasted until April 1814: fourteen years and odd months.

IV.26 *(in Provençal, for no known reason)*
Lou grand eyssame se leuera d'abelhos,
Que non sauran don te siegen venguddos;
De nuech l'embousque, lou gach dessous las treilhos
Cieutad trahido per cinq lengose non nudos.

The great swarm of bees will arise,
Such that one will not know whence they have come;
By night the ambush, the sentinel under the vines,
City delivered by five babblers not naked.

The coup of Brumaire, further. The swarm of bees is an image defining Napoleon and his entourage. The bee (somewhat later, admittedly) became his personal emblem, conspicuous in the Tuileries palace and at Fontainebleau and Malmaison.

With his brothers Joseph and Lucien, he plotted the removal of the Directory, which had little left to offer but talk. A Council of Five Hundred, the nearest equivalent to a parliament, met in the Orangerie at Saint Cloud. Lucien Bonaparte was a member and had just been elected as its president. Napoleon walked in on the Council and tried to dominate it. The deputies, taken by surprise, raised a menacing uproar.

Lucien managed to bring the situation under control. Napoleon was supported by a large body of soldiers, and their leader, Joachim Murat, led them into the building. Most of the deputies fled at once, leaving the Orangerie by the nearest exits and scattering in the gardens outside. By half-past seven in the evening the rest had followed and it was dark. The soldiers who had been standing guard, organized by Lucien, caught and rounded up

Napoleon kings

sixty-one of the 500. About nine o'clock they were assembled. Converted or coerced, they voted to end the existing constitution. The formation of a provisional authority went on through the night and Napoleon's coup was completed by about four o'clock in the morning.

The five Directors handed over the capital without a struggle. Sieyès had been part of the conspiracy all along. Barras had been offered a bribe to resign, but agreed to resign without it. *Non nudos*, applied to the five surrendering 'babblers', can be taken as an allusion to corruption in office. They had done very well for themselves and were anything but naked.

IV.37

Gaulois par sauts, monts viendra pénétrer:
Occupera le grand lieu de l'Insubre:
Au plus profound son ost fera entrer,
Gennes, Monech pousseront classe rubre.

The Gaul will come to penetrate the mountains by leaps:
He will occupy the great place of Insubria:
He will make his army enter to the greatest depth,
Genoa and Monaco will drive back the red fleet.

'Gaul', of course, need not mean an ancient Gaul. The word could be used poetically for a Frenchman – Wordsworth does, for instance – and Napoleon was French by adoption.

In February 1800 a plebiscite, manipulated by Lucien, endorsed the new Consulate, and Sieyès drew up a constitution that gave Napoleon a free hand. France was at war with Britain still and also with a resurgent Austria. A British fleet under Admiral Keith, who had taken part in the Toulon affair, was blockading the French and Italian Riviera. On 23 May his ships attacked Monaco (France had absorbed the small principality). A French force was holding Genoa. The Austrians, who controlled most of northern Italy, besieged it with a view to linking up with Keith for combined operations.

Napoleon startled everyone by a dramatic crossing of the Alps, leading an army of 40,000 over the Great St Bernard Pass. Jacques

David's well-known equestrian painting romanticizes his feat. 'Insubria' is an old name for part of Lombardy, and 'the great place of Insubria' is a circumlocution for Milan, which he captured on 2 June. Keith meanwhile had arrived at Genoa, and it fell to a joint British–Austrian assault, but too late. Napoleon's cross-country offensive was neutralizing the Austrian strategy. The French retook Genoa. Under the terms of an armistice agreed on 14 June they moved in very promptly; Keith had barely time to get his ship out of the harbour. A hostile coastline now extended to the other point of contention, Monaco, and the British fleet withdrew.

Nothing shows why a British fleet should be 'red', unless there is some kind of allusion to the red flag flown by a division of the fleet when in action, its commander being 'Admiral of the Red'. Or, since British soldiers were redcoats, the adjective might have been extended to the armed forces in general. However, one simple fact is that Nostradamus needed a rhyme.

IV.54

Du nom qui onc ne fut au Roi Gaulois
Jamais ne fut un foudre si craintif,
Tremblant l'Italie, l'Espagne et les Anglois;
De femmes étranges grandement attentif.

Of the name which no Gallic king ever had
Never was there so fearful a thunderbolt;
Italy, Spain and the English trembling;
Very attentive to foreign women.

No king of France was ever called Napoleon. The royal names were Louis, Charles, Philip, Henry, Francis and John.

By December 1800 the First Consul seemed invincible. He routed the Austrians at Hohenlinden – or to be precise, his general Moreau did – and peace was concluded in February 1801. With this continental opponent out of the way, he lost no time in bringing pressure to bear on other nations, overawed by his victories. In March he bullied the king of Naples into closing his ports to the British fleet and handing over the island of Elba. In the same month, he intimidated the Spanish into accepting a treaty that bound Spain to France and gave permission for his troops to march through, if he decided to invade Portugal.

Italy and Spain had both 'trembled', the English not exactly, but they were tired of war and anxious for an end to it. They had been fighting France for eight years. The Royal Navy ruled the seas, but without allies to tackle the French on land there was no prospect of winning. William Pitt resigned as Prime Minister and was replaced in 1801 by the more pliable Henry Addington. Negotiations led to the Treaty of Amiens in March 1802. Britain kept some overseas conquests, such as Trinidad and Ceylon, and relinquished others, such as the Cape of Good Hope. Napoleon hung on to most of his gains. The original British aim of overthrowing the French Republic and restoring the monarchy was (for the moment) no longer talked about. This was the nearest Napoleon ever came to inducing a surrender by perfidious Albion. When the war resumed, and he made ostentatious preparations to invade England, the mood changed.

The fourth line is unexpected. There is a little uncertainty over the wording, but the essential point about 'foreign women' is clear and very apt to Napoleon. Best known of the women in his life are Josephine, a Creole, Marie Walewska, a Pole, and Marie Louise, an Austrian.

> VIII.57
> De soldat simple parviendra en empire,
> De robe courte parviendra à la longue;
> Vaillant aux armes en Énglise où plus pire,
> Vexer les prêtres comme l'eau fait l'éponge.

> From simple soldier he will attain to empire,
> From short robe he will attain to the long:
> Valiant in arms in the Church the very worst,
> To vex the priests as water does the sponge.

The first line needs no comment, except that 'empire' with a small *e* denotes imperial power, not a political entity. Napoleon crowned himself in 1804. His official garment as First Consul had been short, his robe as Emperor was long. It was on this occasion that he made himself out to be the new Charlemagne, expressing the claim in the insignia on his coach and carrying Charlemagne's sceptre, or what was alleged to be his sceptre, at the ceremony. Subsequently, in a letter to his uncle Cardinal Fesch in which he asserted his right to dominate the Church, he wrote: 'I am Charlemagne.'

The third line refers to his courage in battle, which was never in doubt. He accompanied his soldiers on many campaigns and was wounded himself. At Waterloo he was not afraid to take up a position where enemy guns could shoot at him, although Wellington thought it would not be playing the game to do so.

A claim that the first line would apply also to Hitler is fair, but the second and third lines nullify it. Hitler did not wear ceremonial garments of either length; certainly not a long robe. Despite his rather mysterious Iron Cross, he showed no great courage in battle during the First World War. When he was Führer the issue never arose, whereas it did with Napoleon throughout his reign. As in I.60, the rival candidate is not really an acceptable choice.

Beyond the brief remark here, Nostradamus ignores Napoleon's dealings with the Church. One explanation of the 'sponge' image is that he has in mind a sponge's expansion and contraction as water goes in and out and implies that Napoleon will show alternate goodwill and enmity. But he sees the Emperor's record as bad on the whole. A survey of the course of events shows that his judgement, however arrived at, is on the right lines.

Napoleon's relationship with the Church was quite friendly at first. In 1801 he was showing it favour, although from political rather than religious motives. He negotiated a Concordat with Pope Pius VII. Then he annoyed the pope by making unilateral changes. In 1804 he brought him to Paris for the coronation and treated him disrespectfully. In 1808 French troops occupied Rome. In May 1809 Napoleon annexed what was left of the papal territories, and Pius retorted on 11 June by excommunicating him. Napoleon kidnapped the pontiff and shifted him from place to place, ending up at Fontainebleau.

The 'vexing' was extended. Napoleon divorced Josephine amid ecclesiastical rumblings and married the archduchess Marie Louise. Still prepared to be friendly with his own clergy, he invited thirty-two cardinals to the wedding in April 1810. Many were no longer prepared to be friendly with the Emperor, however, and only eleven attended. Noticing the empty reserved seats, he was furious and imprisoned several of the absentees, seizing property that belonged to them. After their release he forbade them to wear red, disgracing them visibly as 'Black Cardinals'.

It was not long before he wanted the captive pope to accept a new Concordat, crown Marie Louise and recognize their son's title 'King of Rome'. Pius signed in January 1813 but queried the agreement when he learned that Napoleon had announced it as a *fait accompli* before signature. Pius declared his opposition to the Concordat in March, saying it 'tore his spirit', and resisted further Napoleonic manoeuvres, including an attempt to transfer the Vatican to Paris.

IV.75
Prêt à combattre fera défection,
Chef adversaire obtiendra la victoire:
L'arrière-garde fera défension,
Les défaillants morts au blanc territoire.

Ready to fight, one will desert,
The chief adversary will obtain the victory:
The rearguard will make a defence,
The faltering ones dead in the white territory.

The quatrains about Napoleon, after the prefatory I.60, fall into two groups. The first traces his rise and culminates in 1804 with his coronation. The second begins some years later with the quatrain above, IV.75, and traces his decline. Nothing anywhere in the Centuries can be convincingly fitted to events in between, during his years of triumphalism. A few passing phrases, such as the one about foreign women, refer to this period, but there is no whole quatrain that does; none is applicable to the government of

France, the battles of Austerlitz and Jena or the attempts to organize Europe. Perhaps Nostradamus became disillusioned with the Second Charlemagne and lost interest in him, recovering it only when he could follow him on the way out.

This quatrain's Napoleonic aptitude becomes clearer as it goes along. The most appropriate deserter is Marshal Bernadotte. After fighting for Napoleon, zealously if not always competently, he accepted an invitation to become Crown Prince of Sweden and took up his post in September 1810. Napoleon was displeased. He preferred to make his own royal appointments. The Swedish king's health failed and Bernadotte became the *de facto* ruler. He took to calling himself Karl Johan.

His defection occurred in 1812, the fatal year to which this quatrain applies. Napoleon turned against Russia. Bernadotte declined to turn with him, and made his peace with Tsar Alexander at a meeting in Finland during the summer. As a result, Russian troops did not have to stay in the north to guard the frontier, and the tsar moved them southwards to oppose the Grande Armée as it invaded Russia, now, for the moment, the Emperor's 'chief adversary'.

After a close-run and costly battle at Borodino, Napoleon took Moscow, but the Russians rejected his overtures for peace and he was forced into retreat. On 3 November snow began to fall, and the wintry conditions grew swiftly worse. A historic rearguard action by Marshals Ney and Victor kept the enemy off, while what was left of Napoleon's forces escaped over the icy Berezina. Innumerable men dropped out during the retreat, and collapsed and died in the snowbound landscape – the 'white territory'. The Grande Armée was almost destroyed.

Bernadotte carried his defection further. In October 1813 he played a major part in Napoleon's defeat at the battle of Leipzig, which doomed the Empire. In exile on St Helena, Napoleon said: 'A Frenchman held the destiny of the world in his hands. He was one of the principal direct causes of our misfortunes.'

One or two commentators have gone astray over this quatrain by making a false start. Overanxious to find something about Waterloo, they have identified the deserter as Marshal Grouchy, who failed to arrive with reinforcements. But Grouchy was not a candidate. He was loyal, and his non-arrival was due to misguided strategy and misleading orders. An interpretation starting from Grouchy must collapse in any case on the 'white territory'.

Napoleon himself, by the way, had a precognitive warning of the Russian disaster. In 1808, during a conference with the tsar at Erfurt, he had a nightmare in which he was devoured by a bear. The natural explanation is that this was an understandable anxiety dream. Alexander had recently been fighting against him, and although the two had reached an agreement, it was beginning to emerge at Erfurt that the tsar might revert to hostility. But the dream did not, in fact, reflect any conscious concern at all. Napoleon spoke of it at various times and tried to interpret it, but was apparently blind to the bear's obvious symbolism: the image had come to him as images sometimes came to biblical prophets, without meaning until they were given an explanation. For Napoleon, the explanation was not forthcoming.

X.34

Gaulois qu'empire par guerre occupera
Par son beau-frère mineur sera trahi:
Par cheval rude voltigeant traînera,
Du fait le frère longtemps sera haï.

The Gaul who will hold empire through war
Will be betrayed by his lesser brother-in-law:
He will be dragged by a fierce prancing horse,
The brother will be hated for the deed for a long time.

The word 'empire' means imperial power, as in VIII.57. Napoleon's power depended on military ascendancy, and when that ended, it crumbled. His subordinate kingdoms were lost to him. One of these was in southern Italy. His sister Caroline was married to Joachim Murat, the man who dispersed the deputies in the coup of Brumaire, a fine leader of the cavalry but not much more than that. Napoleon had created him king of Naples. He accompanied the Emperor on the Russian campaign, and took charge of the remnant of the Grande Armée after Napoleon left it.

Joachim Murat

On 11 January 1814, judging that all was lost, Murat changed sides and declared war on France. Napoleon called his act 'infamous' and said he hoped to live long enough to take vengeance.

The horse metaphor may echo Murat's fame as a cavalry leader. He was notoriously a 'fierce prancing' character. He agonized over the betrayal. It saved his crown for little more than a year, and his erratic behaviour made him enemies everywhere. When Napoleon returned from his first exile, Murat professed loyalty again and launched a campaign against the Austrians, who, however, won. Napoleon refused to have anything more to do with him. Having lost his Neapolitan kingdom, he made a bid to recover it, but was now so unpopular that he got no support, and was arrested and shot. The 'long time' in the quatrain seems exaggerated. Still, it could apply to Napoleon's resentment for the rest of his own life or to the lasting animosity of Bonapartists.

IV.70
Bien contigué des grands monts Pyrenées,
Un contre l'Aigle grande copie adresser:
Ouvertes veines, forces exterminées,
Que jusqu'à Pau le chef viendra chasser.

Quite contiguous to the great Pyrenees mountains,
One to direct a great army against the Eagle:
Veins opened, forces exterminated,
Which the leader will come to chase as far as Pau.

The Eagle in juxtaposition to the Pyrenees is clearly the familiar symbol of Napoleon's France, which surmounted his standards. The enemy leader operating in this area has to be Wellington, and the time is early 1814, towards the close of the Peninsular War. There is a slight textual uncertainty in the fourth line, but the sense seems to be as indicated.

Having expelled the Eagle from Spain, Wellington passed the Pyrenees near Bayonne. He drove back Soult, the French commander, to Orthez beside the Gave de Pau – in Pyrenean terminology, the River of Pau. Soult made a stand on 27 February, but without success, and during March he retreated eastward by way of Pau itself. The quatrain is correct as far as it goes, and the mention of Pau is impressive, since this was not a place much associated with warfare. It would be better, though, if Wellington's pursuit had stopped there. Actually he pushed on to Toulouse, where a final battle was fought – tragically, because Napoleon had abdicated, but no trustworthy report had got through.

The phrase 'veins opened' may allude in a general way to the bloodshed of war. However, a specific explanation is possible, and surprising. The men of the 29th Foot, a component of Wellington's army in the Peninsula, were nicknamed 'The Vein Openers'. This nickname dated from 1770. Later, when the 29th Foot became the Worcestershire Regiment, it passed out of use.

I.32
Le grand Empire sera tôt translaté
En lieu petit qui bien tôt viendra croître:
Lieu bien infime d'exiguë comté
Où au milieu viendra poser son sceptre.

The great Empire will soon be transferred
To a little place which will very soon come to grow:
A very lowly place in a tiny domain
Where in the middle he will come to lay down his sceptre.

This quatrain applies, neatly if elliptically, to both Napoleon's exiles.

When he abdicated in April 1814 his 'great Empire' was finished. The Powers that had conquered him – Britain, Austria, Prussia and Russia – hustled him off to rule a Mediterranean island, Elba. Thanks to the tsar's persuasion, they allowed him to retain his imperial title, so the Napoleonic Empire survived in a much reduced form, 'transferred to a little place'. Back in France, Louis XVIII was enthroned but quickly lost support. On 1 March 1815 Napoleon escaped and returned. Within three weeks Louis had fled, and Napoleon was again Emperor of the French. His mini-Empire had grown.

The Powers refused to tolerate him. At Waterloo in June,

Wellington and Blücher defeated him finally. He abdicated again and surrendered to the captain of a British warship, hoping that Britain would grant him asylum. He was, however, shipped off to the small Atlantic island of St Helena and kept there. The operation was supervised by his old adversary Admiral Keith. St Helena was the property of the East India Company, which placed it at the disposal of His Majesty's Government. It was allotted a governor and a garrison.

In the third line we seem to be missing a word or words to mark what is clearly a transition. After the 'growth' the place referred to cannot be Elba again, an Elba that has been left behind. While on Elba, moreover, Napoleon never 'laid down his sceptre'. He always assumed that his stay was temporary and that he would get back, as he did.

So we are on St Helena if we are anywhere. The old word *comté* meant a territorial unit smaller than a country, usually much smaller. In this context I think it can be rendered 'domain', especially as the island was a domain of the East India Company and not a colony. The 'tiny domain' is contrasted with the 'great Empire'. Given that the tiny domain is St Helena, the very lowly place has to be in it. The obvious identification is Longwood, where Napoleon was lodged. This building housed him and his permitted staff. Tales of squalid conditions were largely invented by propagandists fabricating a martyrdom, but it was very lowly indeed after his palaces. In the fourth line, the redundant-looking *au milieu* is not altogether so. If he was not at the island's geographic centre, he was at least compelled to live inland, at a distance from the coast where a boat might have taken him away.

The final metaphor is correct, and does not work anywhere else. On St Helena Napoleon was forced to accept that he would never escape, never return. At Longwood he at last gave up his pretensions, 'laid down his sceptre', and took to dictating memoirs and creating his own legend.

After 1815 comes a stretch of years in which none of Nostradamus's quatrains fit anything convincingly. Napoleon died in 1821; his son Napoleon II, who never reigned, died in 1832. As a result, the Emperor's nephew Louis Napoleon became the

Bonapartist claimant. For the moment, Louis-Philippe was king of France, but in 1848 he was forced to abdicate and another Republic came into being. The pretender saw his opportunity. He put himself up as a candidate for the presidency, and won by a huge margin. Let Nostradamus take up the story.

VIII.41

Élu sera Renard ne sonnant mot,
Faisant le saint public vivant pain d'orge,
Tyranniser après tout à un cop,
Mettant à pied des plus grands sur la gorge.

A Fox will be elected without saying a word,
Playing the saint in public, living on barley bread;
Afterwards he will very suddenly tyrannize,
Putting his foot on the throats of the greatest men.

Louis Napoleon was as crafty as foxes are proverbially supposed to be. Also, he did not talk much, and was nicknamed *Le Taciturne*. As campaigner and as President he talked of peace and prosperity and popular rights. But on 2 December 1851, by a sudden *coup d'état*, he abolished the republican constitution and launched a regime of absolutism and repression. A year later he proclaimed himself Napoleon III.

The word *cop*, retained for the rhyme, is the same as *coup*. 'Living on barley bread' has a metaphorical meaning, 'feathering one's nest', which is apt enough. But this Napoleon is said to have had, literally, a fondness for barley bread. If so, the *double entendre* would clinch the identification.

VIII.43

Par le décide de deux choses bâtards,
Neveu du sang occupera le regne,
Dedans lectoyre seront les coups de dards,
Neveu par peur pliera l'enseigne.

Through the fall of two illegitimate things,
The Nephew by blood will occupy the realm;

Within *lectoyre* there will be blows by lances,
The Nephew through fear will fold up his standard.

The repeated 'Nephew' is emphatic and would not be a natural or logical label for many men who attained power. Louis Napoleon's main appeal in the 1848 election was that the great Napoleon was his uncle.

The two previous regimes, the government of Louis-Philippe and the Second Republic, would both have been illegitimate in Nostradamus's eyes, because France had a genuine royal heir, the Comte de Chambord. Both 'fell': Louis-Philippe's when he was driven out, the Republic when it was overthrown by the Nephew himself, blood-relative of the first Napoleon.

In this group as in the other, there are no prophecies about the Empire's years of success. Nostradamus goes straight to the end. The second 'Nephew' line parallels the first and constitutes the 'down' phase where the first was the 'up' phase. In the Franco-Prussian War of 1870, for which Napoleon III bears the principal blame, he was defeated at the key city of Sedan. Sick and unable to go on, he lost his nerve and, figuratively at least, folded up his standard, hoisting a white flag instead.

Lectoyre has been explained as an anagram of Le Torcey – more correctly, Torcy – a western suburb of Sedan, distinguished from the town in the 1870 map, but afterwards absorbed. If the anagram is acceptable, it confirms the location.

IV.65
Au déserteur de la grande forteresse,
Après qu'aura son lieu abandonné,
Son adversaire fera si grand prouesse,
L'Empereur tôt mort sera condamné.

Towards the deserter of the great fortress,
After he will have abandoned his place,
His adversary will exhibit such great prowess,
The Emperor soon dead will be condemned.

'Emperor' is the clincher. The quatrain has no possible application to the first Napoleon, and other emperors such as the Austrian are irrelevant.

Sedan was not a great fortress, but the chances of war had given it decisive importance, and Napoleon raised his white flag over the citadel. He surrendered himself to the Prussians at Donchery, a short way out beyond Torcy. Once he had 'deserted' Sedan and renounced his authority, their ascendancy was plain. They detained him in Germany until France had to accept defeat and a humiliating treaty. Released in March 1871, he went to England. France was now a republic again and opinion was embittered against him. He died in 1873.

With the Bonaparte series as with the miscellaneous series, the actual number of predictions will depend on how the count is made. The following list of fifty-five seems reasonable.

I.60
Napoleon's birth near Italy
His imperial title
His abolition of the Holy Roman Empire
The carnage caused by his political and military system

VII.13
Foreign dominance of Toulon
Napoleon's becoming a too-powerful subject through victory
    there
His conflict with the Directory
His political haircut
His fourteen-year rule

IV.26
Emblematic bees
The coup of Brumaire
Nocturnal round-up of deputies in the gardens
Capitulation by the five rich Directors

IV.37
Napoleon's crossing of the Alps
His capture of Milan
His march across northern Italy
Repulse of the British fleet at Genoa

IV.54
Napoleon's unprecedented name as ruler of France
His unequalled military success
His intimidation of Naples
His intimidation of Spain
His pressure on England, bringing the Treaty of Amiens
His attachment to foreign women

VIII.57
His rising from the ranks to imperial power
His change from a short official garment to a long one
His personal courage in war
His troubles with the Church

IV.75
Bernadotte's defection
The Russian defeat of Napoleon's invasion
The rearguard action by Ney and Victor
Soldiers dying in the snow

X.34
Napoleon's dependence on military success
His betrayal by his brother-in-law Murat
Murat's association with cavalry
His unpopularity as a result of the betrayal

IV.70
Wellington's passing of the Pyrenees
His pursuit of Soult to Pau with the 29th Foot

I.32
Napoleon's first exile, to Elba
His return and reconstitution of his Empire
His second exile, to St Helena
His final renunciation of power

VIII.41
Louis Napoleon's craftiness
His taciturnity

His public-spirited pose
His exploitation of his position for personal gain
His sudden *coup d'état*
His autocratic rule

VIII.43
Availability of power to 'the Nephew' through the fall of two
    previous regimes
His defeat, as Napoleon III, by the Prussians
His loss of nerve and capitulation
(Possible allusion to Torcy, a suburb of Sedan)

IV.65
Napoleon III's surrender of Sedan
His end as Emperor
Prussian military ascendancy
His death soon after
Public condemnation

As with the previous Class A series, all the fulfilments are packed
into thirteen quatrains.

With what I called the Class B quatrains, arguments in their
favour exist and have a degree of plausibility, more in some cases,
less in others. Despite the attention that a few of them have
received, it would be giving them too much weight to go into
detail or attempt a count of predictions. They may be summarized
briefly, with reference numbers for anyone who may wish to
follow them up. The more optimistic interpretations are in Erika
Cheetham's book *The Prophecies of Nostradamus*. Leoni tentatively
approves some of them.

Earliest in reputed fulfilment is the one about the death of the
king of France, already discussed (I.35). It made the prophet's
reputation, but is not as exact as many have taken it to be. After
this we have a possible allusion to the Casket Letters that were
used against Mary, Queen of Scots (VIII.23), and a better one to
the battle of Lepanto in 1571, when Don John of Austria defeated
the Turks (IX.42). There is a fairly credible quatrain about the

French royal family in 1575–88 (VI.11), another that may relate to France in 1580 and 1703 (VI.2), and another that may fit the accession of Henry of Navarre (IX.50).

Next come some possible references to events in Britain – to the death of Elizabeth I (VI.74), to flooding in the West Country (III.70) and to the career of Cromwell, including his victories at Dunbar and Worcester (V.60, VIII.76, VIII.56, X.4). A dubious quatrain about a French naval disaster in 1655 (III.87) is followed by two English ones, referring perhaps to the Plague in 1665 (IX.11) and the Great Fire of London in 1666 (II.51). The latter has often been cited as a good prediction, but it is not convincing. At least five may concern happenings in the French Revolution: the issue of a new currency (I.53), the attempted escape of Louis XVI and its sequel (IX.34), his beheading (I.57), atrocities at Nantes (V.33) and attacks on the Church (I.44). Other quatrains have been applied to the French Revolution – by Colin Wilson in *The Occult*, for instance – but the Centuries contain so many prophecies of death and disaster that it is too easy to find the Revolution, if one really wishes to. A further quatrain has been supposed, dubiously, to foreshadow the death of Pope Pius VI at Valence (II.97), and another could fit Louis XVIII, but this is very imprecise (X.16).

That makes twenty-two Class B quatrains; I said twenty-four. Two more need special scrutiny. They illustrate the strange fondness of Nostradamus enthusiasts for picking out, as prize exhibits, prophecies that are not among his best. Both are paraded like the one about the French king's death, and both, like that, are open to serious objections. One, III.77, is frankly weird.

Le tiers climat sous Aries compris
L'an mil sept cent vingt et sept en Octobre,
Le Roi de Perse par ceux d'Egypte pris:
Conflit, mort, perte: à la croix grand opprobre.

The third climate included under Aries,
The year 1727 in October,

    The King of Persia captured by those of Egypt:
    Conflict, death, loss: to the cross great shame.

To get not only a year but a month is wholly exceptional. It seems too good to be true. Yet in October 1727 a peace was concluded that ended a conflict in the Middle East, a region supposed to come under the sign of Aries. The trouble is that Nostradamus is totally wrong about the war. One of the combatants was indeed the Shah of Persia, a usurper named Ashraf. His opponent, however, was the Turkish Sultan. While Egypt was a province of the Ottoman Empire, 'those of Egypt' can hardly mean 'Turks'. The war did not end because the Shah was captured – no Shah ever was – or even defeated. He had had the advantage in the fighting, although he restored some territory, to secure peace and Turkish recognition for himself and his dynasty. As for 'to the cross great shame', it is simply irrelevant. Neither the Persians nor the Turks were Christians. This quatrain is in a class by itself, incredibly right in one way, absolutely wrong in another. Is it an amazing guess? Or could it be a correct prevision mysteriously garbled? I see no obvious answer.

    The other quatrain, IX.20, is much better known.

    De nuit viendra par la forêt de Reines,
    Deux pars voltorte Herne la pierre blanche,
    Le moine noir en gris dedans Varennes:
    Élu cap. cause tempête, feu, sang, tranche.

    By night will come through the forest of Reines
    Two couples roundabout route Queen, the white stone,
    The monk king in grey at Varennes:
    Elected Capet causes tempest, fire, blood, slice.

The reason why this has received so much emphasis is that the placename in the third line points to the flight of Louis XVI and Marie Antoinette, on 21 June 1791, when they tried to escape to Montmédy, near the frontier, and were stopped at Varennes. France has other towns called Varennes, but this is the famous one. To sustain the interpretation, the whole quatrain has to fit, but not all of it does. It is a curious muddle, which can be made to look excellent but is full of pitfalls.

To begin with, there is no forest of Reines through which the royal vehicle would have passed. A Forêt de la Reine is on the far side of Varennes and some way off to the southeast. Although the travellers did take a somewhat roundabout route, it was not as roundabout as that. *Deux pars* means two couples, despite the singular verb in the first line. Perhaps the queen's friends, Mme de Tourzel and Count Fersen, who assisted the flight, may count as a couple. Neither king nor queen is mentioned explicitly. *Herne* has to be an approximate anagram for *reine*, and *noir* for *roi*. Leoni allows that the manipulation is fair and in keeping with Nostradamus's practice in other places, but manipulation it is.

The white stone can be explained, but seems inappropriate. A 'day marked with a white stone' meant one to be remembered as good, an allusion to a Roman custom of marking lucky days on the calendar with a white stone or chalk. In this case, however, the day was far from lucky for the fugitives, unless the longest of the year was seen as auspicious for their cross-country journey, a decided misjudgement.

There is no obvious reason for Louis being called a monk. He was disguised as a valet and did wear a plain suit, which may have been grey – but it may equally have been brown.

The last line is clearer than the rest. Louis was a Capet and in a sense elected, as previous kings of France had not been: the revolutionary assembly had recognized his royal status while trying to make him constitutional. The words tempest, fire and blood suggest the violence that the Revolution unleashed. *Tranche* could carry a hint of the guillotine.

Nostradamus's time-range can be defined, provisionally at least. The Class B quatrains cover much the same period as the miscellaneous Class A quatrains. They end in the same year, 1793, apart from the two very doubtful ones about Pius VI and Louis XVIII, and if those are admitted they go only a little further. The Class A Napoleonic series extends to 1873, but after the Bonapartes are out of the picture there are no intelligible predictions. Nostradamus's apparent prevision stops there, unless we count his line in X.100 about the life expectancy of the British Empire, and it still does not point to terminal happenings in the twentieth century.

A quatrain with an undeniable later reference has this only because the prophet does something that he does very seldom, and in most cases erroneously. He gives a date.

> X.72
> L'an mil neuf cent nonante neuf sept mois,
> De ciel viendra un grand Roi deffrayeur:
> Ressusciter le grand Roi d'Angolmois,
> Avant après Mars regne par bonheur.

> The year 1999 seven months
> From the sky will come a great King of Terror:
> To bring back to life the great King of the Angolmois,
> Before and after Mars to reign by good luck.

The first line allows a little leeway. It might mean the seventh month of 1999 or, with 'and' understood, seven months after 1999, in 2000. The seventh month would be July as the year is reckoned now, or September in the calendar Nostradamus may have used. In 1999 this quatrain inspired forecasts of the end of the world, which it obviously does not predict. It is hard to tell what Nostradamus had in mind when he wrote it. The fourth line implies war, which the war-god Mars will regard as good luck. There is no evident clue to the airborne King of Terror. While *Angolmois* indicates Angoulême in southwest France, it has been explained as a scrambled version of *Mongolois*. If so, the king to be resuscitated, symbolically no doubt, would probably be Genghis Khan, and the quatrain could prognosticate some Asian upsurge.

Enthusiasts would deny that the nineteenth and twentieth centuries are so nearly blank. They have found fulfilments going on, a flood of further B cases. They credit Nostradamus with foretelling Pasteur, the Dreyfus affair, Rasputin, many episodes of the World Wars, the rise and decline of Communism, the career of Hitler (supposedly meant by 'Hister' in II.24, IV.68 and V.29), the Japanese attack on Pearl Harbor, the assassinations of the Kennedy brothers and an orbiting space station manned by an astronaut named Sam R. O'Brien ('Samarobrin' in VI.5). This kind of interpretation can be fun, but it has hurt Nostradamus by distracting attention from what is genuinely interesting. It is always fanciful, and it lacks clinching details like the duration of Napoleon's reign or his betrayal by his brother-in-law. One proof of its futility is that attempts to predict the future from Nostradamus's verses have practically always failed.

However, one such attempt did have a sort of success that gave it historical interest. Among many quatrains that are challenging yet obscure is III.57.

Sept fois changer verrez gent Britannique,
Teints en sang en deux cent nonante ans:
Franche non point appui Germanique,
Aries doute son pôle Bastarnan.

Seven times will you see the British nation change,
Steeped in blood in 290 years:
Free not at all its support Germanic,
Aries doubts his Bastarnian pole.

Charles Nicollaud set the ball rolling in 1914 with an explanation of the first and second lines. Nostradamus, he said, predicted that during a period of 290 years Britain would experience seven changes of government or dynasty. The period could not start until after 1603 when King James united England and Scotland as Great Britain. Nicollaud fixed on the execution of Charles I as the first change, added 290 to 1649 and arrived at 1939 for the seventh. This can be made to work after a fashion: abolition of monarchy, 1649; restoration of monarchy, 1660; ousting of James II by William of Orange, 1689; Stuart restoration by Anne, 1702; House of Hanover, 1714; House of Saxe-Coburg-Gotha, afterwards Windsor, 1901; and the hypothetical seventh in 1939.

In 1921 C.L. Loog, a German civil servant, brought out a study in which he followed Nicollaud and tried to explain the fourth line (the third remained cryptic). The ancient Bastarnae were a tribe inhabiting Poland. Loog made out that in 1939 the zodiacal sign Aries, presiding over the Poles at that time, would be deeply disquieted and a crisis would involve both Britain and Poland. 'Steeped in blood' looked ominous.

It was all arbitrary, and Nostradamus very likely meant nothing of the kind. Yet in 1939 Loog's crisis, or part of it, arrived. There was no British change of dynasty, but Germany invaded Poland and Britain declared war in Poland's support. Soon afterwards Frau Goebbels, the wife of Hitler's propaganda minister, happened to be reading a book that mentioned Loog. In bed at the time, she was so impressed by the prediction that she woke her husband and drew his attention to it. Several Germans sent him copies of the same book, with the same prediction underlined. It struck him that the pronouncements of Nostradamus and other astrologers might be used for propaganda, and he employed a Swiss astrologer, Karl Ernst Krafft, with unhappy consequences for Krafft, as we shall see.

Neither Loog's ingenuity nor his luck can make III.57 a Class A quatrain, or even, I would say, a Class B. The essential point remains unaffected. Nostradamus's gift, whatever its nature, has a time limit, and this limitation is adverse to the notion of guesswork. If his bull's-eyes were random shots, we would expect them to go on after Napoleon I or, for that matter, after Napoleon III, not cluster around the two Bonapartes and otherwise fade out.

Moreover, in addition to his time limit, he has a geographical limitation. Out of the twenty-six Class A quatrains, twenty have a French locale or connection and five of the remaining six are English. (Nostradamus tends to do rather well when he crosses the Channel.) Individual phrases and lines reach out beyond or refer to happenings elsewhere, but the concern with France or England is nearly always present, and it is the main element even when other countries are mentioned. The same is true of the B cases, although a few are Scottish rather than English.

Even the exceptions are curious, because they both involve the same person, Don John of Austria. In Class A, VIII.50 is about his capture of Tunis, and in Class B, IX.42 is – or may be – about his victory at Lepanto. It is amusing (probably no more than amusing) that he has an odd might-have-been connection with Mary, Queen of Scots. After the annulment of her catastrophic marriage to Bothwell, a plot was formed for Don John to rescue her from her English imprisonment, marry her himself and be Consort in England as well as Scotland. Nothing came of it. Her son King James, who was a spare-time versifier, wrote a poem about the battle of Lepanto, although a reader of his preface gathers that Don John would not have been welcome as a stepfather. G.K. Chesterton wrote a better poem on the same subject and an essay in 'alternative history' speculating on what would have happened if the marriage with Mary had taken place.

Apart from the irregularity with Don John, all the rest of Nostradamus's good quatrains refer to either France or Britain. Yet a survey of the whole corpus, the whole 942 quatrains, shows that a majority concern other countries or have no geographical connection or, at least, none that can be asserted with confidence. Often, where no country is clearly indicated, a French locale may be intended, but no impartial count could lift the French–British combination above minority status. Outside that combination, Nostradamus has hundreds of opportunities for scoring and never does. Or to be precise, he *may* score in some of his quatrains, but if they are judged by the standards defined here, they fail.

His success is regional; there is no random scatter. It is not a case of Nostradamus pouring out a mass of quatrains, and the Class A ones simply turning up anywhere and anyhow. They do not. All but one of the twenty-six belong to the minority that concern France and Britain. The same is true in principle of Class B, although the Class B quatrains are not so clear cut. To suppose that this just 'happened' is to suppose a statistical monstrosity. Furthermore, there is a monstrosity within the monstrosity. Thirteen of the twenty-six in Class A have the Bonaparte connection. They apply not simply to France, but to France in two short periods of time, under two exceptional regimes.

No scepticism can shift the irreducible minimum of fact. To reject all the prophecies, dismissing even the best as lucky hits, is still to confront the skewed distribution. With such a huge number of quatrains and a majority that concern neither France nor Britain, there ought to be a scatter of lucky hits for other countries. There is not. I do not believe, anyhow, that dismissal is an option. We really do have a match between a significant number of Nostradamus's verses and events long after his lifetime. Nothing is apparent as to the way in which this comes about. He may have a technique, but it doesn't, in itself, show him the future. In an epistle to King Henry II that accompanies the Centuries he offers a survey of the next few hundred years, which is supposed to give them a framework. It is largely incomprehensible and utterly wrong.

Astrology is certainly not the answer. On the most favourable view, it might account for such broad items as the rise and duration of the British Empire in X.100. How could it have forecast details like Napoleon's haircut? In cases like that, technique is surely secondary. It may focus the mind, keep it occupied and make it receptive. We can picture the seer getting into the mood, even consulting astrological charts. But whatever delivers his illuminations is something . . . other.

Chapter Ten

How is it Done?

With Nostradamus duly considered, it is time to take stock provisionally and ask what sort of sense can be made of the data. One conclusion has emerged, and it will be confirmed, not modified, by other cases to come. Successful prediction does appear to happen, but 'happen' is the word. It is highly exceptional and there is no sign of a technique for making it happen.

A backward glance at the Bible can be helpful. The early Christians claimed to discover prophetic 'types' in the Old Testament foreshadowing Christ and anticipating events in his life. Perhaps they were right, but the passages where these 'types' occur are not really predictive. They can be understood in a Christian sense only in retrospect. If we set aside the puzzling manipulation of dates in Daniel, the Old Testament has only one outright prophecy of Christ, Second Isaiah's. It fits the Christ of the *kerygma* and it stands alone. In the concluding book of the New Testament, John's previsions of the great persecution, the solar cult and the fall of Rome are very striking indeed. However, they are confined to two chapters out of twenty-two, in a book probably intended as myth and symbol rather than literal prediction.

Nostradamus multiplies prophecies as the scriptural writers do not and scores enough hits to deserve attention. But his good quatrains comprise only a small percentage of the total. A good one is very much the exception, not the rule. If his incantations and calculations had amounted to a real technique, he would surely have done better.

Yet the phenomena, however rare, are too impressive to ignore, and minor instances like the Prophecies of St Malachy confirm the impression. The usual refutation is that prophets pour out a random mass of vagueness and ambiguity, and the fulfilments, vague and ambiguous themselves, are due to chance. I recall the dictum of some television pundit: 'If you say there will be a queen named Mary, sooner or later there will be a queen named Mary.' In an age with few royals, I am not sure that his example was wisely chosen, but let that pass. The refutation works for (say) newspaper astrology. In the cases reviewed here, it fails. Second Isaiah does not pour out a mass of predictions, nor is chapter 53 ambiguous. The Servant of the Lord is Christ if he is anybody; he has defeated all attempts to explain him as someone else. John in Revelation identifies Rome by its seven hills and its empire by seven emperors; his words can have no other meaning. Nostradamus's good quatrains have enough detail to rule out alternatives: they are not random hits, their distribution is wildly skewed, and the Napoleonic sequence, in a stretch of time where no ingenuity has found any other fulfilments, defies chance.

It is easy to jump to the conclusion that these authors 'saw the future'. That is a conclusion not to be jumped to. Objective probing may well support the common-sense view that precognition is paradoxical. The short dismissal of it is that nobody can see the future because the future doesn't exist to be seen. To put it in the past tense, the scriptural writers and Nostradamus couldn't have seen what was future for them, because it didn't exist, not at the time.

Suppose, however, that in some sense the future does exist. Would 'seeing' it take us any further with the phenomena? Consider Second Isaiah, who anticipates the Christians' account of Christ. Let us go to the extremes of credulity and regard him as an inspired crystal-gazer, having clairvoyant visions of events in Jerusalem about AD30. He sees a man addressing crowds. He sees the same man being brought before some kind of official, flogged, crucified and laid in a tomb. Let us go to the very limit and accept the Resurrection as a literal fact. He sees the same man talking with a woman in a garden and is probably more perplexed than anything, because he was sure the man was dead. Has he made a mistake? Even with all this, merely seeing would not give him the Christians' interpretation of what he sees. Much the same difficulty arises in other cases. If someone 'saw the future', what did that person actually see? How did that person know enough to interpret what was seen?

Take it further still. Imagine that the time-travelling prophet hears as well as sees. He listens to one of the early Christian preachers. Does hearing help? The preacher's language is Aramaic or colloquial Greek; Second Isaiah can make nothing of either. Even if the preacher happens to use Hebrew, they are separated by more than 500 years and by many shifts and upheavals of population. Pronunciation, idiom and vocabulary have changed. I doubt if the prophet would feel much confidence in his understanding of what he heard.

Or what about the Book of Revelation? Let us grant John the same clairvoyant gift. Transported forward in time and seeing a scene of persecution, he can recognize it for what it is – he has witnessed the same himself – but he has no way of realizing the persecution's scope or extent unless he can range widely over the Roman Empire. He cannot see the imperial solar cult or grasp its connection. Travelling further still, into the fifth century, he may have sightings of barbarians, but nothing will tell him who they are, where they came from or what has enabled them to be there. He will have to fly thousands of miles from his Aegean retreat and have glimpses of the future covering fifty years or more, including the Visigoths' sack of Rome in 410 and the Vandals' in 455. No wonder he introduces angels commenting and explaining. They reflect his awareness of the problems he has created himself by saying that he 'saw' everything.

With Nostradamus the same applies, and more so, in view of the larger number of prophecies. Consider only two of his quatrains. In IV.54 a leader with a name borne by no French king wins unparalleled victories, intimidates Italians and Spaniards, puts pressure on England and is attentive to foreign women. Can we really suppose that Nostradamus, in whatever out-of-body state, saw Napoleon campaigning and took the point about his name, observed his diplomacy behind closed doors and watched him with Josephine, Marie Walewska and Marie Louise, at widely separated places and times, even learning their national origins? In IV.75 Bernadotte betrays Napoleon and makes a deal with the tsar, the Russians win, Ney and Victor conduct a rearguard action, and soldiers die in the snow. Can we suppose that Nostradamus saw Bernadotte and the tsar confer in Finland, knew who they were and followed what they were saying? Or that he saw Ney and Victor fighting Russians and knew it was a rearguard action? Hovering over a country so far from home, how would he have grasped what was going on? How could he have connected the Bernadotte–Alexander parley with men freezing to death in far-off Muscovy, their presence unexplained?

Arthur Conan Doyle happens to make the essential point in a short story, 'The Silver Mirror'. An accountant is working twelve-hour days on the ledgers of a businessman suspected of fraud. Near him is an antique, silver-framed mirror. Increasingly fatigued, he begins to see it growing misty from time to time and then slowly clearing. The mist is not uniform. Gaps open in it and images show through that are not reflections. First, he sees a woman's face with an expression of horror. Then, a few days later, he sees her at full length, vivid in a black velvet dress and seated in a chair. A man can be made out, crouching beside her and clinging to her dress. He looks frightened. After a few more days he, too, becomes fully visible. He is small and has a pointed beard. Other men, less distinct, are threatening him. In a final scene with complete clarity, they drag him from the woman and stab him. All is silent throughout, although she is obviously screaming.

The accountant's task is finished, but the exhaustion and the apparitions have been too much for him and he goes to rest in a private nursing home. He has told the doctor about his visions, and now he describes them fully. The doctor, recognizing details, infers from an inscription on the back of the mirror that it belonged to Mary, Queen of Scots, and somehow retained an impression of the murder of Rizzio, her secretary. The accountant knew nothing of Scottish history. Overwork caused an unusual physical and mental condition, and he saw, and saw accurately, but without understanding. Before his talk with the doctor, the drama was meaningless. In this story it is the past that is being seen, and at least the doctor is there to elucidate. Anybody seeing a totally unfamiliar future, with no one to explain it, would be more thoroughly mystified than the accountant.

Second-sight may be real. There may be people who see future events and know, unaided, what they are seeing – a death, for example. But in such cases the event is generally simple and the evidence, it must be admitted, is generally hearsay. What we have to cope with is far more complex and challenging: an array of published previsions where there seems to be no way in which the prophet could have done it alone, because no imaginable 'sight' could have supplied what is on record in the prophecy. Nor, by the way, could the short-term precognition that may or may not have been proved by ESP experimentation.

Perhaps then we are edging towards another hypothesis, the involvement of someone else or, to revive what is after all the traditional conception, some other entity. At Delphi, the 'other' was Apollo. Prophets in the Old Testament claimed inspiration from God, directly or through an intermediary, probably an angel. In Revelation John has his angelic interpreters. Nostradamus has his 'divine being', whoever or whatever that is. And Geoffrey of Monmouth feels bound to imagine Merlin as having a controlling spirit who speaks through him. Belief in the 'other' is normal. The question is whether the 'other' can be defined in an acceptable way.

Should all prophecy be ascribed, in biblical style, to God? In Genesis he enables Joseph, who is not a prophet and even practises divination, to make predictions by interpreting dreams. Theologians, seeking to give prophecy a philosophical basis, have maintained that God foresees everything. Strictly speaking the word 'foresee' is inaccurate, since it implies that he exists like ourselves in linear time and looks along it. But he exists in eternity, outside time as it is humanly experienced. His standpoint is different. He knows events that are unknowable to mortals because, from the mortals' standpoint, they are still to come, and he sometimes communicates his knowledge.

This view may be logically sound, but, irrespective of religious belief, it can hardly be invoked to cover all cases. Prophecy in the Bible is special. Even Joseph's feats are divinely ordained as steps towards his fame and his destiny. The whole idea of the Supreme Being would be vitiated if we were to imagine him dictating conundrums to Nostradamus. Could we take a step downward in the celestial hierarchy and bring in angels, inspiring prophecy on their own initiative? St Thomas Aquinas, the theologian who says more about them than anyone else, would object. According to him, they do not share God's eternity outside time. They do not know the future – not, at least, as God does. They are better than humans at intelligent anticipation, because they are more intelligent, but that is all. An angel hovering in the sixteenth century could not have told Nostradamus about Napoleon. As for 'controlling spirits' and 'divine beings', there seems to be no way of defining them that doesn't simply make them angels over again, more or less. (Augustine's assertion that *evil* angels – devils – can sometimes see the future may be set aside; the notion would be irrelevant here in any case.)

Can we conceive the Other, the Informant so to speak, in a human way? Prophecy, however it may be imagined, assumes a trans-temporal leap of some kind. This is usually thought of as a unilateral reaching-out ahead, by a seer or psychic. Which leads to a dead end – 'seeing the future' is evidently far from explaining the facts. Nevertheless, the facts are there, as in Isaiah and Revelation and Nostradamus's Centuries. I suggest that we should try shifting the spotlight from the prophet to the Other and thinking about a different trans-temporal leap; if necessary, a science-fiction leap.

Read again the main portion of the Servant Oracle in Isaiah 53:1–11 (see page 55). Read it without preconceptions, as if there were nothing to show that it is from the Old Testament. What does it look like? Not, surely, a message from an angel. To me at least, it looks like an early Christian sermon or a compressed version of one, a rhetorical reminiscence.

The speaker is a Jew, maybe one of Jesus's neighbours in Nazareth, who knew him before his public ministry and was not impressed. He and his friends were aware of the circumstances of Jesus's death, were perhaps in Jerusalem at the time, but saw all this as a divine judgement on his Messianic pretensions. They 'esteemed him stricken, smitten by God'. Afterwards, however, the speaker met some of the disciples, a group under Paul's influence, and heard their views on the meaning of these events and their account of the Resurrection. Moved by their conviction and the Church's vitality, he was converted and helped to spread the Good News himself. In Isaiah 53:1–11 we have his personal testimony, or, more precisely, a summary that he carries in his head and expands when he addresses an audience. It is based on what he has seen himself and heard from his mentors. We are in the Church's pre-literary youth.

A fancy, no doubt, yet the idea of 'someone else' behind Second Isaiah's words does supply what is needed. It is *as if* he were open to the mind of a Christian more than five centuries later, a mind outside the flow of linear time, even travelling backwards against it. The prophet receives this Christian's testimony, expresses it in his own language and adds the speeches of the Lord. He makes his prophecy by being in contact with a communicator at the far end, the future end. That Other comes to him, not the reverse. The trans-temporal linkage may be a very rare paranormal phenomenon or it may be a miracle divinely ordained. We need not be either adopting Christian belief or parting company with it.

This is not a hypothesis, not so far. I say 'as if' and I mean 'as if'. Yet, if we explore further, the same 'as if' recurs. In Revelation, John's glimpses of the later Empire can be fitted into the same mould, a science-fiction mould if you will. The notion of John venturing forward in the spirit leads to impossibilities. The notion of an informant in the future moving backwards into contact with him makes the whole performance work. It is *as if* he were responding to the mind of a person in the future who knows something of later Roman history, but who does not have to be a specialist and may only have been indulging a general interest. Attentive reading of two or three books would be enough – books covering the solar cult, the times of Diocletian and Constantine, the fifth-century disintegration. By the same rare process as in Isaiah, a trans-temporal rapport is effected with John, and the Roman passages, not paralleled in the rest of his book, are the result.

In this case the cause of the rapport is less evident. The Christian preacher would be in an outgoing frame of mind, the history-browsing Other might not. However, as Second Isaiah would be receptive to Messianic matter, so John would be receptive to disclosures about Rome's destiny. To keep the 'as if' consistent, we should give the prophet due emphasis, not, however, as someone looking *into* the future but as someone open to messages *from* the future, whose stance, whatever it feels like subjectively, is an invitation.

And that is not far from what Nostradamus says. In his first two quatrains he sketches his procedure. When he has assembled his magical gear and gone through a ritual, his 'divine being' is manifested and sits near him. Presumably this being has some kind of existence in the future and conveys information about it, which Nostradamus versifies. The account may be fantasy, but it is fantasy about communication from elsewhere, not about Nostradamus 'seeing the future' himself.

The idea that may be emerging, still very much on an 'as if' basis, is that someone's knowledge of events can be transmitted back in time to someone else who exists before their occurrence so that the recipient can predict them. A spatial analogy may help. Two drivers, Jim and Jane, are going along a road in separate cars. Jim is a few miles ahead of Jane, who is waiting for a passenger. He passes a place where a rock fall has made driving hazardous. Meanwhile Jane has switched on her car phone. Jim comes through and gives her a warning. She takes her passenger on board and says, 'There's a rock fall three miles ahead.' When they come to it, her prior awareness may seem mystifying or even paranormal if the passenger doesn't know about Jim, and it may amuse her to keep up the mystification. But Jim as an informant from further on, together with the means of communication, explains how the thing was done.

With Nostradamus the number of quatrains, the number of countries to which they apply and the number of events they predict might seem to rule out the notion of an informative Other. No 'Jim' could range so widely or know so much. But no such Jim is needed. The vast majority of the quatrains, even where they make sense, are not successful as prophecy. We need to insist only on the ones that are — mainly the twenty-six good ones in Class A — and that restriction narrows the field drastically, because of the skewed distribution. Most of them relate to France. All or nearly all the rest relate to Britain, meaning chiefly England, and those are confined to the seventeenth century, apart from the touch about the duration of the British Empire. The twenty-four Class B quatrains make hardly any difference, although the British share is larger.

The point that stands out, if we reflect on what Nostradamus does foretell, is that we don't require an encyclopedic source of knowledge or an omniscient informant. If the trans-temporal contact of minds were to be possible at all, a quite ordinary person would be sufficient — it could be somebody acquainted with a certain amount of French history, who is interested in the Napoleonic phases and not much after them. This person would need to have taken a mild interest in Britain too but not beyond what might be gleaned from general reading. To be specific, most of what Nostradamus gets right about the first French Emperor is in just two books, Vincent Cronin's *Napoleon* and Alan Schom's *Napoleon Bonaparte*. Communication from a non-specialist browser, more or less as pictured, could account for practically all Nostradamus's successes: for their near-confinement to France, for their subsidiary glances at Britain and for the apparent blank everywhere else or almost everywhere else. In the successful quatrains, it is *as if* he were versifying, in his own riddling style, information received from a plain human about 400 years ahead. His 'divine being', if not a pure figment, may be relaying messages or inventing them, but the plain human would be enough. If the two of them could be brought together, we could imagine them chatting with a manageable number of books on the table. To turn for a moment to 'Malachy', one book might provide everything – say 'The Popes since 1800'. I wonder if it exists?

With Nostradamus, we can take some tentative steps beyond a basic 'as if'. In each case the notion of someone or something other than himself may have a significant bearing on a difficulty. Quatrain IX.18 (see page 160) scores three times with events during the 1630s, one of which is the execution of Montmorency. Much has been made of the words *clere peyne*, 'celebrated punishment', because an early commentator says the executioner's name was Clerepeyne, in which case we have a prophetic pun. The evidence for the name is untrustworthy. And yet . . . those words come at the end of the fourth line, and prevent it from rhyming with the second. Nostradamus has some poor rhymes, and just before this quatrain he has another that rhymes ABAA instead of his normal ABAB. But a total collapse of rhyming at the end of a quatrain is not his style; he isn't in the habit of ruining his verses completely. Why does he write what he does here? And why does it happen with this maybe-significant phrase? He seems to be under a momentary compulsion. Whatever the truth about *clere peyne*, some external agency has exerted pressure to get it in.

Another crux is in quatrain VIII.37 (see page 161), and here the notion of the 'Other' may actually resolve the difficulty. The quatrain applies to the last days of Charles I. A communicator, in some future year, could have been reading English history – there is even an allusion to Charles's documented shirt – but the third line goes astray, not into vagueness or ambiguity, but into factual error. Charles is near a bridge that must be Westminster Bridge. In 1649 Westminster Bridge was not yet there, so how could 'seeing the future' have put a non-existent bridge into the picture? But an ordinary human in years to come could have used a later map as an aid to historical study, noticed the bridge near Whitehall and not thought to find out when it was built, so that the 'story' reached Nostradamus with the misconception embedded in it.

A third quatrain that raises a similar issue is VI.22 (see page 164).

Dedans la terre du grand temple célique,
Neveu à Londres par paix feinte meurtri.

Within the land of the great heavenly temple,
Nephew murdered at London through a false peace.

The second line applies to Monmouth's rebellion in 1685 and its tragic epilogue. It is the first line, connected with it, that is puzzling. The reference to London shows that 'the land of the great heavenly temple' is England. Leoni accepts this in his commentary, but adds: 'The reason is best known to Nostradamus.' It is not apparent to Leoni, who gives up on the phrase.

This temple is distinctive, clearly unique in England and with no counterpart elsewhere. If there were any like it in other countries, it would not define this one, and since it is *the* temple, it must be unparalleled in England itself. Therefore, it cannot be a church. To a modern reader, Stonehenge is the obvious choice, but when Nostradamus wrote Stonehenge was hardly known in its own country, let alone France, and it was not thought of as a temple, if it was thought of at all. The only account of it was by Geoffrey of Monmouth, who said it was a monument marking the grave of a company of Britons killed by Saxons.

The temple has got into the quatrain through association with Monmouth. He was nowhere near Stonehenge, but he raises another possibility. His main support was in the West Country. Somerset was at the heart of his rebellion, and his army camped in the ruins of Glastonbury Abbey. He draws attention to Somerset, and Somerset does, after a fashion, explain the temple, although the fashion is decidedly odd. The line can refer, not to a reality, but to a speculation, a latter-day myth about that myth-making place Glastonbury.

In 1935 Katherine Maltwood, a sculptor, published a small book entitled *A Guide to Glastonbury's Temple of the Stars* in which she claimed that astrological figures were marked out on the face of central Somerset. This zodiac was formed by features of the landscape and was ten miles across, and it dated from the third millennium BC. Her theory flourished for several decades. Readers took it up and developed it, with a wealth of imagined meanings, some of them suggested by further scrutiny of the map. They insisted that the huge figures – the Ram, the Bull and so forth – could be seen from the air if you flew high enough. The theory has psychological interest, but it never made any impression on archaeologists, and few people now believe that the figures objectively exist. To construct them, exponents have to bring in too many kinds of feature – hills, woods, streams, ditches, hedges, roads. Central Somerset is rich in such features, and a variety of images can be traced on it by the same methods. The Temple of the Stars is selective, a product of the will to see it. It is like a Rorschach ink-blot test. Believers do see it, quite sincerely, on maps and aerial photographs. Sceptics don't.

Fanciful as this theory is, it has a right to be mentioned here because it offers a *grand temple célique*, suitably located. However, the Glastonbury zodiac was not part of Nostradamus's world – Katherine Maltwood invented it, and an assertion that it is mentioned by John Dee, the Elizabethan astrologer, has been abandoned. Many of the features that are supposed to form it are fairly recent and did not exist in the sixteenth century, and no one could have constructed the 'Temple'. If Nostradamus has it in mind in this quatrain – and what else could he mean? – it has reached him in a predictive package with Monmouth. Conventional notions of prophecy fail completely. With the *temple célique* 'seeing the future' is no solution at all. If Nostradamus did pay a visionary visit to Somerset during Monmouth's rebellion, he would not have seen the zodiac, because it wasn't there, and he would not have heard it talked about, because nobody had thought of it.

'As if' is still 'as if', yet it may be solidifying a little. It is *as if* there were mind-to-mind communication from someone in the twentieth century who took an interest in Monmouth, and, following the story of his rebellion, picked up a book on Somerset history and topography that happened to give space to the Maltwood theory – I doubt if many do, but I could name at least one – and it all came through together when Nostradamus's mind was open to it. Here, as with *clere peyne* but more intelligibly, the line gives an impression of the Other thrusting in. Nostradamus had no need of a temple, and he was not on the look-out for a temple. The fictitious zodiac is intrusive, an annoyance for commentators.

I make no pretence to understand these results. I have no idea how a mind-to-mind contact could occur over a huge gap of time and against the flow. If anyone concludes that this is all simply impossible, a paradox, I shall not argue, not yet. Yet the facts are the facts, and I hope to show that they lead to further facts, embodied in two literary works that are more important than Nostradamus's Centuries. Their authors do not prophesy, not relevantly at least. To all appearances, however, they make use of knowledge that was not available until many years later, knowledge that would have had to travel back from the future to make its way into their minds.

Chapter Eleven

Dante and Milton: Unrecognized Sources

The two greatest Christian poets – the two, at least, who wrote the greatest poems on Christian themes – are Dante Alighieri and John Milton. In the work of both there appears to be a transcendence of time, which accompanies a departure from Christian norms. The reason why this is so needs some explanation, and the facts are unfamiliar enough to make an explanation worthwhile.

Dante Alighieri (1265–1321) was a native of Florence. He had a troubled career in civic affairs and spent much of his life in exile. His principal work, the *Divine Comedy*, was composed in the early years of the fourteenth century. He had a high opinion of Joachim of Fiore, and he condemns Celestine V, the might-have-been Joachite pontiff, for his 'great refusal'; he also denounces Boniface VIII, who extinguished the hope.

The *Divine Comedy* ('divine' was not part of the author's title) is in three parts: the *Inferno*, *Purgatorio* and *Paradiso*, Hell, Purgatory and Heaven. It takes the form of a first-person narrative in which the poet travels through the three realms. He is conducted, first, by Virgil, the Roman poet who describes Aeneas's visit to the Underworld, and later by Beatrice Portinari, whom he once adored and idealized, but who, at the date of the story, is long since dead and exalted in Heaven. In the course of his journey he meets numerous people no longer in this world and learns their condition in the next. He places Joachim in Heaven among the wisest, as a true prophet.

The *Comedy* can be read in various ways. As an allegory, it is about the poet's spiritual progress. As a story, it has a literal sense but is doubtless not meant to be taken too literally. Dante might have said more or less what C.S. Lewis says in the preface to *The Great Divorce*, his own first-person story of Heaven and Hell:

> I beg readers to remember that this is a fantasy. It has of course – or I intended it to have – a moral. But the trans-mortal conditions are solely an imaginative supposal: they are not even a guess or a speculation as to what may actually await us. The last thing I wish is to arouse factual curiosity about the details of the after-world.

None the less, Dante does give his story a quasi-real setting. He fits it skilfully into the framework of the universe as his contemporaries conceived it, but with a remarkable addition, which raises remarkable issues.

Earth, which is at the centre, is a globe. Dante has no need to argue about that, for educated people were aware of its shape long before Columbus. They made some good guesses at its circumference, ranging from about 20,000 to about 30,000 miles. Dante favoured the lower figure, making our world smaller than it is (as Columbus did) but not much too small. Around it in medieval astronomy, as in the Ptolemaic system from which it derived, were the concentric transparent spheres bearing the planets and stars, as already described. There is a stubborn delusion that the pre-Copernican universe was tiny. By modern standards it was, but it was big enough to reduce Earth to a speck. An author known to Dante, trying to compute actual figures, puts the distance to the sphere of the Moon at 159,000 miles, the distance to the sphere of the Sun at 3,965,000 miles and the distance to the sphere of the stars at 65,357,500, so that the circumference of the visible universe is more than 400 million miles, 20,000 times that of Earth. Another estimate makes the stars farther off and the universe consequently larger.

Alone among medieval authors, Dante presents a spiritual pilgrimage in terms of a journey through this cosmos. The first, earthbound part requires a few understandings about our world as he portrays it. He divides it into a land hemisphere and a water hemisphere. The former contains all the known populated regions: Europe, most of Asia and part of Africa. A tradition dating from at least as far back as the Book of Ezekiel made Jerusalem an equivalent of Delphi, the centre of the world when the world was still supposed to be flat. It continued to be central in medieval diagrams – they were hardly maps – of the inhabited lands. Dante accepts its centrality and adapts this to the round Earth, placing Jerusalem at the centre of the land hemisphere. The other hemisphere, as he imagines it, is completely covered by sea except for an island at its own centre, the antipodes of Jerusalem, a point that can be defined as 144° 47' west, 31° 47' south.

Hell, where his journey starts, is an immense, funnel-shaped hollow. He descends into it with Virgil, visiting the souls on successive levels and conversing with them. It narrows down all the way to the centre of the globe, where the Devil resides. Past that, a passage leads upward (Dante glosses over the distance involved) and comes out into daylight on the antipodean island, near the foot of a huge mountain. The mountain is Purgatory, and Dante and Virgil climb it, experiencing much on the way.

At the summit Dante meets Beatrice, and Virgil vanishes. Under his former love's tutelage, the poet makes a further ascent through the radiant planetary and stellar spheres – the sub-heavens as we might call them – and in each, he encounters members of the Blessed for whom that sphere is appropriate. The degrees of bliss at the different levels are unequal, but they all gladly accept what God has willed for them and all have their places in his true Heaven, which is beyond the system entirely and has no spatial relationship to it. Dante soars ever upward, dazzled by the light but becoming able to endure it, with Beatrice and others resolving his doubts and difficulties. At last, in the Heaven beyond it all, he has a momentary vision of God. That crowning episode carries an implied warning against too much literalism: the poem ends there, with no anticlimactic return.

For the first and third parts of the *Comedy*, customary belief and popular lore gave guidelines. Hell was 'below', Heaven was 'above'. The intermediate region was another matter. Dante had to imagine Purgatory for himself and assign a place to it in the physical scheme of things. Theologians had long held the view that it must exist. Many of the dead were destined for Heaven yet were not ready for it. They were aimed in the right direction, but carried a burden of sin and error and had perhaps only repented at the last moment. There had to be expiation, purification. Hence there had to be Purgatory as a preliminary to Heaven.

Before Dante it was not much more than an inference. When thought of at all, it was apt to be thought of in sombre terms as virtually a department of Hell, a place of punishment with no essential difference except that it had an end. This grim idea lingers in *Hamlet* even after the rejection of the doctrine by Protestantism. The Ghost says to the Prince:

I am thy father's spirit;
Doom'd for a certain term to walk the night,
And for the day confin'd to fast in fires,
Till the foul crimes done in my days of nature
Are burnt and purg'd away. But that I am forbid
To tell the secrets of my prison-house,
I could a tale unfold, whose lightest word
Would harrow up thy soul . . .

Dante thinks otherwise. If Purgatory is a bridge between Earth and Heaven, if its occupants are on their way to beatitude even through penitential pains, it should be, in essence, a happy place, and he makes it so. His Purgatory is not hellish. It is out in the sunshine on the island where he and Virgil emerge from Earth's interior: the colossal mountain they climb, a 'positive counterpart to Hell's empty concavity' (in the words of one scholar), immeasurably higher than any other mountain. Around its base is an ante-Purgatory, where souls who are detained for various reasons await entry. The Mount itself rises above our disturbed atmosphere into clear skies and tranquillity. It tapers upwards and is septenary, having seven terraces encircling it at different levels. The terraces, which are connected by stairways, correspond to the principal sins – pride, envy, wrath, sloth, avarice, gluttony and lust. Souls bearing the stain of these sins live on the terraces, sitting on them and lying on them, or walking and hurrying along them. They endure cleansing pain and endure it gladly, as they progress towards release. Each terrace has a presiding angel. At the top of the Mount is the Earthly Paradise where Adam and Eve first dwelt – in biblical terms, the Garden of Eden. This abode of innocence is where the glorified Beatrice appears, Virgil departs, and the flight to Heaven begins.

Dante's conception is revolutionary. His Purgatory has no Christian precedent. Even apart from its structure, no one before him located the place of purification – or anything at all of an intelligible kind – at the Antipodes. His apparent motive is a wish or need for centrality. When Jerusalem, the holy city, was the centre of a disc-Earth, it was unique. A spherical Earth altered this. With Jerusalem at the centre of the land hemisphere, a second centre was automatically projected opposite, in the water hemisphere. Dante located his island there, with the holy Mount on it.

He had already worked this out when he wrote *Inferno* XXVI:90–142, one of the finest passages in the *Comedy*, developing his cosmic design by an original addition to classical legend. Ulysses tells the tale of his last voyage. He sailed out with his crew to explore 'the world without people', and headed westward and southward through empty ocean for five months. They actually sighted Mount Purgatory, but a divinely ordained storm prevented them from approaching it. The ship spun round, turned on end and sank. This episode is Dante's idea; he refers back to it in *Paradiso* XXVII:82–3. Tennyson makes use of it in his poem 'Ulysses'.

Also without Christian precedent is the location of the Earthly Paradise on top of the Mount. Unlike Purgatory, this was a topic of speculation before Dante. In Genesis 2:8 it is 'a garden in Eden in the east', a phrase that could place it almost anywhere east of the Holy Land where the book was written. The Bible offers one other topographic hint, a passage in Ezekiel (28:13–14) about 'Eden, the garden of God' on 'the holy mountain of God'. Before Dante there was agreement at least that it was high up. This was a matter of logic as well as exegesis. Genesis said four great rivers flowed from it, and since they flowed for long distances, a high-altitude source was needed. Two of them were the Tigris and Euphrates, which do start fairly close together. Unfortunately the other two were the Nile and Ganges, or maybe the Indus. St Augustine suggested that they started from the same area but ran underground through natural tunnels and surfaced in Africa and India.

A few Islamic legends concurred on the main issue, if not on the tunnels. They likewise put the Earthly Paradise on top of a mountain, but they disagreed about where it was. It might be in Syria, Persia or India, although on the whole India was preferred. Christians, too, tried geographical guesses. As Asia came to be better known, it became evident that there were no good clues to the place's whereabouts and that no one had ever found it, although Alexander the Great was reputed to have come close. St Thomas Aquinas, Dante's chief philosophic mentor, decided that it was farther off than the Middle East and shut off from the known world by impassable barriers. The paradisal height was an established motif, but an indistinct one, and Dante's equation of it with his Mount Purgatory combines the themes and wafts the Earthly Paradise to the southern ocean, thousands of miles from the homelands of humanity.

In his fusion of motifs Dante perpetrates a flagrant breach with the Bible. He might almost be contradicting scripture on purpose and in detail. His Earthly Paradise on top of the Mount is not 'a garden in Eden in the east' – it is a woodland – and it is not in Eden because there is no Eden, no surrounding country at all. As for its being in the east, its position on the spherical Earth makes it as much westward as eastward. You could get to it from the Holy Land by going around the globe in either direction. Ulysses, the only voyager who comes anywhere near the Mount, sails west through the Straits of Gibraltar.

The rivers named in Genesis could not flow from this place, because they could not cross the sea; Dante shows no awareness of the tunnel theory. During his imagined visit, the topic of the rivers is raised. He sees two streams, which he thinks are the infant

Tigris and Euphrates, whatever the explanation . . . but no, they are not (*Purgatorio* XXXIII:112–29). Nor is he told how Adam and Eve, after their expulsion, travelled over the watery wilderness to the Middle East or to any other region where their descendants could have multiplied.

Medieval interpretation of scripture was not fundamentalist in the modern sense. Symbolism and allegory were recognized, and Dante could have claimed that the passage in Genesis was symbolic or allegorical, but the literal reading was the standard, and any readings that positively opposed it had to be justified. I question whether Dante would have defied it as he does on the basis of a private fancy alone. It is no use appealing to the originality of genius. In the Middle Ages originality, total originality, was not much valued or cultivated, and writers drew on previous authors and on recognized tradition. They gave the work of their predecessors fresh meanings, but they seldom invented radically or tried to please their readers by doing so. If they had no prior source for what they wrote, they sometimes pretended that they had – Geoffrey of Monmouth does this, and even Chaucer is praised by a French contemporary as a 'great translator'.

Dante judges that he can express what he wants by his conception of the Mount better than he could by orthodox imagery, keeping the ingredients separate. Yet the break with scripture and tradition is so audacious that medieval norms point to something behind it, something compelling. He would not have spun a composite mountain, elaborately un-biblical, out of his own head.

Do the Islamic legends suggest an answer? Some told of mountains of unparalleled height, even mountains where a pilgrim's climb was a spiritual progress or where a bridge led to Heaven from the summit. It seemed to me once that these legends supplied Dante's source-material, but, on reflection, I doubt it. They were little known and scattered over remote lands, there is no evidence that they reached Italy, and Dante would have had to hear not merely one of them but several and put them together, to synthesize even a sketch for his own mountain. Such a contrived bundle of scraps would not have exerted the sort of pressure required to thrust him into his departure from scripture. Moreover, they were Muslim scraps. He would very likely have recoiled from them as infidel superstition. The *Comedy* shows respect for some individual Muslims, but it damns Muhammad as a perverter of truth. A devotee of the Bible would scarcely have defied its text in response to devotees of the Koran.

What is required as an explanation is something ready-made, capable of gripping Dante's imagination by its own power and relevance: a prototype. That would be purely speculative, if it were not for the fact that the prototype exists and is probably at the root of the Muslim lore itself. The problem is not to find it, but to cope with the paradox of Dante's knowledge of it, before anyone in Europe knew. It is a mountain that figures in Hindu mythology and in Buddhist derivatives. Its name is Meru. Buddhists call it Sumeru, meaning the same thing.

Meru is at Earth's centre, the centre of a disc-Earth, admittedly, but centrality is part of its nature. It soars skyward to a gigantic height – thousands of miles, according to some – and, as the hub of the universe, it 'stands carrying the worlds above, below and transversely'. In one way or another (accounts vary) it is septenary: it has seven faces or levels, or it has seven concentric rings of sea around it, separated by seven rings of land. A writer belonging to the Jain sect describes Meru as being composed of truncated cones, one on top of another and of diminishing size, so that it has encircling terraces. It is paradisal. Divine and semi-divine beings frequent it, notably the Seven Rishis, immortal seers identified with the stars of Ursa Major, the Great Bear. On the mountain are 'the gardens of the gods' and beautiful woods. The holy Ganges flows from its summit, which is a dwelling-place and assembly-place of deities.

Indian mythic imagination is flamboyant and inconsistent, but Meru has the key attribute of uniting paradisal motifs with a purifying ascent, not only up the mountain but into the heavens beyond. In the Hindu epic *Mahabharata*, an envoy of the gods discourses to a holy man about the divine regions. He mentions Meru, quoting one of the less extravagant figures for its height.

It is there that the golden Meru sits, king of the mountains, thirty-three leagues high, where the gardens of the gods are situated. . . . There is no hunger or thirst, no fatigue, no concern with cold or heat, no atrocity or unholiness. . . . There is no sorrow, no old age, no effort or complaint. Such, hermit, is the world that is won by the fruits of a man's own deeds, and by virtue of their own good deeds men come to share in it.

Elsewhere in the epic, a brahmin speaks of the mountain to an exiled king, evoking it in imaginative vision.

Behold the pure land, the superb peak of the Meru, where the Grandfather [Brahmā] dwells with the gods. . . . Beyond the seat of Brahmā shines the supreme abode of the lord Narayana [Vishnu, the Supreme Being], God without beginning and end. . . . Even the gods can only with difficulty look at that divine and auspicious place, which is made of light. . . . Ascetics go there to Narayana Hari through their devotion, yoked with the utmost austerity and perfected by their holy deeds. Great-spirited, perfected by yoga, devoid of darkness and delusion, they go there and no more return to this world.

Meru is inaccessible by ordinary means of travel. The king in the epic, on a final pilgrimage with his wife and brothers, comes within sight of the mountain, but they die without reaching it. Temple-builders in historical times made models or representations of it, embodying some of its numinosity. The Khmers of southwest Asia built stepped pyramids. The most impressive of all such images is a Buddhist one, Borobudur in Java, dating from AD 800 or thereabouts. It is not, of course, intended as a model to scale. It is an analogue in Buddhist terms, and in its relevance to Dante it invites special attention.

Its invisible nucleus is a real hill, which it completely encases. The building material is grey stone. A great square plinth forms the base, and on top of this are five square layers or storeys, one above another, diminishing in size so that the structure is a kind of pyramid with terraces going all round. The walls beside the terraces are full of sculptured reliefs in trachyte, a pale volcanic rock, depicting stories of the Buddha. The complete pilgrimage procedure is to climb a flight of steps from ground level to the lowest terrace, running along the top of the basic plinth, and walk all round meditating on the reliefs. Then another flight ascends to the next terrace. The pilgrim circumambulates that in the same way and continues upward.

Borobudur has five terraces with sculptured panels, close to 1500 in all. The scenes they illustrate conduct the pilgrim through the realms of material being. Those on the lowest level have themes of evil and warning. Those on the levels above make a gradual ascent to higher and higher good. A sixth terrace, without imagery, is transitional. The next layer or storey is round instead of square, so that the pilgrim climbs to a seventh, circular terrace. Above are two more storeys with two more circular terraces. This upper portion of Borobudur stands for the spiritual realm and corresponds to the mountain's summit paradise. Around the last three terraces are stupas or bell-shaped shrines. Surmounting the whole edifice is a much larger stupa with a spire at its apex. On the highest terrace, you are walking around the rim of this bell. It represents the goal of the human quest, nirvana, liberation.

The Meru or Sumeru that Borobudur imitates is not an isolated concept: it underlies a cruder 'World-Mountain' that occurs in other Asian mythologies, a cosmic pillar connecting earth and sky. It may have been directly, it may have been through these derivative myths, that Meru influenced the mountain-lore of Islam – if it did. But no one could have reconstituted the mighty original out of such fragments. To all appearances, Dante's septenary Mount Purgatory is Meru made Christian, with angels taking the place of gods.

He has echoes even in detail. As the characters in the Indian epic die within sight of an unattainable Meru, so Dante's Ulysses dies within sight of the unattainable Mount. He seems to recall the Seven Rishis, the stars of Ursa Major, with allusions to the constellation. He imagines himself climbing stairs from each girdling terrace to the next, as at Borobudur, and walking along the terraces. The lowest has narrative bas-reliefs, again as at Borobudur, and also pictures on the floor (*Purgatorio* X:28–29 and XII:13–69) with biblical and legendary subjects for reflection. As with Hindus and Buddhists, the ascent is a progression. It has been remarked that the spiritual development of Dante's penitent souls, working their way along the terraces, 'takes place in response to narrative', as with the Borobudur pilgrim meditating on the stories of Buddha.

Dante's ascent culminates in entry into the paradisal realm at the summit. The celestial region above it, portrayed in the *Paradiso* with imagery of dazzling light, could – if one cared to press the point – be a Christian elaboration of Vishnu's radiant abode beyond Meru, where the gods themselves have visual difficulty such as Dante describes (e.g. *Paradiso* III:127–9).

I see no reason why Dante should not have adopted and adapted Meru and taken a good deal of the plan of Purgatory from its analogue at Borobudur . . . if he had known. He respected such non-Christian mythology as he did know, not holding its gods up to obloquy as fallen angels and diabolic deceivers. It has been said that he 'uses classical models to articulate Christian truth'. Four poets from pagan antiquity have roles in the *Comedy*. Virgil, his guide through Hell and Purgatory, is the most important. The sixth book of the *Aeneid*, describing Aeneas's visit to the Underworld, is in the background of the *Inferno*. Dante endorses the belief that Virgil, living before Christ, was inspired to foretell him in the Fourth Eclogue, and he depicts another Roman poet, Statius, as converted to Christianity by this prophecy. The work of two further Romans, Ovid and Lucan, also makes its mark. Dante suggests that pagan poets may have had inklings of revealed truth and when they sang of a lost golden age, they may have been dimly aware of the lost Earthly Paradise and the happiness of Adam and Eve before they fell (*Purgatorio* XXVIII:139–41).

Dante would probably have had an open mind for matter from beyond Christendom as long as it was not tainted, like Islamic lore, with outright hostility. He could have looked as far away as India without disquiet. In a passage where he wonders about divine justice, when a good pagan who has never heard of Christ is debarred from salvation, his hypothetical good pagan is an Indian (*Paradiso* XIX:70–78).

At this point, however, we run full tilt into the paradox. If there were a book Dante could have read giving information on Meru and Borobudur, modern commentators would most certainly acknowledge it as a major source, a manifest key to the problems his vision of Purgatory raises. But there was no such book. Medieval Europeans knew little of India and nothing of its mythology. The texts were in Sanskrit, a language undiscovered and untranslated. Western acquaintance with the subcontinent did not begin on a large scale until long after Dante, and study of its literature emerged only gradually from the spread of British imperial power. As for Java, Marco Polo proves that travellers' tales of it could have reached Dante, but they would not have been tales of Borobudur. A few decades after it was built, encroachments by Hindu kings condemned this Buddhist monument to disuse and decay. By the year 1000 it was entirely neglected and overgrown with vegetation, and the subsequent advance of Islam through Indonesia prevented any revival. It was rediscovered at last in a poor condition, damaged by erosion and water seepage, and it was not examined and restored until recent years.

Hence the paradox. On the one hand, it looks as if Dante was aware of these things, even in some detail. On the other, there is no way he could have been, in the ordinary course of events. It is *as if* knowledge of them in the mind of a person half a millennium after him, an orientalist perhaps, entered his own mind through a trans-temporal contact against the flow. This is the same kind of 'as if' that was suggested by the prophecies of Nostradamus and others.

By itself, this phenomenon might be dismissed as a curiosity or explained away by some notion of archetypes or secret tradition. However, the other great poet whom I have in mind makes a break with scripture and tradition as Dante does, and in the act of doing so, he too seems to tap knowledge not available in his time.

★

When John Milton (1608–74) confronts us with a similar crux, it is even more difficult to come to terms with it.

From an early stage in his career his ambition was to compose a major work: an epic, or a poetic drama. He considered King Arthur as a subject, but dropped him. One reason was that he felt too unsure of the historical basis. Another, probably, was that he sided with Parliament in the English Civil War – a Roundhead could hardly write a royalist poem. He held an important post in Cromwell's government, but the return of Charles II drove him back into private life and freed him to pursue his aim. He had already made a start on the major work, now definitely an epic. It was *Paradise Lost*, telling the story of the Creation, the fall of Adam and Eve through Satan's wiles and their banishment from the Garden of Eden.

When Milton imagined the world's beginnings, what he was consciously aware of was the Israelite version in Genesis, plus Jewish and Christian expansions. The Israelite creation story had earlier roots. We can see where some of the imagery came from, we can see how the main source may have influenced the expansions, and by examining the process we can see how Milton carried it further and how mysteriously.

The underlying myth is Babylonian. It is embedded in a Creation Epic probably dating from the second millennium BC. This is named from its opening words, *Enuma elish*, 'When on high'. Recorded on cuneiform tablets, it was ritually recited by priests on the fourth day of the New Year festival. After Babylon's decline it lapsed into oblivion and remained unknown until the tablets were dug up and deciphered. Portions were reaching scholars from 1876 onwards. However, decades elapsed before the fragments found on several sites were pieced together into an adequate text.

Enuna elish is surprising. As we work through this Creation Epic we may well wonder when creation is going to begin. The story starts in what Australian Aborigines call the Dream Time. A vast female being named Tiamat, a kind of dragon, has a companion, Apsu; in a vague way Tiamat is the sea and Apsu is fresh water. Through their mingling in primordial chaos the gods are formed within them. The turbulence of these junior beings disturbs the senior ones, and Apsu proposes to destroy them. Tiamat demurs, but finally acquiesces.

The chief god Ea, the All-Wise, realizes what is threatened and kills Apsu. Then he begets a new deity called Marduk, endowing him, as his son, with 'double godhead'. It becomes clear that Marduk and Tiamat are going to be enemies. Some of the gods, resenting Ea's upstart offspring, approach Tiamat and urge her to avenge Apsu's death. She generates demons, including serpents and lesser dragons, to fight against the main body of gods. Now thoroughly malignant, she prepares for battle and is supported by the renegades who have gone over to her. She appoints one of them, Kingu, as her commander-in-chief. The gods who are loyal to Ea decide that Marduk should lead them. After a test of his divine powers, they pay him homage and promise to obey him. He arms himself with the winds and a fearsome bow, and rides out in a chariot to meet Tiamat. When she opens her jaws to swallow him he flings a net over her, distends her with a terrible blast and shoots an arrow into her with fatal effect.

It is only after all this that creation happens. Having disposed of Tiamat's army, Marduk surveys her enormous corpse, recumbent on its back. He forms the notion of recycling it for world-making. Creation is a consequence of the conflict, a divine afterthought. Marduk splits the corpse 'like a shellfish' with a horizontal slash, and divides the upper part from the lower. The upper part becomes the sky, and he attaches the celestial bodies to it; the zenith is in Tiamat's belly. The lower part becomes our environment of land and water. Aided by his father, Ea, Marduk makes the first humans out of the blood of Kingu, Tiamat's commander, ordaining that the new species shall be the gods' servants. Tiamat, with her conqueror secure in power, is now retrospectively a 'rebel'. The gods hail Marduk as 'the Son, our avenger'. Henceforth he is to be the presiding deity of Babylon.

While this myth still flourished, the Israelites adopted some of its imagery, reshaping it in line with their own beliefs. The first chapter of Genesis is fairly late as it stands, but it reflects their ideas over a long stretch of time. They dropped the preliminaries and elder beings. They kept the primeval waters of chaos but did not personify them. The Hebrew word translated as 'the deep' ('darkness was upon the face of the deep') is *tehom*, cognate with 'Tiamat', but the Israelites' version admitted no actual being so called. They assigned Marduk's creative work to the solitary Lord God, acting by his own will 'in the beginning'. They kept the separation of Above and Below, but their Above was the firmament, pure sky, not the upper half of a defunct monster. They kept the creation of humanity as the final act, but treated Adam and Eve with more respect. These changes lifted the myth on to a higher plane. God's first speech, 'Let there be light', was a touch of sublimity unequalled anywhere else.

That might have been the end of the matter. It was not. Even when *Enuma elish* was buried (literally), some of the rejected motifs began to creep back. Israel had tried to eliminate the gods, yet presently the Creator ceased to be thought of as alone. He remained unique and sovereign, but he had an entourage of angels. Like the gods, they had existed before the world. The creation story in Genesis did not mention them, but other scriptural writings did, so it was fair to try to fit them in. They had come into being, perhaps, together with the primal light and certainly before humanity. They were the 'sons of God' in Job 1:6 and 2:1, who shouted for joy when he laid the foundation of the earth (38:4–7). Their home was with him in Heaven.

Granted these immortals, the way was clear for a further step occasioned by the perennial problem of evil. Tiamat could, in a sense, come back, and, with a change of gender, she did. Her role as the Enemy was revived in the person of Lucifer or Satan, the celestial arch-rebel. Once a glorious angel, Satan had turned away from God, and many other angels had joined him. Condemned, he had fallen from Heaven and been deprived of his splendour – the equivalent of Tiamat's downfall, although Satan survived as she did not – and he now roamed the world, troubling and corrupting humanity, together with the deluded spirits who had taken his side.

Satan barely figures in the Old Testament. As the Devil of Christianity, he is more conspicuous in the New. In Revelation

12, where John presents him as a dragon, Tiamat still underlies the conception. John recalls the ancient clash in which he was cast out of Heaven, conquered by the archangel Michael. His defeat at Michael's hands is a Jewish tradition that becomes the standard Christian account. Hell is his home, and while he and his followers are allowed to be active on the world's surface, they can never return to their former place in Heaven. The Babylonian victory of gods over demons has made its way, disguised, into Christian minds. There is no single or simple explanation. Ancestral motifs adrift in the Middle East, especially among the Persians, re-entered a system that had tried to keep them out and passed from Judaism into Christianity.

That was about as far as the process went. The primordial War in Heaven was seldom enlarged upon. Dante imagines Satan and his cohorts as falling through their own perverted will soon after they came into existence. While he acknowledges Michael's role, he only glances at it (*Inferno* VII:11–12) and never pictures anything as crude as a fight, nor does he or any other Christian hint at the Babylonian 'afterthought' notion of the world's being created as a result of the Evil One's demise. In the *Divine Comedy*, when the Devil falls, Earth is already there to engulf him. Some Fathers of the Church speculated that God made human beings as replacements for the banished angels. Responsible Christians came no closer to the 'afterthought' notion in the centuries before Milton. Residual Babylonianism had no power to propel them further, either directly or through intermediaries.

Milton, however, does go further, and entirely on his own. Throughout a substantial portion of *Paradise Lost* he appears to be adapting *Enuma elish*. The case is the same with him as with Dante. On a specific issue, the Earthly Paradise, Dante breaks with scripture and Christian tradition and by doing so he opens the door to Asian mythology. On a specific issue, the War in Heaven, Milton, too, breaks with scripture and Christian tradition and by doing so he opens the door to the Babylonian epic. The question is: how did it ever get through the door when it was unknown? The tablets with the text had lain in oblivion for many centuries, and more centuries were to pass before they were rediscovered.

Milton's break is spelled out in a prose treatise he was composing at the same time as he was working on his poem. *Christian Doctrine* remained forgotten in manuscript until 1823, and had to wait almost another hundred years before it dawned on anyone that it might be relevant to *Paradise Lost*. In it, Milton tries to base Christianity completely and rigidly on biblical texts. One might think that any fundamentalist would do the same, but Milton has a relentless logic which leads him to conclusions that most fundamentalists would be unhappy about, such as the lawfulness of polygamy. So it is all the more remarkable that on one issue he defies scripture, with no explanation or excuse. A large part of his epic versifies that defiance.

He is discussing the archangel Michael and the War in Heaven, and he cites Revelation 12. Michael, he accepts, was the leader of the good angels and the antagonist of the Devil, but he did not defeat Satan's host or cast him out. 'Their respective forces were drawn up in battle array and separated after a fairly even fight.' It was Christ, the Son of God (not yet, of course, incarnate as Jesus), who vanquished the enemy, which is not at all what the verses in Revelation say. There is no hint in them that there was ever a 'fairly even fight' between Michael's army and Satan's, or an ensuing truce or an intervention by Christ. Milton rejects tradition, but even if he had admitted it he would not have found it supporting his assertions.

Why this aberration? The reason lies in Milton's ideas about God's Son. In Christian orthodoxy he is the Second Person of the Trinity, co-equal and co-eternal with the Father. He is 'begotten', but the begetting is a mysterious generation outside time. In *Christian Doctrine*, however, Milton denies the Trinity. He argues that you cannot prove it from biblical texts, and he has no use for any other authority. God the Father, in Milton's opinion, is the one and only Supreme Being. He produced the Son by decree at the beginning of time and endowed him with deity in a series of steps, not all at once. Milton explains the word 'beget' as referring first to the original decree, and then, by a stretch of meaning, to the later acts of 'exaltation' by which the Son's status grew. He became his Father's agent in the work of creation, he became humanity's saviour and so on. Besides these promotions Milton postulates an earlier, pre-cosmic one that led to the Son overthrowing Satan. He sets it forth in the central part of *Paradise Lost*, and the Son is here strangely unlike Jesus and strangely like Marduk, who, in *Enuma elish*, is likewise 'the Son'.

Let us follow the story as Milton tells it. He begins with the fall of Satan and his legions, reserving the events leading up to it for narration later. It is clear from the start that the poet has adopted the War in Heaven with its Babylonian provenance and made it very warlike indeed. Satan fought against God and was expelled with his host, violently.

> He trusted to have equal'd the most High,
> If he oppos'd; and with ambitious aim
> Rais'd impious War in Heav'n and Battel proud
> With vain attempt. Him the Almighty Power
> Hurld headlong flaming from th'Ethereal Skie
> With hideous ruine and combustion down
> To bottomless perdition, there to dwell
> In Adamantine Chains and penal Fire,
> Who durst defie th' Omnipotent to Arms.

The Miltonic Hell is not subterranean. It is wholly distinct from Earth. Lying there collapsed, Satan and his chief lieutenant, Beelzebub, commiserate. Satan laments their discovery, too late, of the fearful weapons at God's command. But a careful reader of the ensuing narrative will notice a certain blurring of verbal distinctions. Miltonic angels are sometimes called 'gods', not often, but often enough to attract notice. When this happens it is apt to be in a speech by Satan or one of his fellow rebels, and the term might be explained as mere diabolic self-inflation. Yet God the Father addresses the heavenly host as 'gods' (III:341). Milton attempts a justification in *Christian Doctrine*. While the point is not very important, gods seem to be present in his thoughts.

Satan rises, assembles his defeated 'gods', and shows his resilience and resourcefulness by proposing a break-out – possibly a counter-stroke. He speaks of a report that was current and known to him in Heaven before the fatal revolt. God, he heard, is planning a new creation with new inhabitants . . . humanity. There may be scope for fresh trouble-making.

> 'Space may produce new Worlds; whereof so rife
> There went a fame in Heav'n that he ere long
> Intended to create, and therein plant
> A generation, whom his choice regard
> Should favour equal to the Sons of Heaven:
> Thither, if but to prie, shall be perhaps
> Our first eruption, thither or elsewhere:
> For this Infernal Pit shall never hold
> Caelestial Spirits in Bondage.'
> (I:650–58)

Satan's words are consistent with traditional Christian belief. The creation of our world was at least planned before the fall of the angels. In Book II, Beelzebub speaks of the report as well founded. The new realm of humanity may already exist.

> 'There is a place
> (If ancient and prophetic fame in Heav'n
> Err not) another World, the happy seat
> Of som new race call'd *Man*, about this time
> To be created like to us, though less
> In power and excellence, but favour'd more
> Of him who rules above; so was his will
> Pronounc'd among the Gods, and by an Oath
> That shook Heav'ns whole circumference, confirm'd.'
> (II:345–53)

In his wording of this speech, Milton is still orthodox . . . but suspend judgement. A twist is coming.

Hoping to harm and maybe colonize the new world, Satan sets

off to look for it. By now God has indeed created it, and after a perilous journey Satan arrives intact. Since a blow at humanity offers the best prospect, he makes his way to the Earthly Paradise, the dwelling-place of Adam and Eve. Milton locates it scripturally in the Middle East, high up, although not as high as in the *Divine Comedy*. As a Protestant he has no need to speculate about Purgatory, which is a popish fiction.

Seeing the first human couple in blissful innocence, Satan considers how to strike at God by corrupting them. Perhaps he can persuade them to eat the forbidden fruit. God, aware of what is happening, sends the archangel Raphael to warn Adam of the danger of disobedience. Raphael does so by giving a detailed account of Satan's rebellion and the doom of the rebels. This long flashback, as we may call it, is Milton's full version of the War in Heaven. Here he develops his departure from scripture, and here Babylonia seems, however impossibly, to return to life and break in.

It transpires that the immediate cause of the rebellion, before the creation of the world, was one of the aforesaid 'begettings' or promotions of the Son of God. That motive is apparently Milton's own idea, and it depends on his special theology and would be hard to reconcile with an orthodox view. God the Father, Raphael says, summoned the angels to a New Year ceremony and introduced his Son to them in a fresh, authoritative role.

> 'This day I have begot whom I declare
> My onely Son, and on this holy Hill
> Him have anointed, whom ye now behold
> At my right hand; your Head I him appoint;
> And by my Self have sworn to him shall bow
> All knees in Heav'n, and shall confess him Lord.'
> (V:603–8)

Similarly, Babylon's chief god Ea invests his son Marduk with full divinity, and Marduk's power is confirmed by an assembly of other gods:

'From this day unchangeable shall be thy pronouncement,
To raise or bring low – these shall be in thy hand.'
(*Enuma elish* IV:7–8)

Not all the Babylonian gods accept Marduk, and in Raphael's narrative not all the Miltonic 'gods' accept the Son in his new dignity. God's demand for obedience to him is too much for Satan, who, in his pride, secedes. Many angels join him, as some of the Babylonian gods, resenting the newly exalted Marduk, desert to Tiamat. Satan wins the allegiance of one-third of the heavenly host. Addressing his own assembly, he makes a startling claim. The angels, of course, are created beings, but he denies it. He is an independent entity, self-begot, and so are his followers: gods in truth. After all, they cannot remember being made. 'We know no time when we were not as now.' Therefore Satan's project of making war on God, even supplanting him, is not absurd. Milton gives him an eloquent speech in support of his delusion, which makes an epic battle, even a deadlocked one, conceivable.

His army marches. For two days of warfare the angels loyal to God, led by Michael, oppose it. Despite having a two-to-one superiority, Michael's force does not win or even gain a decisive advantage. This is the 'fairly even fight' of the cryptic sentence in *Christian Doctrine*. Now the parallels accumulate. As Tiamat's defeat is to be the work of the Son of Ea, so Satan's is to be the work of the Son of God.

Here the gods who support Marduk prepare him for his attack on the monster:

They gave him matchless weapons to ward off the foes:
'Go and cut off the life of Tiamat,
May the winds bear her blood to places undisclosed.'
(*Enuma elish* IV:29–32)

Here is God the Father exhorting his Son at the corresponding juncture:

'Go then thou Mightiest in thy Fathers might,
Ascend my Chariot, guide the rapid Wheeles
That shake Heav'ns basis, bring forth all my Warr,
My Bow and Thunder, my Almightie Arms
Gird on, and Sword upon thy puissant Thigh:
Pursue these sons of Darkness, drive them out
From all Heav'ns bounds into the utter Deep.'
(VI:710–16)

Here, in part, is the description of Marduk's preparations for battle:

Bow and quiver he hung at his side.
In front of him he set the lightning,
With a blazing flame he filled his body . . .
He then made a net to enfold Tiamat therein.
Then the Lord raised up the flood-storm, his mighty weapon.
He mounted the storm-chariot irresistible and terrifying.
He harnessed and yoked to it a team-of-four.
The Killer, the Relentless, the Trampler, the Swift . . .
For a cloak he was wrapped in an armour of terror,
With his fearsome halo his head was turbaned.
The Lord went forth and followed his course,
Toward the raging Tiamat he set his face . . .
Then they milled about him, the gods milled about him.
(*Enuma elish* IV:38–63)

And here is the Miltonic account of the Son's preparations, in the equivalent scene:

Forth rush'd with whirl-wind sound
The Chariot of Paternal Deitie,
Flashing thick flames, Wheele within Wheele undrawn,
It self instinct with Spirit, but conveyed
By four Cherubic shapes, four Faces each
Had wondrous, as with Starrs thir bodies all
And Wings were set with Eyes, with Eyes the Wheels

> Of Beril, and careering Fires between . . .
> Beside him hung his Bow
> And Quiver with three-bolted Thunder stor'd . . .
> Attended with ten thousand thousand Saints
> He onward came, farr off his coming shon.
> (VI:749–56, 763–4, 767–8)

Marduk's approach throws the enemy into confusion. Tiamat taunts him, but his challenge demoralizes her.

> When Tiamat heard this,
> She was like one possessed, she took leave of her senses.
> In fury Tiamat cried out aloud,
> To the roots her legs shook both together.
> (*Enuma elish* IV:87–90)

On the celestial battlefield, the Son tells the loyal angels to fight no more. This is the separation of the armies in the *Christian Doctrine* paragraph. He himself, he says, is the target of the rebels' hate, and he will dispose of them himself.

> Hee on his impious Foes right onward drove,
> Gloomie as Night; under his burning Wheeles
> The stedfast Empyrean shook throughout,
> All but the Throne it self of God. Full soon
> Among them he arriv'd; in his right hand
> Grasping ten thousand Thunders, which he sent
> Before him, such as in thir Soules infix'd
> Plagues; they astonisht all resistance lost,
> All courage; down thir idle weapons drop'd.
> (VI:824–39)

Marduk destroys Tiamat as already described, and casts her attendant demons into fetters. The gods who supported her try to get away, but he captures and imprisons them.

The gods, her helpers who marched at her side,
Trembling with terror, turned their backs about,
In order to save and preserve their lives.
Tightly encircled, they could not escape.
He made them captives and he smashed their weapons.
Thrown into the net, they found themselves ensnared;
Placed in cells, they were filled with wailing;
Bearing his wrath, they were held imprisoned.
(*Enuma elish* IV:107–14)

The Son of God's purpose with the rebel angels is 'not to destroy, but root them out of Heav'n'.

The overthrown he rais'd, and as a Heard
Of Goats or timerous flock together throngd
Drove them before him Thunder-struck, pursu'd
With terrors and with furies to the bounds
And Chrystall wall of Heav'n, which op'ning wide,
Rowld inward, and a spacious Gap disclos'd
Into the wastful Deep; the monstrous sight
Strook them with horror backward, but far worse
Urg'd them behind; headlong themselves they threw
Down from the verge of Heav'n, Eternal wrauth
Burnt after them to the bottomless pit . . .
Hell at last
Yawning receavd them whole, and on them clos'd,
Hell thir fit habitation fraught with fire
Unquenchable, the house of woe and paine.
(VI:856–66, 974–7)

That is not quite the end of the parallelism. After his victory, Marduk has his afterthought and creates the universe. At the same stage, Milton springs a surprise. His parallel to *Enuma elish* goes further still. He not only portrays the Son doing likewise, he makes creation a consequence of the war; even, to employ human language, an afterthought. Thus he contradicts the first part of his poem. There was no pre-existing plan that Satan or Beelzebub could have heard before their fall.

Raphael, the narrating angel, tells Adam what happened after the war was won. God the Father observed that Satan's revolt had drawn off so many angels that he might boast of having 'dispeopled Heaven'. However . . .

> 'I can repair
> That detriment, if such it be to lose
> Self-lost, and in a moment will create
> Another World, out of one man a Race
> Of men innumerable, there to dwell,
> Not here, till by degrees of merit rais'd
> They open to themselves at length the way
> Up hither, under long obedience tri'd,
> And Earth be chang'd to Heav'n, and Heav'n to Earth.'
> (VII:152–60)

At once the Son set forth, girt with paternal omnipotence, to carry out the work of creation. That is why Earth was in place already when Satan made his reconnaissance from Hell, although now Milton has left it unexplained how it occurred to him to look. The rest of *Paradise Lost*, telling the story of the Fall and its sequels, has no relevance here.

To revert to the Son's pre-cosmic victory over the rebels, there is no clear Christian precedent, and we cannot be sure exactly how Milton proceeded. Perhaps he wrote his strange paragraph in *Christian Doctrine* and spun Raphael's narrative out of that, or perhaps it was the other way round – he wrote the epic narrative first, and then wrote the paragraph to 'support' it. But he would have been turning away from scripture and tradition in either case, and the apparent Babylonian intrusion, going far beyond the older influences, would be there just the same.

The result is less than happy. The Son, as we may have trouble remembering, is the divine Person afterwards incarnate as Jesus Christ. For a reader of the Gospels, his Miltonic character and conduct are disturbing. The violence and fury, however splendidly portrayed, go too far; the break with scripture expands into a yawning gap. Even in matters of detail, Christian precedents are not easily come by. Describing the war chariot and the beings accompanying it, Milton takes hints from the visionary chariot in Ezekiel. Jewish tradition, however, regards the interpretation of the chariot as a mystical exercise leading to deeper knowledge of God. It figures in the *Divine Comedy* (*Purgatorio* XXIX:91–111) and still has nothing to do with war. Its militarization is Miltonic, and directly recalls the terrible chariot of Marduk.

We have the same problem with Milton as with Dante. If *Enuma elish* had been known when he wrote, his commentators would recognize it as a major source for the whole central portion of *Paradise Lost*, however strange it might be to find him using it. The trouble is that it was not known, and never had been known in a language he could have understood. The tablets were brought to light only in the late nineteenth century. Yet Milton seems to echo this text, which was not even partially rediscovered till two centuries after his death and not translated into English till after that. It is *as if* his mind were penetrated by someone's knowledge of the Babylonian epic in the twentieth century or later.

Comparison of the two poets brings out one or two significant points. While we cannot be dogmatic about their mental processes, we can define a common factor. Exotic mythology – Indian, Babylonian – intrudes when the poet is doing something original and breaks with scripture and tradition in pursuit of that aim.

Dante has to imagine and locate Purgatory. No one has ever tried it before in a manner he can take seriously. He also has to locate the Earthly Paradise. Previous authors have gone as far as putting it on a very high mountain, but they have left the whereabouts of the mountain in doubt, and have certainly not thought of equating it with Purgatory. What comes to Dante ready-made – in whatever inscrutable way it does come – is the Indian mountain at the world's centre, immeasurably high, associated with spiritual progress, septenary, having a paradise of gods on it and a radiant divine region beyond the summit. Translated into Christian terms, it draws everything together, and Dante adopts it. He invents his own Mount Purgatory, locates it at the centre of the sea-hemisphere and, in defiance of the Bible, puts the Earthly Paradise on top with the realms of glory above. He takes details from the model of the Indian mountain at Borobudur – surrounding terraces, along which the pilgrim passes, communicating stairways and sculptured reliefs.

Milton wants to give narrative form to the War in Heaven. What started it? Theologians say Satan's pride. But what event impelled Satan to assert himself? To set things in motion, Milton applies his own theology and imagines God the Father conferring a new status on his Son. This promotion leads to Satan's resentment and secession and also to the Son's logically becoming his conqueror, with the corollary that Michael, the traditional victor, must fail. Milton might have got so far without *Enuma elish*, but with his break with orthodox opinion the Babylonian epic – in whatever inscrutable way – moves in on him. The Son becomes a new Marduk. Even Ezekiel's venerable chariot is perverted to martial ends.

Another point. The poets are not prophesying. They are not foretelling future events. Yet they raise the same issue that prophecy has raised: receiving messages from the future, that is, from a time future for themselves. It may be grotesque, even ludicrous, to suggest a parallel with Nostradamus's line about the great heavenly temple, yet the parallel does present itself. And as with the temple, as with numerous other cases, 'seeing the future' is irrelevant. In fact it is a *reductio ad absurdum*. Suppose we do picture Dante and Milton making out-of-the-body journeys into the twentieth century. Their astral selves float into libraries and find ideas in books on mythology. Never mind how they pull them off the shelves or understand them when pulled. Why would they go to those particular books? Why should Dante pick out Indian mythology when he knew very little about India and had no interest in it? Why should Milton explore the literature of Babylon, especially as Babylon, to biblically moulded minds, was evil?

No. We are left with the same paradoxical 'as if' that has occurred elsewhere. It is *as if* these poets, like the prophets, were open to minds that were future from their own standpoint, minds acquainted, in this case, with future scholarship and drawn somehow into a contact against the temporal flow. Whether the 'as if' can be translated into anything comprehensible or conceivable remains to be seen. This, however, is the shape of the phenomenon. 'Seeing the future' isn't.

The Jim-and-Jane analogy in the last chapter can still apply. Jim stops at a newsagent and buys a local paper that has just come out. Meanwhile, Jane is miles behind, waiting for her passenger. She switches on her car phone and Jim comes through. He has noticed an article in the paper that would interest her, and he tells her about it. Where she is, the paper isn't available, but thanks to Jim's call, she knows the contents of the article.

Chapter Twelve

Seers and Witches

England produced no counterpart to Nostradamus. However, two prophets living before him left reputations of a sort; and after him, another great literary work gave powerful expression to a new view of prophecy, or rather a very old one revived.

Robert Nixon is a curious case. He has the distinction of being mentioned by Dickens in *The Pickwick Papers*, chapter 43. The dialogue is between Sam Weller and his father.

> 'Vell now,' said Sam, 'you've been a-prophesyin' away, wery fine, like a red-faced Nixon as the sixpenny books gives picters on.'
>
> 'Who was he, Sammy?' inquired Mr Weller.
>
> 'Never mind who he was,' retorted Sam; 'he warn't a coachman; that's enough for you.'
>
> 'I know'd a ostler o' that name,' said Mr Weller, musing.
>
> 'It warn't him,' said Sam. 'This here gen'l'm'n was a prophet.'
>
> 'Wot's a prophet?' inquired Mr Weller, looking sternly on his son.
>
> 'Wy, a man as tells what's a-goin' to happen,' replied Sam.

Nixon is 'red-faced' because of the method of printing in popular chap-books of the time.

According to the usual account, he was born in 1467 at Over Delamere in Cheshire. He began his working life as a ploughboy and seemed stupid, even retarded, but he was able to find employment with the Cholmondeley family. Taciturn for most of the time, he had lucid intervals when he attracted attention by displays of second-sight about local matters. One day he went into a trance and spoke afterwards of a whole series of future happenings, including, it is said, the English Civil War and the deposition of James II. On 22 August 1485, the day of the battle of Bosworth between Richard III and Henry Tudor, he started shouting about a fight between 'Richard' and 'Henry', which Henry won, before news of the battle could have arrived through ordinary channels.

The story goes that the Bosworth victor, as Henry VII, employed Nixon in the royal household. He prophesied an invasion by 'soldiers with snow on their helmets', an unexplained image (not fulfilled by the Russians with snow on their boots, reputedly seen in England in 1914). He ate greedily and stole food. Before 1485 was out, the exasperated cooks locked him in an empty room during Henry's absence and forgot about him. He died of starvation and dehydration.

Dickens shows that accounts of Nixon in 'sixpenny books' were still familiar enough to be known to Mr Pickwick's servant. He seems to have impressed contemporaries as an inspired idiot. Oral traditions of the 'Cheshire Prophet' were handed down. But as to his trance prevision, it is odd that the events he reported did not begin until long after his lifetime. One theory is that he really lived in the early seventeenth century; another, that the prophecies of a seer at that time were wrongly attributed to him. In any case the evidence is too late and filmsy to carry much conviction. The stories of him were not in print until 1714, when John Oldmixon published them. Alexander Pope ridiculed Oldmixon in his satirical poem *The Dunciad*, but, in a way, the publisher had the last laugh. His Nixon book went through many editions and was the basis for the pamphlet that Sam Weller mentions, whereas I doubt if Sam would have read *The Dunciad*.

Mother Shipton is supposed to have been a Yorkshire contemporary of Henry VIII. The only biography is much later, and whatever oral tradition may underlie it is lost. If not trustworthy, it is at least specific. Her name was Ursula Southiel. She was born in 1488 at Knaresborough and married Tobias

Shipton, a carpenter. Legend asserts that her father was a supernatural being who gave her his more-than-human powers and that she was born in a cave near the castle, still called Mother Shipton's Cave. Described as tall, ugly and very intelligent, she is credited with prophecies about public figures of the time, notably Cardinal Wolsey, whose rise and fall she predicted, more or less. Wolsey had her investigated, and she told the fortunes of the men he sent to investigate.

Some alleged prognostications of hers were published in 1641. Five years later the astrologer William Lilly brought out *Collections of Prophecies* containing eighteen attributed to her. The majority were prophecy-after-the-event. It was really not much use to claim that she had foretold the Spanish Armada in 1588. There was, however, an arguable prediction of a great fire in London.

The implausible 'Life', written by Richard Head, was published in 1677. The difficulty with Mother Shipton is much the same as with Nixon and, indeed, with other popular prophets such as Thomas the Rhymer, the Scottish Covenanter Alexander Peden and the 'Brahan Seer', also in Scotland, who made forecasts about prominent Scottish families. There is no solid documentation. Mother Shipton may have existed more or less as described, perhaps with a reputation for soothsaying. She certainly fits into a well-attested context of prophecy during Henry VIII's reign, which caused unrest and annoyed the king. The activities of the 'Maid of Kent' got Sir Thomas More into trouble. However, belief in Mother Shipton's share is a matter of opinion. Lilly, who publicized her prophecy of the Great Fire of London, made the same prediction himself and could have invented Shipton's to reinforce his own. Still, it was recognized as hers at the time. When the Fire broke out in 1666, Charles II's cousin Prince Rupert was in a boat on the Thames and observed that Mother Shipton had been vindicated. Pepys mentions this remark in his Diary.

She had a later burst of fame because of a reprint of Head's 'Life', which was published in 1862 by Charles Hindley, a bookseller. He put in the prophecies ascribed to her and some verses said to have been copied from a long-lost manuscript.

These foretold 'thoughts flying round the earth', presumably by electric telegraph, 'carriages without horses', presumably railway trains, tunnels through hills, ironclad ships and other nineteenth-century phenomena . . . plus the end of the world in 1881. In 1873 Hindley confessed that he had written the verses himself. Yet they went on being quoted into recent times by people who did not know of his confession and soft-pedalled the end of the world. A small British moth, with wing-markings supposed to look like a witch's face, is named after Mother Shipton. Her date of death is given as 1561.

America supplies a case-history that is somewhat better attested. It concerns two famous Shawnees. The chief Tecumseh (*c.*1768–1813) had a brother known as 'the Prophet'. In a prophetic episode that involved them both, Tecumseh was right, the Prophet was wrong. Tecumseh hoped to organize Native American resistance to the white advance, and in 1811 he tried to enlist the help of other tribes. He met their chiefs and gave them bundles of red sticks, telling them to throw away one stick every day. At certain points in this process, signs would be manifested. They were, in the shape of a comet and an earthquake. But the Prophet, claiming superior powers, incited the Shawnee to make a premature attack on General Harrison's camp. His promise that the enemy would be paralysed by his magic was not fulfilled, and the defeat wrecked Tecumseh's plan. There are different versions of the build-up with sticks, but the comet and earthquake at least were real, and recognized as signs at the time.

When Nostradamus invoked spirits he was following a time-honoured procedure. During most of the Middle Ages, ritual or ceremonial magic was a recognized art, which could be used for various purposes, of which inquiry into the future was only one. While it was suspect in the eyes of the Church and theoretically forbidden, its practitioners for the most part were left alone. By Nostradamus's time a change had set in. The sky had darkened. When he claimed that his work was divinely sanctioned, he was protecting himself against the charge that, by invoking spirits, he was making himself an agent of evil powers. Encouraged by a papal pronouncement in 1484, the great European witch-hunt had been gathering momentum.

Witchcraft had existed from time immemorial. There were village wise-women and healers. There were superstitions about witches who had the evil eye or cast harmful spells. This sort of thing seldom attracted much attention from ecclesiastics or those in power. Dante, in the *Inferno* (XX:121–3), devotes just three scornful lines to 'wretched women' who neglect ordinary household tasks to busy themselves with wax images and herbal potions. Mother Shipton may have been a witch in that traditional sense. Joan of Arc, by the way, was not even accused of being one, in that sense or any other. Her trial in 1431 was forced by the occupying English, and she was burned for heresy and sorcery.

It was during the later decades of the fifteenth century that witchcraft acquired a wider diabolic meaning. In the ensuing period of the Reformation the ascendant opinion, both Catholic and Protestant, was that all sorts of activities savouring of magic – including many of those of the village wise-women – were components of a conspiracy masterminded by Satan for the affliction of humanity and the ruin of souls. Since facilities for travel were poor, it might have been thought that the conspiring witches would have found it hard to get together. That difficulty was resolved by reviving an ancient belief that witches could fly. Dismissed in the Middle Ages as fantasy, this was now taken literally. They rode through the air on broomsticks or otherwise and met the Devil and his cohorts, to whom they had sworn allegiance. At these gatherings, the Witches' Sabbaths, they reported on the mischief they had been doing and engaged in erotic orgies and blacker things, such as the ritual killing and eating of children.

A witch now meant anyone involved in the imagined conspiracy. In 1486 a handbook of witch-hunting had appeared under the title *Malleus Maleficarum*, the Hammer of Witches. Its authors were two priests of the Dominican order, Jacob Sprenger and Heinrich Kramer. They listed numerous ways in which Satan's host of devils could operate through consenting humans, usually women, enabling them to work all manner of harm. Many diseases, accidents and misfortunes could be blamed on such practices. In that belief thousands of suspects were arrested, tortured until they confessed, and executed. The persecution reached its height only in the second half of the sixteenth century, but, overall, it went on for more than 200 years.

Although the great witch-hunt had roots in the Middle Ages, it was definitely not medieval. An alleged fourteenth-century outbreak in southern France is fictitious. It was post-medieval and symptomatic of a new paranoia. Understanding of it has been hindered by modern theories that capitulate to the witch-hunters, and accept that there really was a conspiracy or at least a society of witches. According to one theory, witchcraft was the 'old religion', popular paganism surviving. According to another, it was a sort of proto-feminism, and the great witch-hunt was a male attack on women. Misogyny undoubtedly played a part, and women victims outnumbered men by a wide margin, but they were far from being the only ones. A feminist estimate of nine million put to death is still current in some circles. It is utterly impossible. The actual total was probably 40,000 to 50,000, perhaps 10,000 of these being men. Such a number is appalling, but it is not nine million.

There was nothing like the unrelenting pressure and terror that Jews, for example, experienced under Nazism. Persecution was not continuous – it broke out sporadically, often in response to local conditions – and it was not universal – it never spread to eastern Europe, and in some countries, such as Holland and the Republic of Venice, victims were few. Nor was it unanimous; even the Spanish Inquisition warned against a too-ready belief in *Malleus Maleficarum*, and individual protesters dared to speak up, including Friedrich von Spee, a German Jesuit, who said he had talked with hundreds of convicted witches and decided that not one of them was guilty as charged. What persisted, whether or not anything was actually happening, was the attitude that made persecution possible. It was there all the time, increasingly, and it was always a threat.

A major factor was a simple religious one. The Bible said witches existed, therefore they did, and it was anti-Christian to express scepticism. The Bible said, 'Thou shalt not suffer a witch to live,' therefore they could and should be killed, and it was anti-Christian to question the propriety of doing so. The biblical authors meant something different. Their witches were mediums and diviners. They did not see them as agents of Satan, because they had never heard of Satan. But in the sixteenth and seventeenth centuries witches had to exist and had to be diabolic. This notion persisted until long afterwards. John Wesley wrote in 1768: 'The giving up of witchcraft is, in effect, giving up the Bible.' He reaffirmed that position even later.

Since the Devil and his minions made use of witches, anything witches said was suspect. In particular, Augustine's opinion of prophecy resurfaced. There was true prophecy inspired by God, but any other kind was likely to be inspired by demons to deceive humanity. *Malleus Maleficarum*, listing witches' unholy deeds, says that they 'show to others occult things and certain future events, by the information of devils'. This type of iniquity is not stressed, and the authors accept, as Augustine does, that prevision 'may sometimes have a natural cause'. Nevertheless, Nostradamus was wise to insist that although he employed astrology and other arts, God was his ultimate inspirer. In the prevailing atmosphere, a charge of prophecy by unholy means was always a danger. A mob had wanted to lynch him after the death of the French king.

The 'Life' of Mother Shipton by Richard Head marks the movement of ideas. In Head's account she is abducted by the Devil and gives birth to an imp. Such flights of fancy were perhaps not meant to be taken too seriously. In England the witch-mania was never as virulent as it was in some other countries and burning at the stake was not the normal method of execution. Many of the trials were due to people exploiting the climate of opinion to make trouble for enemies by accusing them of witchcraft. There was only one full-scale hunt, by Matthew Hopkins in East Anglia in 1645–7.

But Scotland was more witch-conscious. James Stuart, King James VI, was an expert on the subject and wrote books on it. In 1603, when he became James I of England and moved south, he acquired a company of players, henceforth known as the King's

Men, one of whom was William Shakespeare. *Macbeth*, written in
1606 or thereabouts, is his only play with a Scottish setting. It was
doubtless planned with performance at court in mind. The story
of Macbeth involved prophecies and made the topic of witchcraft
unavoidable. How to handle it for a royal patron who was a firm
believer?

Shakespeare had confronted the issue in an early play, perhaps his
first, *Henry VI* Part One. Reading up on English fortunes in
France after Henry V's death, he encountered the problem of 'La
Pucelle', Joan of Arc. She won victories for the French, and his
English audience would want an explanation of that. He made
her, unhistorically, a witch in the current sense, a wonder-
working agent of Hell. In the play she quickly convinces the
French leaders of her holiness and supernatural powers. One of
them, introducing her, says:

> The spirit of deep prophecy she hath,
> Exceeding the nine sibyls of old Rome:
> What's past and what's to come she can descry.

The Dauphin Charles falls under her spell, and she wins battles for
him. He promises that when she is dead, she shall be France's
patron saint – a prescient touch on Shakespeare's part. The
principal English commander, Talbot, sees that she is a witch, but
Shakespeare never directly portrays her thus until near the end.
Alone after a French reverse, she appeals desperately to 'fiends'
who have been helping her. They desert her. She is captured, and
ends her career ignominiously.

In *Henry VI* Shakespeare hardly comes to grips with witchcraft.
He finds Joan too interesting, an unscrupulous genius. The little
he shows of her relationship with the 'fiends' is ambiguous. She
addresses them as

> Ye choice spirits that admonish me
> And give me signs of future accidents.

This is close to *Malleus Maleficarum*, but she is under the delusion that she can make use of them. Their real dominance is revealed only when they refuse her offers of body and soul, and their departure leaves her powerless.

In *Macbeth*, after long experience as a successful dramatist, Shakespeare approached the topic more thoughtfully. James undoubtedly knew the story, or legend, which was about a real Scottish monarch in the eleventh century. Milton himself was later to consider it as a theme, but dropped Macbeth as he dropped Arthur. The main source was Holinshed's *Chronicle*, which relates how Macbeth met three mysterious women, who told him he would be king. Holinshed is uncertain who or what they were – Gaelic goddesses of destiny maybe, 'or else some nymphs or fairies'. After an accession and reign with dramatic potentialities, Macbeth was beguiled by the original prophetic success into trusting deceptive promises by soothsayers, and he came to grief.

No one knows whether Shakespeare agreed with James about witchcraft, but he transformed Holinshed's ill-defined trio into the most famous witches in English literature. To read *Macbeth* focusing on their role in it, rather than on the principal characters, is to see how well it illustrates the demonization of prophecy.

They are called 'the weird sisters'. At one level they are simply malignant hags, killing livestock and stirring up storms. Shakespeare remains in touch with village folklore. The first scene, however, shows their deeper commitment to evil. 'Fair is foul, and foul is fair.' It also shows that they have plans for someone named Macbeth. In the next scene the audience learns who he is: a leader of the army of the Scottish king, Duncan. Together with his colleague, Banquo, he has just routed several enemies. On the way home, the two commanders meet the witches, who salute Macbeth as Thane of Glamis and Thane of Cawdor and tell him he will be king. They tell Banquo that while he will not be king himself, his descendants will be. Macbeth is already Thane (feudal lord) of Glamis, but he professes bewilderment at the other titles and wants to know more. The witches, however, vanish.

A moment later Macbeth learns that the Thane of Cawdor has

been condemned as a traitor, and Duncan has transferred the title to him. The witches could have known this by ordinary means but, for the sake of the third prophecy, he wants to believe that 'they have more in them than mortal knowledge'. In a sense, they have: they have penetrated his secret thoughts. It transpires that he has already had notions of killing Duncan and claiming the crown in virtue of cousinship. So temptation is setting in. Banquo, by contrast, has seen the witches for what they are. When the message about the thaneship arrives, he says aside, 'Can the devil speak true?' And a little later he says:

> Oftentimes, to win us to our harm,
> The instruments of darkness tell us truths,
> Win us with honest trifles, to betray's
> In deepest consequence.

Lady Macbeth urges her husband on to the royal murder. With many misgivings and mental torments, he carries it out and becomes king. Duncan's son Malcolm, on whom he pins the blame, flees to England. By awakening the darker side of Macbeth's nature, the prophecy has created its own fulfilment. But this is only the beginning. As king he enjoys no peace of mind. He and his wife have terrible dreams. He trusts none of the men around him and employs spies to watch them. Banquo's untarnished honour is a standing reproach, and the next prophecy becomes a torture: if Banquo's descendants will rule, Macbeth's reign will be a dead end. Although there is no reason to fear him as an immediate threat, Macbeth hires murderers to dispose of him and his son. The son escapes, so the apprehension is not laid to rest. When Banquo's ghost appears, throwing him into panic, Macbeth decides to consult the witches again. He is aware of the kind of step he is taking.

> I am bent to know,
> By the worst means, the worst.

It is seldom noticed that a crucial shift has occurred. At the first meeting, the witches appear and vanish unbidden. Now, Macbeth can find them when he wants to. He has been drawn closer to them.

When he arrives, they have been filling a cauldron with repulsive ingredients. He begins to question them, and they invoke their 'masters' to reply. Mere soothsaying has been left behind, and we are now in the diabolic world of the witch-hunters. Questioning is unnecessary, because the controlling demons know what Macbeth has come to ask. They speak in the guise of apparitions.

First is 'an armed head'. He, or it, warns Macbeth against one of his nobles, Macduff. As before, his own thoughts are echoed. He fears Macduff and intends him to be the next victim. The second apparition, 'a bloody child', addresses Macbeth at slightly more length:

> Be bloody, bold, and resolute; laugh to scorn
> The power of man, for none of woman born
> Shall harm Macbeth.

This is in a long-standing tradition of oracular cheating and is evidently not going to work. Macbeth takes it at face value. He thinks 'none of woman born' is simply a way of saying 'no one', so he can do whatever he likes with impunity. A third apparition is 'a child crowned with a tree in his hand':

> Be lion-mettled, proud; and take no care
> Who chafes, who frets, or where conspirers are:
> Macbeth shall never vanquished be, until
> Great Birnam Wood to high Dunsinane hill
> Shall come against him.

The same applies. Macbeth takes this as a way of saying 'never'. The prophecy is correct but catastrophic. The witches have given him a false sense of security. They have another prophecy for him. He still wants to know about Banquo's descendants, and they horrify him with a vision of them as future kings, the Stuarts, the royal house of King James himself.

News is brought to Macbeth that Macduff has fled to England, beyond his reach. Senselessly, he has Macduff's family slaughtered. When Macduff hears, he vows vengeance and joins the self-exiled heir Malcolm in planning a move to dethrone Macbeth. They will return to Scotland with an English army to support a revolt. In the last phase Macbeth has become a ruthless tyrant, uninterested in earning his subjects' loyalty, because he trusts in the safety promised (as he imagines) by 'the spirits that know all mortal consequences' – that is what the demons have convinced him they are. He moves into a stronghold at Dunsinane, where his wife's mind gives way and she dies, apparently a suicide.

The demons have tricked him. Birnam Wood does come to Dunsinane when Malcolm's troops camouflage themselves with branches. This was the meaning of the crowned child holding a tree: Birnam Wood, carried, will put the prince – whom Macbeth sneers at as 'the boy Malcolm' – on the Scottish throne. Macbeth comes out of his castle, but many of his soldiers are unwilling to fight for him and the battle is lost. Confronting Macduff, he can still boast of his invulnerability because 'none of woman born' can harm him. Macduff replies that he was ripped from his mother's womb in a Caesarian section. Hence the bloody child. Macduff was not of woman *born*; the prophecy did not mean what Macbeth supposed, because the natural emphasis was not on the key word. Macbeth retorts with a curse:

> . . . And be these juggling fiends no more believed,
> That palter with us in a double sense;
> That keep the word of promise to our ear,
> And break it to our hope!

He has seen through them at last, yet his only reaction is fury. He could surrender and win time for repentance, but refuses. He has passed a point of no return; he has no capacity for repentance left. Macduff kills him and cuts off his head, as the first of the apparitions foreshadowed. Malcolm is king. The weird sisters and the devils they serve have used prophecy to ruin Macbeth and succeeded.

Once again, while we do not know whether Shakespeare shared the current view of witchcraft, *Macbeth* illustrates that view and especially the belief in evil prophecy inspired by evil beings. When the persecutions were past, Robert Burns could write *Tam o' Shanter* and make witches funny. Shakespeare's are not funny. If they sometimes appear so, that is because we don't look at them with contemporary eyes. The theatrical superstition that it is bad luck to speak of *Macbeth* by name and it must be referred to as 'the Scottish play' may owe something to its being accident-prone; but it does carry an air of nightmare.

Chapter Thirteen

The Cazotte Prophecy

During the eighteenth century, a more rational mood was setting in. Its effects were not confined to ending the witch-mania; it was arousing hopes for social and political change, which would destroy outworn institutions and bring the reign of Reason over humanity. Such hopes were strong among the French intelligentsia, under the influence of Voltaire. Yet it was France that produced the century's best-known prophecy, and this was not an anticipation of Reason's triumph but a very specific warning against it.

The chief witness is Jean de La Harpe, a critic and dramatist. Here is the story as he tells it. Early in 1788, a little over a year before the outbreak of the French Revolution, he attended a dinner party in Paris. Among the guests were the Marquis de Condorcet, a mathematician and politician, inventor of the idea of Progress; Sébastien de Chamfort, a fashionable writer; Félix Vicq-d'Azyr, the queen's doctor; Chrétien de Malesherbes, who had held major government posts; and Jean Sylvain Bailly, France's leading astronomer.

Also present was the novelist Jacques Cazotte. Born in 1719, Cazotte retained Catholic sympathies but had indulged in a mild form of occultism, and he was reputed to have clairvoyant gifts. He was the author of a fantastic novel, *Le Diable Amoureux*, a title not quite accurately translated as *The Devil in Love*. Students of English Romanticism see it as a precursor of Matthew Gregory Lewis's lurid tale *The Monk*. Despite his eccentricities, Cazotte was liked and respected. Another author, Charles Nodier, met him in childhood (he was a friend of Nodier's father) and remembered him long afterwards with affection.

> In addition to the extreme kindness that was visible in his handsome, happy face and the tenderness that his still very lively blue eyes expressed in a most captivating way, M. Cazotte had the precious talent of telling stories better than any man in the world. . . . Whenever M. Cazotte would appear in his three-cornered hat, his long redingote of green camlet fringed with a little braid, his square-toed shoes with their big buckles rather far forward, and with his tall cane with its golden knob, I never failed to run to him with every outward sign of foolish joy.

At the dinner party, says Jean de La Harpe, the wine flowed freely. Chamfort read some improper stories he had written, and the ladies didn't even pretend to be shocked. In the post-prandial relaxation there was much joking about religion. The Church was still established and rich, just as the monarchy was still strong, although hard pressed financially. With one exception, the guests agreed that 'superstition and fanaticism must make way for philosophy'. Thanks to Voltaire, the reign of Reason was coming, and it would be glorious.

Cazotte was the exception. He did not share the others' enthusiasm, and he made a few quiet jokes of his own about it. He was senior to most of them, but some, as eager as anyone for the reign of Reason, were old enough to regret that they would not live to see it. Suddenly he spoke up, in a tone that compelled attention. The guests, he said, knew his prophetic reputation, and he assured them that they would see the revolution they longed for. Some retorted that he didn't have to be a magician to make a guess like that. No, said Cazotte, but it might be helpful to learn what the revolution would be like. He began to talk. The reign of Reason was coming, and soon; but it would be frightful.

Condorcet wanted particulars. Cazotte told him that 'the joy of those times' would drive him to carry poison to cheat the executioner, and he would die on the floor of a prison cell. The listeners were taken aback, but recalled Cazotte's penchant for fantasy and began laughing again. This wasn't as amusing as *Le Diable Amoureux*. What could it have to do with the reign of Reason?

He stuck to his guns. Dreadful things would be done in the name of philosophy and liberty. Reason would reign, would even have temples. Chamfort would be a priest of Reason, and he would slash his wrists in despair, although he would not die for several months. More predictions followed. Dr Vicq-d'Azyr would allow his veins to be opened and die in the night. Malesherbes and Bailly would perish on the scaffold, and so would two other guests, Aimar de Nicolaï and Jean-Antoine Roucher, a poet. All would suffer at the hands of people talking 'philosophy' exactly as they had been talking themselves.

Unable to take such a prospect seriously, the guests tried to shrug off the prophecy as a joke in poor taste, but Cazotte's manner was grave and calm. Chamfort wanted to know when these things would happen; Cazotte replied that they would happen within six years. La Harpe, the narrator of the story, says he put in a word himself at this point. The events sounded to him like sheer miracles. Would he have a part in them? Cazotte promised that he would have a special miracle. He would become a Christian believer. Since La Harpe was a convinced atheist, this was such manifest nonsense that it lightened the atmosphere for a moment. However, all was not over. The Duchesse de Gramont remarked that women didn't seem to be in danger. After all, they didn't get too deeply involved in revolutions. Cazotte assured her that women, too, would be put to death, including herself. Under the reign of Reason, they would be treated just the same as men. The greatest ladies in France would not be spared, princesses and 'even greater' . . .

This was a plain hint at the queen, Marie Antoinette. Cazotte was going too far, and the host became uneasy. When the hints extended to the king, Louis XVI, he politely asked the prophet to cease. He would be causing trouble. As Cazotte was preparing to leave, the duchesse put one more question. Had he any predictions for himself? He referred her to a passage in the Jewish historian Josephus, about the Romans' siege of Jerusalem. A man walked round the ramparts for seven consecutive days, shouting 'Woe to Jerusalem!' and 'Woe to me!' On the seventh day a stone from a Roman catapult struck him and shattered him. That was Cazotte's parting word. He bowed to the assembly and was gone.

La Harpe's narrative ends here. It is thought to be based on notes that he wrote on his return home, perhaps with a view to producing them when six years had elapsed and the prophecy would surely have been falsified. In view of his beliefs at the time, he may have had hopes of discrediting Cazotte.

The Revolution broke out in 1789. Several of the guests at the party were active supporters. It did bring the reign of Reason, or what purported to be that. One of its features was the enthronement of an actress impersonating the Goddess of Reason in Notre Dame Cathedral, which thus became a 'temple' such as Cazotte had spoken of. Presently came the Terror. Bailly was guillotined in 1793. Marlesherbes, Nicolaï and Roucher followed in 1794. In the same year Condorcet took poison under the circumstances foretold, and Chamfort slashed his wrists clumsily and died two months later owing to bad medical treatment. Vicq-d'Azyr was an exception, but only a partial one. Threatened by revolutionaries, and shaken by the course of events, he contracted a fever and died in delirium.

As for Cazotte himself, the missile had struck already, in September 1792. He had not been against the Revolution at first, but he turned against it and was drawn into a plot to rescue the king. His daughter's pleas brought a stay of execution. The sentence, however, was upheld and he died courageously. La Harpe was imprisoned. While in jail he had a spiritual experience that converted him. After his release he was firmly loyal to Church and Crown. He died in retirement in 1803. His account of the dinner party, composed at a date unknown, was published in 1806.

Did this happen? The deaths happened, La Harpe's conversion happened, but did Cazotte foretell them?

The natural supposition is that the story is a royalist fiction, a prophecy-after-the-event, which La Harpe concocted when the people he named were all dead and in no position to contradict. As the famous literary critic Sainte-Beuve remarked, it doesn't read like a memorandum written in full when the memory was fresh. It is carefully crafted with dramatic effect, arguably the best thing its author ever did. Still, other guests at the party survived, and none of those contradicted the account. Several letters and memoirs attest that La Harpe talked about the prophecy quite soon after the date assigned to it, and Cazotte referred to it in conversation. Few of these allusions can be proved earlier than the Terror, but they converge, with a cumulative impact. The question is not so much whether the prophecy was uttered as whether La Harpe improved it in retrospect, and if so, how radically?

Someone who takes us close to Cazotte is Mme d'Hautefeuille, the author of a memoir of the novelist and his family. She believes in his gift, and quotes other predictions, including one that could fit Napoleon. She has no doubt about his prophecy of the Terror and says many people knew and spoke of it, although without attaching much credence until after its fulfilment. Cazotte's eldest son, Scévole, endorsed her book as reliable. However, it confirms the prophecy in general terms only.

Most of the other testimonies come from high-society figures who detested the Revolution and were impressed by Cazotte's diagnosis of its tendency. The most informative is the Comtesse d'Adhémar, who attended the French court and published her recollections of Marie Antoinette. She says that Cazotte's mysterious pursuits and pronouncements were known in royal circles. More than once the queen told her to ask him for his latest predictions, and they were good enough to be surprising. Mme d'Adhémar was present at the fateful dinner. According to her, there were about sixty guests, and she names thirty-three, including most of those mentioned by La Harpe. It may be inferred that she had, and kept, a list; in other words, she had at least something that was written down at the time. Her version confirms La Harpe's in its main drift, even naming another victim, Le Peletier de Saint-Fargeau. She adds that the prophecy was reported to the queen, although, understandably, in 'veiled terms'.

The comtesse raises a couple of questions. She dates the party near the beginning of 1787, not 1788. The discrepancy has been cited as adverse to credibility, either hers or La Harpe's. Yet it cuts the other way, too. She is not copying him, and her version has independent value. One of them had a slight lapse of memory, that is all. Another query arises from the number of guests. La Harpe says there were 'many', but still gives the impression of a gathering where the conversation was general; with sixty it could not have been so. They would have had to sit at several tables. The host might have called for silence so that Chamfort could read aloud to the whole assembly, but he wouldn't have done the same for Cazotte. The prophecy was not a lecture. Taken together, the accounts suggest an after-dinner situation when people had risen and were strolling about chatting, and gravitated towards a group round Cazotte when he was seen to be a focus of interest.

The Duchesse de Gramont, also present, left nothing in writing about the prophecy. However, she talked. The former royal mistress Mme du Barry, whose testimony cannot be later than 1793 (she was guillotined in that year), says the duchesse quoted Cazotte as foretelling a 'bloody death' for guests of both sexes – as, according to La Harpe, he did. The duchesse also talked to the Marquise de Crequy, who kept a record. Another titled lady who was not present but contributed to the evidence was Henriette-Louise, Baronne d'Oberkirch. She says in her memoirs that as the Revolution approached, prophecies were circulating. In January 1789 we find her reading 'the famous prophecy of M. Cazotte'. This must be the dinner-party prophecy, since La Harpe was her source for it. He had sent an account to a correspondent in Russia, from whom it had got back to Henriette-Louise.

Charles Nodier, who cherished that pleasant childhood memory, recalled that Cazotte spoke of the prophecy himself. Nodier was twelve years old at most and probably did not take much in. Later in life, when he had read the final version, he did not question it but denied any paranormal implications. In 1788, he thought, it was 'probably not difficult to foresee that the coming revolution would select its victims from the highest society of the age and then devour those who had created it'.

More testimony was gathered by the English author J.M. Neale. He started out as a sceptic, but his inquiries led him to believe that the prophecy was truly uttered. Some of his information came from the Comte de Montesquieu, some came from the celebrated Mme de Genlis, the former governess of royal children, among them the future king Louis-Philippe. In a letter written in November 1825, she mentioned that before the Revolution she had heard La Harpe narrate the prophecy very much as he did in his final version. Neale also drew on a surviving acquaintance of Vicq-d'Azyr and on Cazotte's son, Scévole. Scévole had no doubt as to the main fact, although he was unwilling to confirm the details. Finally, Neale got what purported to be a corroboration by one of the dinner guests. It depended, however, on the word of the Baron de Lamothe-Langon, a grossly unreliable person who turns up (oddly enough) as an authority, or rather a non-authority, on witchcraft. Fortunately, Neale's conclusions were satisfying without him. He put them in a book called *The Unseen World*.

These items are more impressive together than they are singly. We glimpse a number of individuals testifying in similar terms, not in touch with each other and not specially anxious to prove anything. One or two cavils amount to very little. No one has found a reference to the prophecy in a newspaper. Why should there have been any? No reporters were at the party. The Comtesse d'Adhémar and Mme d'Hautefeuille disagree as to its venue, and Alexandre Dumas, who wrote on the incident, disagrees with both. But only the comtesse was actually there. The other two had nothing to go on but hearsay, Dumas long afterwards.

The gap in the evidence is the shortage of particulars. Except in La Harpe's account, and in materials that could have been copied from it, the victims are not named and their fates are not specified. Moreover, once again, his narrative is too good: not perhaps too good to be true, but too good to be convincing. Whether or not he took notes at the time, his final text is a literary production. He improved the original event, and once we admit that he improved it at all, it is hard to be sure what is improvement and what isn't.

The irreducible fact seems to be that Cazotte did in some sense foretell the Terror. There is no reason to doubt that La Harpe kept a memo of the prophecy, talked about it and sent a summary to his correspondent in Russia. Years later he worked up whatever notes he had into the existing version, making it more personal and closer to the course of events in the interval. Some of the guests had died in the evil days Cazotte had anticipated. That degree of fulfilment excused naming them, even if they were not named originally. This was not exactly misrepresenting the prophet, it was making him say what, in La Harpe's opinion, he could and should have said. The end product may have been a purely private exercise. It does not appear that La Harpe had any notion of publishing it himself.

Numerous people saw the Revolution coming, but Cazotte was exceptional, perhaps unique, in foretelling the homicidal phase through which it would pass. He was so far out of line that he shocked his audience, and rumours of his prophecy may have grown in the telling, even apart from La Harpe's activities. But if accusations of spreading alarm were false, we would expect to find him denying or protesting, if only in his letters. We never do.

Can the story be demystified? Conjectures would be in order, even if the full La Harpe version were correct. Possibly, Condorcet and Chamfort became mentally unbalanced and did what Cazotte had said they would, so that the prophecy created its own fulfilment. La Harpe's conversion might have been precipitated in the same way, without the mental disturbance; he was recoiling from the Revolution in any case. However, the four who went to the guillotine would hardly have arranged their own executions.

If, as is obviously more likely, the prophecy was in fairly general terms, Nodier's rationalization is at first sight attractive. Cazotte foresaw, by his own natural good sense, that the Revolution would (as the phrase goes) devour its children. That is all the more plausible today. Nodier, however, was talking with hindsight, when the Terror had become a notorious fact of history. To echo him now is to talk with double hindsight, after the experience of Russia as well as France. In 1788 the prospect was different. There had been many wars and persecutions, but the reign of Reason was going to end such things. Nothing like the revolutionary slaughter had ever been known, certainly not in the Cromwellian revolution in England, which French hopefuls looked to as a precedent. Nor, by the way, was there any reason to expect women to be treated with the same ruthlessness as men. That is a touch in the prophecy that looks authentic.

Cazotte predicted something beyond the guests' mental grasp, something wholly unthinkable. It was all very well for Nodier to argue, long afterwards, that it was 'not difficult to foresee' the Terror. If it was 'not difficult' why did nobody else foresee it? Those who looked forward to the reign of Reason assumed that it would be benign. We can sample their way of thinking in a book by one of them, Louis-Sébastien Mercier, entitled *L'An 2440* ('The Year 2440'). This is a bland fantasy of an enlightened future when all the world is moral and peaceable and constitutional government is universal. Nothing indicates prior birth-pangs of transition. It all seems to have just happened and to have continued for centuries without major setbacks.

Cazotte challenged such daydreams with a nightmare of disillusionment, which no one else was evoking. He had no facts to go on, no precedents to guide his thinking. Simply as a rational forecaster, he would have needed a rare acumen. And here we encounter an obstacle. In his writings, there is no trace of such a quality, and he strays into some strange vagaries. As the Revolution unfolds, his letters at first show a certain optimism. Then he is against it, and his royalism builds up into absurd outpourings about the coming deliverance of Louis XVI and his future glories when it's all over. If Louis's supporters do their duty, with divine aid, the king will outshine the glories of Solomon, he will be a model and a beacon for Europe. Cazotte puts some of his fancies into another 'prophecy', taking up Revelation like so many other cranks and giving John's imagery wild interpretations in terms of current events.

Of course, he had every right to switch his attention from revolutionary peril to royalist hope, but the hope expressed in his late writings is so wishful, so woolly minded, so utterly mistaken. If he had talked like this at the party, on any theme at all, he would have made no impression on that élite company. The Cazotte whose 'famous prophecy' was remembered has to be, in effect, a different person. Nor is it unfair to go back before 1788 and ask whether his earlier output shows the requisite gifts. I don't think it does. *Le Diable Amoureux* nowhere suggests the kind of insight required.

I feel also that the prophecy is out of character from a purely social point of view. If La Harpe's account is anywhere near the truth, Cazotte's conduct was deplorable. To take part in a convivial evening, to contribute quietly to the fun and then, without warning, to launch into horrible predictions about one's fellow guests . . . it won't do. He might have passed it off as a joke, if a rather sick one, by his expression. 'When you say that, smile,' in the words (more or less) of Owen Wister's Virginian. Apparently he didn't. If we take the minimal view and suppose that, without picking on individuals, he simply foretold the Terror – even making it less terrible than it was – it would still have been a disagreeable performance in that company, discourteous to his host and liable to make him unpopular afterwards. He wasn't like that.

The insight that is displayed in the prophecy, and the aggressiveness of displaying it thus, both seem foreign to Cazotte. There are grounds for wondering about a prophetic intrusion into his mind, an external inspiration that briefly changed him. His beliefs and interests would have made him receptive to it, and just possibly a little more was involved than passive receptivity.

In a biography published in 1845, Gérard de Nerval, another writer of fantasy, reproduces La Harpe's account of the prophecy. He gives it 'only relative credence' and approves Nodier's dubious verdict that it would not have been difficult to foresee such events. However, he also draws attention to a bizarre passage in *Ollivier*, a narrative poem by Cazotte published in 1763. He suggests that a reader may discern in this, however vaguely, a 'prophetic hallucination'.

The woman who tells the story is travelling with a companion, and they are lured by the magic of the 'fay Bagassa' into her palace. They fall down a pit where a wheel armed with sharp blades cuts them into pieces, yet in some inexplicable way they remain alive. After a while the narrator opens her eyes and finds that her separated head, the conscious part of her, has been placed with 800 other heads of both sexes, of all ages and all colourings. The others are alive like herself. They are bored and quarrelsome, they yawn a great deal, they complain of being without their limbs, and they have a bitter humour but no hope.

Nerval comments:

> Is it not curious to find in a mock-heroic poem of the author's youth this bloody dream of heads and limbs severed from their bodies, this strange association of ideas that brings together courtiers, soldiers, women and gallants, expounding and jesting upon the details of their torture, just as the nobles, ladies and poets of Cazotte's mature years will later do, among whose number he will come bearing his own head and trying like the others to smile and make light of the whims of this bloodthirsty fay who, unbeknownst to him, would one day be called the Revolution?

Well, yes, perhaps it is curious, just a little. Does any other author imagine a mass assembly of severed heads? When Cazotte wrote *Ollivier* the guillotine was unknown in France. It made its début when the Revolution required a swift method of decapitation.

Chapter Fourteen

More Astrologers

Christians never quite abandoned astrology, even in the early centuries when it was opposed by Augustine and other ecclesiastics. Their word, after all, was not final. No condemnation could get rid of the Magi, the Wise Men from the East, who saw the star and came to Bethlehem. It had always been supposed that they were astrologers, yet they were manifestly good in God's sight, and their homage to Jesus was important as the first proof that he was for Gentiles as well as Jews. While planets could no longer be gods, they might be allowed to influence and indicate. As a 'scientific' technique, astrology began to revive in the tenth century. Arabs may have played a part in its rescue, but scholars in the Church, especially Benedictines, saved it from going on the list of forbidden arts. During the Middle Ages astrologers practised without hindrance, although they laid more stress on character-reading and medical diagnosis than on prediction.

Under the later Tudors the versatile John Dee, who, like Nostradamus, had connections at court, cast the horoscopes of Queen Mary, her husband Philip of Spain, and the Princess Elizabeth. He was in temporary disfavour in 1555, possibly because he had said Mary would have no children (she did not), but when Elizabeth became queen, all was forgiven, and he was allowed to fix a date for her coronation. He wrote of astrology theoretically, but not much is on record about his actually practising it; he was more interested in alchemy and an early form of Spiritualism. His ideas about English expansion overseas were prompted partly by political and commercial considerations and partly by his belief in the wide extent of King Arthur's domains, which Elizabeth, as the restorer of Arthurian Britain, had every right to reconstitute.

On the Continent, astrology declined with the decline of Earth-centred astronomy. In England it retained some vitality into the seventeenth century. The new interest in Merlin sustained respect for prophecy in a general way, despite the prestige of Francis Bacon, who declared in a dismissive essay that prophecies 'ought all to be despised' and are remembered only when they turn out right. Today, with a vast number that didn't turn out right preserved and reprinted, the gibe has lost some of its force.

William Lilly (1602–81) was a professional. He made money not only by casting horoscopes but by teaching the art to pupils. His almanac of forecasts appeared annually under the pseudonym Merlinus Anglicus Junior from 1644 until his death. He gave Charles I advice, which the king ignored, and ended up siding with Parliament in the Civil War, although he was in trouble during both the Cromwellian regime and the Restoration. As the first publicist of Mother Shipton, he did as much as anyone to establish her fame. In 1648 and again in 1651 he foretold disasters in London around 1665, including 'sundry fires and a consuming plague'. The Great Plague came in 1665 and the Great Fire in 1666. Lilly was suspected of starting the fire himself or at least of knowing about arsonists, and Samuel Pepys mentions him disrespectfully in his Diary.

The Arthurian prophet's name was used again by John Partridge (1644–1715), who put out an almanac as Merlinus Liberatus. Impressive as an autodidact but bogus as an astrologer, he was annihilated by Jonathan Swift. Francis Moore (c.1657–1715) launched another almanac in 1700 that survives to this day as 'Old Moore'.

Very little happened in the eighteenth century. One or two handbooks came out, and a few astrologers set up as consultants, among them John Varley (1778–1842), who is more memorable as an artist and friend of William Blake. Predictive almanacs began appearing again in the 1830s; the authors' pseudonyms were

Raphael and Zadkiel. It does not appear that any astrologer, in all this time, was conspicuously successful as a prophet.

Astrology's real revival began as a by-product of Theosophy, the movement founded by Mme Blavatsky, who endorsed it in 1877 in her book *Isis Unveiled*. A Theosophist named Alan Leo (the pseudonym of William Frederick Allen, 1860–1917) was its first popularizer, and he published a textbook, *Astrology for All*. A more prominent American counterpart was Evangeline Adams (d.1932), a descendant of John Quincy Adams, the sixth president. She had social contacts and was consulted by celebrities, including John Pierpont Morgan Jr and Mary Pickford. In the early days of radio broadcasting her voice was heard over the air, and her popular manual, *Astrology for Everyone*, was published in 1931. Outside of private consultation her predictive successes were not numerous. In 1931, besides producing the manual, she foretold that the US would be at war within eleven years – right and mildly interesting, since eleven is a curious number to think of and the natural 'ten' would not have been quite enough. She also predicted that Edward, Prince of Wales, would run into difficulties because of his fondness for married women who would not be able to share his throne; and so it turned out, when the prince became Edward VIII and shipwrecked on his amour with Mrs Simpson.

Evangeline Adams's vogue contributed to the birth of newspaper astrology. In August 1930 the British *Sunday Express* began to run predictions by R.H. Naylor. His breakthrough came that October when he made a fairly convincing forecast of the crash of the airship R-101. From then on he wrote a regular Sunday feature. He and others hired to do likewise worked under the disadvantage of being forced to make frequent pronouncements that could easily be proved wrong. Naylor had the post-mortem distinction of appearing in Stephen Pile's second book of 'Heroic Failures' as 'The Least Correct Astrologer'. Within a few weeks during his heyday in the late 1930s he declared that General Franco would never rule Spain (he did, for thirty-six years); that Ireland's unification was imminent (not even yet); and that 'war is not scheduled for 1939' (it broke out that September). Hitler's horoscope showed that he was 'not a war maker', although he 'might at some point show an interest in regaining Togoland', a former German colony. Naylor also said that 'aircraft which cannot hover will soon be deemed utterly useless' and that 'Iceland will become a key area'. As far as I know, no mass-circulation astrologer has ever done much better. The standard defence is a statement of medieval origin: 'The stars influence but do not compel.'

There was a moderate revival in France during the 1890s, associated with occultism. Charles Nicollaud, the Nostradamus expert, writing under the pseudonym Fomalhaut (the name of a star), scored a remarkable hit: 'There is a planet beyond the orbit of Neptune and its name is Pluto.' Correct, more than thirty years before Pluto's discovery. Unless this is a real case of precognition, it would be interesting to know why, in 1930, the name was chosen. The choice may have been merely a strange coincidence. Or – unlikely as it seems – someone may have read Nicollaud's pronouncement. About that time, the fantasy writer H.P. Lovecraft (1890–1937) imagined a trans–Neptunian planet. He called it Yuggoth. Possibly, Lovecraft knew of Nicollaud: he mentions the star Fomalhaut from which the Frenchman took his pseudonym. But, admittedly, 'Yuggoth' is not 'Pluto'.

It was only in Germany after the First World War that astrology became a high-level concern, and it was only there that it achieved, or appeared to achieve, a predictive triumph. Again, an early impulse came from Theosophy. Another came from the related Anthroposophy of Rudolf Steiner (1861–1925). Further factors, not operative in other countries, or less so, had special weight. The interest shown in astrology by Carl Gustav Jung gave it prestige. The sufferings of Germans in 1923–4, during the period of great inflation, created a yearning for a doctrine that would make sense of life and perhaps promise a brighter day ahead. Germany's chief astrological revivalist, Hugo Vollrath, had been preparing the ground; he was a Theosophist and also friendly with Steiner. An Astrological Congress in Munich was the first in a series. Attempts were soon under way to make astrology an authentic and reputable science.

It hovered around the Nazi movement from an early stage. In 1923, the year of Hitler's abortive *putsch*, two of its exponents were drifting in his direction. Rudolf von Sebottendorf taught astrology to the public while preaching German nationalism. Elsbeth Ebertin talked about a coming Führer. Vollrath himself presently became a supporter of Hitler and tried to give astrology a Nazi bias. Trouble, however, lay ahead. In 1929 a new character enters the scene, Erik Jan Hanussen.

Hanussen, whose real name was Steinschneider, was Austrian and part-Jewish. Professionally he was an entertainer, well paid for exhibitions of hypnotism and mind-reading in Berlin theatres, and he also gave psychic counselling as a private consultant, finding out facts about his clients by bugging, then little known. There are signs, however, that he had a genuine clairvoyant gift. The novelist Arthur Koestler, then working as a journalist in Berlin, describes him as 'a stocky, dark-haired man with quick movements, full of dynamic energy and not without charm'. Koestler subjected him to a test and regarded the result as a failure, but his own account shows that it was actually a success, in an unexpected and rather amusing way. Koestler's resolute disbelief made him miss the point.

Hanussen had Nazi contacts and was on friendly terms with the head of the Storm Troops in Berlin. He coached Hitler in public speaking and publicly predicted his accession to power. Astrology was not among his major interests, but, seeing the market for it, he brought out a popular astrological weekly. On 1 January 1933 he cast Hitler's horoscope and foretold correctly that he would attain power on the 30th. Critics accused him of having inside information. It was rumoured, however, that the horoscope not only indicated the date but also went on to predict disaster after a phase of spectacular success. It is even said to have put Hitler's end in the spring of 1945 – also correctly, as it turned out.

The Gestapo discovered Hanussen's Jewish background, and in February he went too far. He sometimes worked with a medium, Maria Paudler, who, in a trance and before witnesses, described what was recognized as the burning of the Reichstag. That notorious fire was planned by the Nazis themselves, with the object of putting the blame on the Communists and crushing them. On 26 February newspapers carried an officially inspired account of the séance, according to which it was Hanussen himself who had gone into a trance. He had had a most convenient revelation: 'I see a blood-curdling crime committed by the Communists. I see blazing flames. I see a terrible firebrand that lights up the world.'

The fire broke out the following evening. It is impossible to be sure what Hanussen knew, how he knew it or what he or his medium really said. In the unlikely event that he was in on the plot, he would surely have kept quiet and done nothing to give it away. More probably he was aware of it or had strong suspicions and said too much or allowed too much to be said. Soon afterwards, before one of his stage performances, he was hustled into his own car and driven off. His body, riddled with bullets, was found in a wood on the outskirts of Berlin. Years later, when many things had changed, Hanussen became a minor cult figure, and a film made in 1988 accepted the reality of his psychic gift and connected it with a war wound in the head, although no attempt was made to explain or rationalize it. The film attributed his murder, plausibly enough, to his hinting too openly at Nazi responsibility for the fire.

In the frenetic atmosphere of the early 1930s it was to be expected that other astrologers would draw up horoscopes for Hitler. The process had begun when his importance was growing obvious, and several were circulating during his first year in office. They disagreed, because of doubts as to the time of his birth. Some were far from encouraging – even critical and ominous – and one of the astrologers, Josef Schultz, dared to predict the Führer's ultimate downfall. Before long official disapproval made itself felt. More than disapproval: another astrologer, Karl Guenther Heimsoth, was killed in the purge of June 1934, although perhaps more for his association with Röhm, the purge's principal victim. The Nazi regime began to suppress astrological publications, and after 1936, no more congresses were held.

Hitler did not believe in astrology. The canard that he did and that he employed an astrologer as adviser was put about in England during the Second World War by Louis de Wohl. An astrologer himself, he tried to convince the British government that Hitler made use of the technique; by doing so he hoped to get a job in Intelligence, forecasting what the astrologically advised Führer would do next. He submitted samples without success. It is hard to see how he could have kept such a job for long, unless his forecasts happened to be extremely lucky. Anyhow, the government had better sources of information.

Louis de Wohl underwent a repentance and wrote several historical novels focused on saints. *The Quiet Light*, about Thomas Aquinas, is quite good, and his achievement in making the theologian a fictional hero is unusual. The only basis for his less competent wartime fiction was Germany's employment of a Swiss astrologer, not for advice but for propaganda. As we saw, an interpretation of one of the Nostradamus quatrains intrigued several German readers, including Frau Goebbels. Her husband, Joseph, in charge of 'public enlightenment', had no more belief in astrology than Hitler, but since Nostradamus was regarded chiefly as an astrologer and since he could evidently impress people, it appeared that he and his art might have a place in the war effort. Goebbels consulted the author of the book that his wife had read, who drew his attention to Karl Ernst Krafft (1900–45). This man seemed to have good prophetic credentials – he had recently warned of an attempt to assassinate the Führer – and in December 1939 Goebbels put him on the payroll.

Krafft, a Swiss of German descent, was an eccentric. He had invented several pseudo-sciences with names like Cosmobiology, which purported to give psychological insights. For a while he worked in a department store, applying his notions to personnel selection. In 1933 he received a legacy and lost most of the money in investments based on his own theories, which had come to include ideas about sun-spots. He published many articles, but never made any converts of standing. An attempt to interest Jung led nowhere.

When Goebbels hired him, he had been living in Germany for

two years. He had already given lectures on Nostradamus, and his main assignment now was to work out pro-German interpretations. Besides giving further lectures, he wrote a commentary that was published in French and Portuguese under German auspices. Fake Nostradamus predictions were printed as leaflets and dropped in France during the 1940 campaign. Krafft made some predictions of his own, but he had a certain fatal integrity. In 1940, when Germans hoped and expected that the war would end soon, he said it would go on and should not be allowed to continue beyond the winter of 1942–3 – apparently because he foresaw a great German defeat during that winter, which, of course, happened at Stalingrad. Ordered to draw up horoscopes that could be used, Krafft concocted one for President Roosevelt that put him in a bad light but, referring to the war in North Africa, he insisted that the chart of the German commander Rommel was inferior to that of his British opponent Montgomery. Imprisoned in 1943, and very ill, he died towards the end of the war *en route* to the Buchenwald concentration camp. His last prediction was that British bombs would hit Goebbels's Propaganda Ministry in retribution. They did.

Mystery surrounds a horoscope said to date from long before Hitler's rise to power, and it is because of this that German astrology has more than historical interest. Reputedly drawn up on 9 November 1918, at the end of the First World War, it was a horoscope of the German Republic proclaimed when the Kaiser abdicated.

No one seems to have remembered who drew it up. It was certainly in existence at the outbreak of the Second World War, when someone who had seen it spoke of 'two strong Mars directions for 1939–40'. That was manifestly apt. There are various indications that it pointed to German success up to 1941 and then a turning of the tide. In May of that year, Hitler's deputy Rudolf Hess made a sensational solo flight to Britain in the hope of negotiating peace. He had an entirely straightforward motive. Hitler was about to launch Operation Barbarossa, the invasion of Russia, and Hess, who was apprehensive, hoped to avoid a war on two fronts. But he believed on astrological grounds that Germany and its Führer had reached a zenith and deterioration was liable to follow if nothing was done about it. A horoscope of Hitler himself suggested a downturn, and according to *The Times*, Hess had warned him of this. Albrecht Haushofer, the son of a Nazi theorist who was one of Hess's principal mentors, said Hess acted as he did because Hitler's aspects were 'malefic' in early May.

Nothing came of Hess's mission, and the official German version was that he had gone mad. It did, however, acknowledge the influence of astrologers. More was involved than one man's insanity. Hitler complained of 'astrological cliques' and 'stargazers' who must be suppressed. What was known as the *Aktion Hess*, beginning on 9 June, was a sweeping clampdown not only on astrologers who still practised but on spiritualists and occultists of various kinds. It was proof that confidence was being sapped, and not because of rational fears about Operation Barbarossa, which had not yet got under way and was a well-kept secret. The astrologers were right. The turning-point came in December 1941 with the first failure in Russia and the involvement of America.

Germany's horoscope, together with Hitler's, surfaces again more fully in the last phase of the war. Its sequel to 1941 now emerges. Goebbels kept a diary until near the end, and in the entry for 29 March 1945 he gives a glimpse not only of the horoscopes but of himself, still not believing in astrology but still hoping to make use of it.

Some voluminous material has been submitted to me intended to initiate astrological or spiritualistic propaganda; it includes the so-called horoscope of the German Republic of 9 November 1918 and also the Führer's horoscope. The two horoscopes are in striking agreement. I can understand why the Führer has forbidden people to concern themselves with such uncontrollable matters. Nevertheless it is interesting that both the Republic's horoscope and that of the Führer predict some relief of our military situation for the second half of April; on the other hand the position will deteriorate in May, June and July, whereas apparently hostilities should cease by mid–August. May God grant that this is so. Admittedly we should be facing some difficult months; nevertheless if one knew that the worst period of the war would be over this year, these months would be considerably more tolerable than they will be in fact. For me these astrological prophecies are of no significance whatever. I intend, however, to use them in anonymous camouflaged propaganda, since, in these critical times, most people will snatch at any straw.

And he did use them. He could not have deciphered a horoscope himself, let alone compared two, and the unnamed person who sent the material must have sent an interpretation with it.

Goebbels says no more in his diary, but Hitler's entourage included another diary-keeper, Schwerin von Krosigk, the Finance Minister. From him we learn that the two horoscopes were in the research files of Heinrich Himmler, the chief of the SS and Gestapo. Apparently Goebbels had not known of them before they were drawn to his attention. Soon after he saw them (or copies, or whatever he did see), they were brought out and studied. According to the diarist, that for the Republic had been cast on 9 September 1918 – a slip, since the monarchy did not fall until November. Goebbels gives the true date. The horoscope of Hitler had been cast on 30 January 1933, the day he became Chancellor. This may or may not have been the one drawn up by Hanussen. Supposedly he cast his on 1 January, not the 30th, but he may have repeated the exercise or added a new interpretation when his prediction of Hitler's rise to power was fulfilled. The testimony of Schwerin von Krosigk makes the horoscope sound as if it might have been Hanussen's.

He confirms the probabilities as to what was in the earlier part. Both horoscopes pointed to war in 1939, German success until 1941, then reverses until early 1945. There would be a sudden victory in the second half of April. Peace would follow in August. After three difficult years Germany would rise again. This is clearly the same interpretation that Goebbels refers to, picking out only part of it, although wishful thinking by Schwerin von

Krosigk, or whoever did the interpreting for him, improved 'some relief of our military situation' into a victory.

Everything up to the date of this entry, in early April 1945, could have been rewritten or faked. The last portion, after early April, could not, nor could the corresponding entry in Goebbels's diary. It is predictive on any showing and good, although not as Goebbels would have wished. The swing in Germany's favour in April did happen, but in a non-military sense. When President Roosevelt died on the 13th, Hitler saw this briefly as bringing the change. While it did not save his regime, it brought the change. Roosevelt had approved a programme devised by Henry Morgenthau, his Secretary of the Treasury, for the post-war destruction of Germany as an industrial country. With Roosevelt's death the presidency passed to Truman, who had a low opinion of Morgenthau and in July, to his annoyance, did not take him to the Potsdam Conference on Germany's future. The Morgenthau Plan faded out and German recovery became possible. General peace ensued precisely in Goebbels's mid-August, against all expectation, with the surrender of Japan. Three tough years followed, after which the Western Allies agreed to the formation of the Federal German Republic. It rose strongly and quickly from the ruins, and eventually took over the eastern Communist zone.

Hitler's horoscope was probably a supplement. The most significant parts of the prophecy concern Germany only. It looks like a brilliant astrological feat. The difficulty in knowing what to make of it lies in the dearth of such feats. This is not just an outstanding instance of a recurring phenomenon. It would be hard to find any real parallels at all, not only because of the accurate sequence of predictions but because the sequence, at least as reported, is the whole message, not a mere fortunate hit embedded in failures.

In the absence of parallels, the prophecy must be considered alone and apart from astrology. As far as I can see, there is no convincing evidence that astrology reveals the future. Prediction, in the words of its historian Ellic Howe, is its Achilles' heel. Both in the West and in Asian countries its success, to the extent that it has any, is more with individual readings of character and potential destiny. In that field a few astrologers have done well. Jung judged horoscopes to be worth using as therapeutic aids. But as with other respectable kinds of fortune-telling, an acquaintance with actual cases is apt to suggest that the technique is not the secret. A horoscope may focus the mind, keep it busy or supply talking-points, but success is due more to insights and inspirations on the astrologer's part; it depends on a personal factor.

Two considerations support this view. First, computerized horoscopes, without a personal factor, are not conspicuously good. Second, research actually has revealed correlations between human aptitudes and planetary positions at birth, however these should be explained; but the statistical proof has nothing to do with traditional astrology and I don't think astrologers have made any use of it. Objective fact is not what they want, nor is it what they can work with.

As for the German prophecy, not much more can be said except that it is open to the same explanation, or quasi-explanation, as the better quatrains of Nostradamus. It is *as if* information about Germany, in the mind of someone during (say) the latter part of the twentieth century, made a trans-temporal entry into the minds of the astrologers who drew up the horoscopes decades earlier. True, no such message from the future could have affected the astrological data, but it could have moulded the interpretations. As with Nostradamus, no great knowledge would have been required on the part of the 'informant'. All this is schoolbook stuff except the abandonment of the Morgenthau Plan. A book on post-war Allied policy, or a biography of Truman, would supply that.

Chapter Fifteen

Premonitions and Previsions

On 21 October 1966, at the Welsh village of Aberfan, a mass of mine waste slid downhill, causing 144 deaths. Many of the inhabitants of the village claimed that they had foreseen the tragedy. Some had had dreams about it. An investigation by a psychologist, J.C. Barker, covered sixty claims. Twenty-two people turned out to have voiced their forebodings to others who could confirm them. Two more had written them down in advance. Still, people living on mining land might have known enough about slag heaps to see reasons for apprehension. Is there likely to have been more to it than that?

The early history of the United States furnishes a case where the facts are beyond dispute. Benjamin Rush, a signatory of the Declaration of Independence, corresponded during 1805–13 with ex-President John Adams. Thomas Jefferson and Adams were then deeply estranged. In October 1809, after Jefferson's term of office had expired, Rush reported to Adams that he had had a dream about them. They would be reconciled, and would die at 'nearly the same time'. The reconciliation happened in 1812, and Adams congratulated Rush on a prophecy fulfilled. But the fulfilment of the rest was spectacular. Adams and Jefferson died within five hours of each other, on 4 July 1826, the fiftieth anniversary of the Declaration of Independence. As Joseph J. Ellis says in his book *Founding Brothers*, 'no serious novelist would ever dare to make this up'.

A point of interest is that the double event in 1826 casts doubt on J.W. Dunne's theory of precognitive dreaming, mentioned in the Preface. Dunne implies that dreams cannot anticipate anything beyond the dreamer's lifetime. But Rush died long before the two ex-Presidents did. His dream reached beyond his own lifetime.

In 1968 Robert Nelson founded the Central Premonition Registry in New York and invited the public to contribute. Over the next dozen years he received approximately 5000 predictions of public happenings of which about fifty were on target. Such a small number might be dismissed as lucky guesses, were it not for one oddity. They did not come in a random scatter. Half of the good ones were sent by only five people, each of whom scored several times, whereas the enormous majority never scored at all. As with Nostradamus, if less vividly, the distribution was skewed.

Perhaps, then, there are individuals who can be labelled 'psychic', whether the word applies to them all the time or only occasionally: individuals for whom previsions and anticipations happen often enough or impressively enough to suggest some special gift. Several for whom this might be so have been noticed in England. One who flourished during the Second World War was Cyril Macklin, whose most celebrated feat was foreseeing three enemy air raids and in each case arranging to be somewhere else. In more recent times, media attention has been paid to Chris Robinson, who has had many dream-presentiments of accidents and other misfortunes and has warned the police or the prospective sufferers accurately enough to gain respect. Warnings obviously imply that a threatened evil can be averted – in other words, that an event apparently foreseen can be cancelled – in which case a question arises as to what the seer saw in the first place. That question can wait a little longer. The immediate issue is the claim made by, or for, 'psychic' individuals. It can be tested to a certain extent by looking at a few publicized anticipators.

William John Warner (1866–1936), alias Count Louis Hamon, began a career as a society fortune-teller in the 1890s. He used palmistry and derived his professional name 'Cheiro' from the Greek for 'hand', but he also used numerology and astrology. He made predictions for Oscar Wilde (whom he warned correctly of potential disgrace), Arthur James Balfour of the Balfour Declaration (whose premiership he foretold), Mark Twain (for whom he forecast a financial upturn) and the spy Mata Hari (for whom he foresaw a crisis in 1917, the year in which she was shot). In 1930 he moved to Hollywood and became popular with film stars, among them Mary Pickford, who also cultivated the astrologer Evangeline Adams. However, Cheiro's reputation led his admirers to claim too much, with results that cast doubt generally.

Some of Cheiro's predictions for his clients need not imply anything more than keen perception. Some perhaps do. He told Lord Kitchener that he would be in danger of dying in his sixty-sixth year, not on land as a soldier but at sea: a surprising idea to hit upon and correct. It is hard to believe that he said Rasputin would be poisoned and knifed and shot, and would then die in the River Neva. Too good to be true! He made predictions about public events, and is alleged to have foretold the First World War, the Russian Revolution, the Jewish return to Palestine, the independence and partition of India. These events were foreseen by others with no psychic pretensions, although admittedly Cheiro would have needed more acumen than most commentators to foresee all of them. Details in one of his prophecies, that a Russian invasion of Palestine would lead to Armageddon, show that this at least was not paranormal. It was based on the British-Israelites' interpretation of Ezekiel 38. In the upshot he is interesting but not outstandingly so, and there is insufficient proof that he did as well as he is supposed to have done.

Another seer who foretold public events was Anton Johanson, a Norwegian, who was a few years senior to Cheiro but did not begin having precognitions until later. He sometimes saw visions, sometimes had intuitions, sometimes heard a voice, which he believed to be Christ's. He is said to have foreseen the Martinique eruption in 1902 and the San Francisco earthquake in 1906. A prolonged experience on 14 November 1907 ranged over two future periods, 1914–21 and 1947–53. Several forecasts in the earlier group were printed in Scandinavian papers during 1913. Johanson predicted the First World War, the military stalemate, and the flu epidemic and German upheaval at the end. He was less successful with his second period, but spoke of the foundation of the Jewish state in Palestine. His bull's-eyes with natural disasters are impressive if authentic. But again a good deal can be explained by an intelligent appraisal of current affairs.

The anticipations of the *Titanic* sinking in 1912 put other case-histories in the shade. They involve both Johanson and Cheiro, although only marginally. The story begins in 1886, when W.T. Stead (1849–1912), then editor of the *Pall Mall Gazette*, published an imaginary description of the loss of a great passenger ship with heavy mortality. Stead appended a footnote of his own: 'This is exactly what might take place and what will take place if the liners are set free short of boats.' In the following year a book of poems by Celia Thaxter included one entitled 'A Tryst', which took up the theme.

Stead was converted to Spiritualism. In November 1893 he visited America, and the *Chicago Sunday Tribune* carried a long interview with him. Recalling the assassination of the city's mayor, Carter Harrison, he said: 'He had, I am told, a premonition of his violent taking off. I have had a similar warning. I am to die a violent death.' Later, speaking of telepathy and related topics, he said: 'I get communications from our living friends and also those which purport to come from friends who have quitted this earth. They are often more useful, because they often contain an element of prophecy.' Years afterwards he was still talking of his violent death, although it does not appear that he connected it, so far, with his fears about ships.

The next step was taken by Morgan Robertson, a former seaman in the United States merchant marine. He left the service and wrote competent sea stories for magazines. Then he started a longer work of fiction, with the help, he claimed, of an 'astral writing partner'. Published in 1898, it was called *Futility*. Although it attracted very little attention, it was highly original, perhaps almost unique in its time; nothing like the modern 'disaster movie' had yet become popular. It was about a British luxury liner named (of all things) the *Titan*, which struck an iceberg on her maiden voyage. Robertson's maritime experience enabled him to give details of his imagined ship. The *Titan* was 800 feet long, bigger than anything actually on the sea, and alleged to be unsinkable thanks to nineteen watertight compartments. She had three propellers and twenty-four lifeboats, and carried 3000 passengers and crew. In the story, she struck the iceberg at twenty-five knots and sank with great loss of life because there were not enough boats.

Robertson wrote little more of consequence and never talked again of an astral collaborator. For a time he was mentally unbalanced. Anton Johanson, meanwhile, had a prevision of a great ship going down, one of the passengers who drowned being a member of the Astor family. Soon the *Titanic* was built, and the public saw her as a supreme achievement of Western technology and progress. She came close to fulfilling the specifications of the *Titan* in Robertson's forgotten novel. She was 882.5 feet long and alleged to be unsinkable, with sixteen watertight compartments. She had three propellers and twenty lifeboats. On her maiden voyage in 1912 she carried 2235 passengers and crew. W.T. Stead was aboard. Cheiro had warned him not to travel by water during that month, but the warning was ineffectual. Shortly before the voyage, another piece of fiction was going into print for a magazine. Its author was Mayn Clew Garnett, its title was *The White Ghost of Disaster*, and it was about an 800-foot liner striking an iceberg and sinking, losing half the people aboard because there were not enough boats. Garnett was rumoured to have dreamed the story while at sea on *Titanic*'s sister ship the *Olympic*.

On 10 April 1912 the *Titanic* sailed. On 15 April she struck an iceberg at about twenty-three knots and sank with great loss of life because there were not enough boats. Stead and John Jacob Astor were among those who perished. The Western world's confidence never quite recovered. In the words of Wyn Craig Wade: 'It was almost as if the catastrophe was prophecy fulfilled – an inevitable toppling of Titans by an outraged Divine Power.'

After the *Titanic*, other 'psychic' case-histories are somewhat anticlimactic, but two individuals deserve notice if only on account of their persistent fame.

Edgar Cayce (1877–1945), nicknamed the Sleeping Prophet, was born in Kentucky and was primarily a healer. When he received a patient he went into a self-induced trance, in which state he diagnosed the complaint and prescribed treatment, often of a homely folk-medicine type. After a while his trance experiences extended to other topics, and he gave 'readings' of wider scope. They began to suggest reincarnation and previous lives. A conventional Christian, he was disturbed by these, although he did his best to accommodate them, a sign of his honesty. He talked of Atlantis and ancient Egypt, and he also talked of events yet to come. A few of his predictions were good. In April 1929 he foretold the Wall Street Crash six months later (although it was not totally unexpected: an investment adviser, Roger Babson, became well known for a similar prediction). He made rather ill-defined forecasts about the Second World War, the deaths of Presidents Roosevelt and Kennedy, and the independence of India. He spoke of an important religious development originating in Russia, a remarkable thing to think of during the Stalinist era, but his prevision has yet to be confirmed. Unfortunately, he also made predictions about natural cataclysms changing the map, and gave dates for them – California, for instance, was to fall into the sea in 1969.

A prophecy to do with Atlantis is still worth pausing over. Cayce declared that the lost land had indeed existed and extended into the West Indies, and that late in the 1960s a portion of it would reappear in the Bahamas. The first point of interest is the location. Plato, the Greek authority for the legend, put Atlantis in the ocean not far west of Europe. Cayce might have known this, and he might have read modern authors who accepted Plato's account. However, these sources would not have given him a West Indian connection. As it happens, the only real evidence for any such sunken Atlantic country does place it nearer America and in the region of the West Indies; the clues are in books that Cayce almost certainly never read.

The second point of interest is that in 1968, on schedule, divers in the Bahamas found what looked like a ruined building on the sea-bed near the island of Andros and what looked like a paved road near Bimini. Geologists dismissed these remnants of Atlantis as illusory. Nevertheless, foreknowledge of what the divers claimed would still have been foreknowledge. Again we have a hint at transmission against the time-flow. It is *as if* someone in

1968 read a newspaper report of the 'find' and that person's consciousness of the report entered Cayce's mind decades before, unaccompanied by the geologists' scepticism, which did not reach the media until afterwards.

Best known of a number of 'psychic' journalists is Jeane Dixon (1918–97). Her reputation, like that of the astrologer Naylor, was built mainly on a single success. In 1952 she had a vision of the White House with the digits 1 9 6 0 above. She prophesied that a young Democrat would be elected in 1960. In an interview, she repeated her forecast and spoke of a danger of assassination. The election of Kennedy seemed to bear her out. As a matter of fact, however, she had gone into reverse and said Nixon, the Republican candidate, would win. She explained the mistake by echoing Republican charges of electoral fraud and insisted that Nixon 'really' won. With that upset out of the way, she was right about Kennedy's assassination and reputedly knew of it on the day it happened. It is worth noting that Robert Ripley, author of a famous 'Believe It or Not' newspaper feature, had pointed out long before that presidents elected every twenty years from 1840 on had died in office, so 1960 was ominous for its victorious candidate.

Over a stretch of more than forty years, Jeane Dixon scored with the deaths of a few other prominent people, but most of her predictions were obscure or obvious or wrong. Her book *My Life and Prophecies* contains plenty of material that can now be checked. She attached immense importance to an unidentified child born on 5 February 1962, but envisaged him first as a sort of Messiah, later as Antichrist. She expected an early end to the papacy in its present form; but that could have been an echo of Joachim or Pseudo-Malachy. She made apocalyptic pronouncements about 1999; but she could have taken a hint from Nostradamus.

Jeane Dixon maintained that her visions were invariably correct. Errors were due to her own misreading of them. She retains a certain interest. The same cannot be said of other media 'psychics', whose records, under scrutiny, are almost uniformly poor.

★

One more prophecy remains, which I place here not because it was 'psychic' – it was nothing of the kind – but because of a certain parallelism with some of the 'psychic' prophecies. It may close this survey with a triumph and a mystery. When I first heard the story, the way in which it was told did not dispose me in its favour. However, I saw the place where it happened and met a participant, and since then a further fulfilment, an astonishing one, has left no alternative to saying whatever can be said.

The village of Fatima is in Portugal, at no great distance from Lisbon. On 13 May 1917 a girl aged ten, Lucia dos Santos, was walking in the neighbourhood with two younger cousins who partly shared the experience that followed. She had a vision of a radiant Lady who was identified – not at once – as the Virgin Mary. Lucia heard her speak, and they had a brief dialogue. The Lady promised to reappear on the 13th of each successive month, and she duly reappeared. At that time Portugal had a strongly anti-clerical government, and in August, when reports of the apparitions began to draw visitors, the district administrator tried to call a halt. Lucia was virtually arrested and subjected to interrogation and threats, but she would not recant.

Despite her firmness, the story thus far does not read very convincingly. The Lady's reported words are almost confined to assurances of the children's salvation and requests for prayer, especially prayer for the end of the war, in which Portugal was a belligerent. The natural inference would be that this was all a fantasy, hatched in the mind of a child who had heard of Lourdes. Lucia's family were very sceptical, and her elder sister Maria, when I talked with her long afterwards, told me that she did not believe any of it.

In September, however, the Lady made a new commitment: on 13 October, at noon, she would give a public 'sign'. Fatima now snowballed. The appointed day was dull and wet, but a crowd estimated at 70,000 people converged on the scene of the apparitions. A notable arrival was the atheist editor of the chief anti-clerical paper, *O Século*. He had given Fatima full coverage in the expectation of a fiasco, and he came to witness this and report on it. Lucia's family accompanied her to the spot, in terror that a failure would expose them to mob violence.

At this point it is vital to stress that the young visionary had not given the slightest hint of the sign's nature. No one was looking for anything in particular. About midday the rain stopped, the clouds parted and Lucia – who had seen the Lady again and was to speak of other visions – suddenly exclaimed, 'Look at the sun!' The voice of a child, outdoors in a huge crowd, would have been heard only by the nearest bystanders, and mass suggestion can have had no part in what ensued. The sun was shining through the gap in the clouds. It appeared to lose brightness, emit rays of different colours and rotate. Then it spiralled downwards and up again, returning to its place. The phenomenon lasted for several minutes and caused a panic. Photographs show people staring up at the sky, unquestionably looking at something.

Of the many witnesses, five carry special weight. The atheist editor admitted reluctantly that the thing had happened and was honest enough to publish an account in his paper, calling the sun's behaviour a 'macabre dance'. The spectacle was visible at a school six miles away, where nobody had been taking much notice of Fatima. One of the boys recalled later that it touched off an end-of-the-world scare. Here, any notion that the event was due to the crowd having a mass hallucination obviously collapses – the schoolboys were nowhere near the crowd. The same follows from the testimony of an author, Alfonso Vieira, who lived farther away than the school. He, too, had taken little interest in Fatima and made no connection, yet he saw the sight and thought it was beautiful. The limit of visibility seems to have been somewhere about twenty miles; Lisbon Observatory noticed nothing unusual.

To return to Fatima itself, an English maidservant accompanying a Portuguese couple wrote home with an amusing back-handed confirmation. She supposed that this was something that happened in Portugal but it was disappointing! Maria, the elder sister, told me as she told others that she had not believed in the apparitions before the sign, but after it she did . . . and she traced a spiral in the air with her finger.

Apparent solar eccentricities can be caused by freak cloud

movements or peculiar atmospheric conditions. The Fatima sign is not entirely unparalleled. Witnesses gave slightly discrepant descriptions, and two women told an investigator that they saw nothing. This is in keeping with the fact that people respond to optical illusions differently or not at all. The point is not so much that the sign happened, in whatever way, as that it happened at the place predicted and on the day predicted and roughly at the time predicted. For those who were willing to believe in the Lady, it proved that she spoke the truth and her appearances were real, whether as external manifestations or as mental images due to an external cause. Certainly no juvenile fancy could have projected a rare aberrration into the sky or anticipated it with a long-range forecast.

But if the prophesied solar gyration was a sign, what was it a sign *of*? Fatima became a venue of pilgrimage, yet even on a believer's assumptions, what was it all about? There was nothing in the Lady's words, as first reported, to justify drawing attention to them with such a spectacular demonstration. They were exhortations to penitence and spiritual amendment such as might have been heard from many pulpits. A fuller meaning emerged, but it took a long time to do so. When I first heard of Fatima, it was harnessed to unappealing propaganda and to support for the Salazar dictatorship, which then governed Portugal. What had happened was that Lucia, who had entered a Carmelite convent, had given two accounts of her experience, adding to earlier versions. They were written in 1936–7 and 1941–2, and published, although not in full. As things have turned out, they were much more interesting than the pious messages based on them.

Looking back, Lucia verbalized her revelations in conventional metaphors and phrases, making Mary speak, for instance, of her Immaculate Heart. That was understandable, no matter what the Lady actually said or appeared to say. But definite predictions came through. 'If men do not cease from offending God, a new and worse war will begin in the pontificate of Pius XI.' It nearly did, although not quite, unless the Spanish Civil War counts as its prologue; in any case it began a few months into the next pontificate. Further: 'Russia will spread her errors through the world, arousing wars and persecutions.' This fitted the Russian Revolution and its effects. During the months of the apparitions it was moving towards the ascendancy of Lenin, the formation of the Soviet Union and the launching of international Communism under Russian direction. But Mary promised or was said to have promised, if certain acts of devotion and consecration were performed in the Church, that 'Russia would be converted' and the menace would pass.

All this accorded so well with the Catholic Church's passionate anti-Communism, and with the right-wing views that were then heard most loudly in it, that Lucia's belated announcements looked dubious. What was she actually remembering? As a child, could she have understood such a message before the Bolsheviks took power and before Russia had even started 'spreading errors'? However, prayers for the conversion of Russia began to be recited at the end of Mass, and the popes complied with Mary's reported wishes in other respects. Not everyone was impressed. In 1965 a Catholic historian of the Marian cult, Hilda Graef, who would have liked to debunk Fatima, observed loftily that 'the promised effects . . . have not become apparent'.

But now, of course, they have. The downfall of the Soviet system in 1991 was not altogether a conversion, but the sudden demise of Communism was surely enough of a conversion to count, and its end as an international movement meant that the spreading of Russia's 'errors' ceased. It does not make much difference how far Lucia's later statements really recall what she understood the Lady to say at the time. Argument about this is hardly relevant any more. No matter how it was done, the Portuguese village seer turned out to be a better prophet than almost anyone among the well informed and sophisticated. I know of only one 'rational' commentator who did anything like as well in foreseeing the Soviet collapse, and that is the sociologist and novelist Andrew M. Greeley, himself a Catholic, whose forecast is on record in Wallechinsky's *Book of Predictions*. Impressive as this was, he made it after decades of world disillusionment with Communism, not early in its career.

An additional message was sealed, to be left unopened until 1960. As that year approached, rumours spread that it prophesied a third world war. These had some serio-comic consequences. Several wealthy Catholics reputedly transferred assets to Portugal, under the impression that it was the only country with a celestial guarantee against devastation. Pope John XXIII read the message, but he disappointed the hopes of many by deciding not to publish it, and two successors concurred. A purported text printed in a German paper in 1963, on 'third world war' lines, was recognized to be spurious.

It was revealed finally, in May 2000, that Lucia had had another vision of the persecution of Christians by 'atheistic systems'. This added more emphasis to the Russian prophecy, but with an added feature, that she saw a bishop dressed in white who was shot and fell to the ground. The image was interpreted as foreshadowing the attempted assassination of Pope John Paul II in 1981. However, it was not really a prediction, and Rome's long reluctance to publicize it was probably due to the danger of its being mistakenly read as such.

Chapter Sixteen

Answers?

Foreseeings, anticipations, irregularities in the time-flow do happen. The only basis for denial is a mere dogma that they do not. With most of the principal cases in this book, the objection that they are merely hearsay does not apply – they were on record long before whatever was foreseen or anticipated. But the facts furnish no explanation. There seems to be no technique that, in itself, reveals the future. Astrology is the front-runner, but since the demise of Ptolemaic astronomy, it has certainly been hard to see how the positions of planets could influence earthly events or how these could be predicted from future celestial aspects. Nevertheless, a modern astrologer might speak of correlations or synchronisms rather than influence. If the claim were borne out by results, it would deserve to be examined, but few astrological predictions have ever been good enough. The German instance is so exceptional that it is best considered separately.

Technique, astrological or otherwise, may be of help to prophets in a catalytic way. It may increase receptiveness to whatever it is that they receive, but the fact that the phenomena simply happen highlights the difficulty of studying them. At present it appears that prophecy cannot be made to happen experimentally, under controlled and repeatable conditions. But the same applies to many things, such as falling in love and composing great music, which also cannot be made to happen experimentally, under controlled and repeatable conditions . . . yet have happened, countless times. With prophecy, we can accumulate case-histories. Do they suggest any generalizations or explanations?

I would suggest that precognition (or whatever we call it) is confined to individuals with a special gift or aptitude and is uncommon even with them. Both statements would have been challenged by J.W. Dunne, the author of *An Experiment with Time*, to whom we may now at last return. He believed that many people have precognitive dreams and presentiments of other kinds, only they do not remember the dream or presentiment or recognize the fulfilment when it comes. He also believed that the phenomenon may happen often for the same person.

It should be stressed that his theory is narrowly restricted in scope. There are many prophecies in this book which it would not cover. The dreams and presentiments that Dunne discusses foreshadow only personal experiences of those who have them. Moreover, they usually only look a little way ahead, and never extend to anything after the death of the person.

Within those limits, what about Dunne's first claim? The nearest he came to a systematic study was his project with six volunteers and himself, all of whom wrote down their dreams. The results did not really bear him out. He got images relating to the past, which he called P-resemblances, and images fulfilled in the future, which he called F-resemblances. He classified these as 'good', 'moderate' and 'indifferent'. The eighty-eight recorded dreams gave fourteen P-resemblances and twenty F-resemblances, from which he inferred not only that precognitive dreams occur, but that dreamers who have them are in no way special. The first inference tallied with the facts as far as they went. The second did not. Dunne himself got five F-resemblances. Volunteers B, C and F got none, A got three, D got two, and E got ten. Furthermore, E got three 'good' ones and the rest of the volunteers got only one among them. Dunne got one. The logical conclusion was that the whole team could be eliminated except E. Dunne rejected it. He insisted that E had no 'special faculty for precognition'. She did better on P-resemblances too; it was just that 'her dreams were more clearly related to distinctive episodes of waking life'. The fact remains that she was the only real scorer.

Dunne himself had been experimenting for years and was adept at matching his waking images to dreams. It is said that he attended a séance in his youth and the medium told him he would be the greatest medium of all. So far as I know, he never tried to function as such, but, for what the insight may have been worth, it suggests that he was exceptional psychologically. As for E, she was so far ahead of her colleagues that she, too, was clearly unusual and may well have been attracted to the project because she was.

Something like Dunne's position was asserted in 1955 by Louisa E. Rhine, but I have my doubts. The experiment at the Maimonides Center in 1969–70 gave no results comparable to Dunne's because the one test subject was hand picked. Suppose we range more widely than Dunne's theory allows. With premonitions and dream-warnings of public events, such as those collected by Robert Nelson's New York bureau, the percentage of persons who have valid ones is still small. Nelson did discover a few who stood out a little, like E.

If there are not many for whom such things happen, at any rate conspicuously enough to be noticed, what about Dunne's other claim? Do they happen often for any individuals at all, even those who possess the gift? The difficulty is the one that he was aware of. They may happen often, only to be left unrecorded and forgotten. Where records exist, the evidence is ambiguous. Nelson's few contributors who scored significantly did manage it often enough to be interesting. The same is true of Chris Robinson. It is implied in the traditions of characters like the Cheshire Prophet. On the other hand, Nostradamus is a case-history on a much larger scale, and he dictates a certain caution. He wrote down his quatrains and published them and went on doing it for years. He scored, sometimes spectacularly, but he did not score often. We can allow him five per cent or so. That contrasts favourably with the record of most modern 'psychics'. Here, however, is someone who had the gift if anyone ever had, yet he averaged no more than four or five interesting quatrains a year and of those, only two or three were really good, Class A. His twenty-six Class A quatrains are not isolated hits; taken together they cohere and are packed with multiple meaning and are frankly extraordinary; but twenty-six is not a large number.

No, it doesn't happen often, for anybody. Jacques Cazotte had the reputation of a clairvoyant, yet only his prophecy of the Terror stands up, at least in a documented sense. His other long prophecies are absurd. Morgan Robertson wrote many stories without anything prophetic in them. He had no random scatter of anticipations. They were concentrated in one story, written with the aid of his 'astral writing partner', the story foreshadowing the sinking of the *Titanic*.

The thing happens, so far as the proven record goes, for a minority only, and it happens infrequently. But what is it that happens? 'Seeing the future' is a cliché, and I have put forward reasons for rejecting it. The obvious one is that seeing the future is a contradiction in terms, because, from our standpoint at least, the future doesn't exist to be seen. That would apply to all persons, exceptional or not, and to all future events. We have enough case-histories to refute such an absolute dismissal. A more serious objection is that if we review these, 'seeing the future' often explains nothing or very little. The seer would seldom have had enough understanding of what was seen. To take one of Nostradamus's more interesting quatrains, if he did eavesdrop on Bernadotte's conference with the tsar in 1812, he would not have known what they were discussing, or related it to the images in the other three lines. With Dante and Milton we have a *reductio ad absurdum* of 'seeing the future': we would have to picture them going forward several centuries, astrally entering libraries and picking out books on Asian and Babylonian mythology, which would probably be quite incomprehensible to them.

Moreover, 'seeing the future' leads to one of the well-known paradoxes of time-travel. I dream of an accident. I go to the place where it is about to happen and intervene to prevent it. So the accident doesn't happen. So what did I see in the first place? If the accident doesn't happen I can't have seen it. But if I didn't see it, I won't have done anything to prevent it. So it does happen. So I see it and go there to intervene . . . and so on in a circle.

Cases have been recorded in which prevention of events seen

in dreams is said to have worked. If so, the dreamers who 'saw' the undesired happenings, and took steps to prevent them, cannot actually have seen. The only escape from the paradox, apart from total denial, is to drop the notion of 'seeing the future' and infer that the dreamers were getting warnings in visual forms of events that *might* happen. Sometimes these could have been due to ordinary anxiety, if the dreamers were aware of a dangerous situation. If they were not, if the warnings concerned the unfamiliar and unexpected, the question of their source arises.

And we confront an issue that we have confronted repeatedly, the issue of the recurrent 'as if'. With every prevision, it is *as if* the mind of some future individual were making a trans-temporal contact, were communicating backwards against the flow. What strikes me as interesting is that the 'as if' applies not only to prediction but to cases that are not predictive. Dante and Milton did not prophesy, but it is *as if* they received knowledge existing in human minds centuries after them. Morgan Robertson had no notion of literally foretelling the loss of a great ship, he was only writing a story, but it is *as if* information about the *Titanic* reached him from a time after the event and moulded what he wrote, even suggesting the ship's name. So, likewise, with any warning dreams where more is implied than simple anxiety: it is *as if* the dreamer received a visual message from someone in the future, perhaps the very near future, who is aware of a danger but not of anything actually happening: the dreamer can avert it and there is no paradox.

A conjectural figure emerges dimly, the Other, the Informant in the future. Prevision in its various forms is perhaps not *seeing* the future but receiving information *from* the future, from an Informant in another time-frame for whom it is already a realized fact, the Jim of the Jim-and-Jane analogy. As we saw, this would account for one or two oddities in Nostradamus, such as his apparent allusion to the fictitious Glastonbury zodiac – his Informant could have been fallible and believed the zodiac to be real. There is nothing original in the notion of the Other, as such. It is a norm in the literature that prophets do not prophesy by their own unaided ability. They prophesy because some being inspires them. In the Bible this is the Lord, directly or indirectly. At Delphi the Informant was Apollo. Merlin had his controlling spirit. Nostradamus had the mysterious being whom he summoned. Morgan Robertson had his astral writing partner who collaborated just once and, without conscious intent on Robertson's part, created a prophetic story. Such ideas reflect a realization that the phenomena can be invited but not commanded, that they do not come purely from within the individual. But can we take a further step, and, with the recurrent 'as if' in mind, construct a model of prophecy that will handle everything on a human level?

Surprisingly, the Old Testament's most powerful prophecy, Isaiah 53, is supportive. It foreshadows Christ, and yet, subject to a few minor ambiguities, the speaker in verses 1–9 talks of him in the past tense. This is not Second Isaiah's usual practice. Most of his work is a mixture of prediction and exhortation. But here Christ is foreshadowed by the entry of a speaker reminiscing about him, and interpreting events that, for the speaker, have already happened. The voice could be that of an early Christian. To say so is not to exclude God – the trans-temporal contact between the speaker and the prophet could be divinely inspired, divinely ordained – but I sense the speaker's presence, 600 years after Second Isaiah.

As a matter of courtesy, I would like to record how this idea first came to me. It came from a classic of science-fiction, Olaf Stapledon's *Last and First Men*, which was published in 1930 and which influenced me deeply. I had some correspondence with Stapledon and eventually met him. One of many reasons for respecting him still is his description of the appearance of an atomic explosion, fifteen years in advance, as a 'gigantic mushroom'. *Last and First Men* projects humanity into a future stretching millions of years ahead. Various human species come and go, and the book purports to be transmitted back to Stapledon by one of the Last Men, giving him glimpses of events which, for him, are in the future. Among other matters the narrator tells how human beings in that far-off era have learned to

observe the past. Now, he says, they are learning also to intervene
in it.

> We have long been able to enter into past minds and participate
> in their experience. Hitherto we have been passive spectators
> merely, but recently we have acquired the power of influencing
> past minds. This seems an impossibility; for a past event is what it
> is, and how can it conceivably be altered at a subsequent date,
> even in the minutest respect?
>
> Now it is true that past events are what they are, irrevocably;
> but in certain cases some feature of a past event may depend on an
> event in the far future. The past event would never have been as
> it actually was (and is, eternally) if there had not been going to be
> a certain future event, which, though not contemporaneous with
> the past event, influences it directly in the sphere of eternal
> being. . . . In certain rare cases mental events far separated in time
> determine one another directly by way of eternity.
>
> Our own minds have often been profoundly influenced by
> direct inspection of past minds; and now we find that certain
> events of certain past minds are determined by present events in
> our own present minds . . .
>
> Our historians and psychologists, engaged on direct inspection
> of past minds, had often complained of certain 'singular' points in
> past minds, where the ordinary laws of psychology fail to give a
> full explanation of the course of mental events; where, in fact,
> some wholly unknown influence seemed to be at work. Later it
> was found that, in some cases at least, this disturbance of the
> ordinary principles of psychology corresponded with certain
> thoughts or desires in the mind of the observer, living in our own
> age. . . . We now found ourselves in possession of an amazing
> power of communicating with the past, and contributing to its
> thought and action . . .
>
> Our first inexperienced efforts were disastrous. Many of the
> fatuities which primitive minds in all ages have been prone to
> attribute to the influence of disembodied spirits, whether deities,
> fiends, or the dead, are but the gibberish which resulted from our
> earliest experiments. And this book, so admirable in our

conception, has issued from the brain of the writer, your
contemporary, in such disorder as to be mostly rubbish.
(Chapter 16)

That passage was written almost a lifetime ago, but much more
recently TV viewers have seen Stephen Hawking, no less,
debating the possibility of moving backwards in time. People in
the future, he said, may learn to do it. The main reason for doubt
is that if they are doing it, we ought to see them around us, and
we don't. Still, maybe they are and we don't recognize them; or
maybe they travel back in another form. When wondering about
a model for prophecy, I thought first in Stapledon's terms. Since
the result was a science-fiction model, it could, in the present day,
demand priority. It conjured up entertaining notions. Imagine
scientists in some future year who have found a way – an
experimental, tentative way – to contact minds in times that, for
them, are past. One of the team, a communicator whom we may
call C, explores a past period and identifies someone there, R, as a
promising recipient of messages. They study historical records,
pick out an event that is still future for R and plant visual or verbal
imagery of it in R's mind. R doesn't know what has happened,
but talks about this implant and is credited with prophecy when,
in due course, the event happens. By monitoring R and noting
the prophecy, the team has feedback and verification. Knowledge
has been demonstrated that could not have come to R in any
other way. The technique has worked!

One or two facts are genuinely in favour of such a science-
fiction notion. Precognition is rare – well then, it could be
because good recipients are rare themselves. Or it could be as
Stapledon's character said: the technique has been very hit-or-
miss and has seldom given clear results. If we picture the team
working on Nostradamus, his ultimate five-per cent score is in
line with that possibility. The five per cent got through, nothing
else did, and a good deal of the Centuries is, to use Stapledon's
word, gibberish. Again, it has become clear that the source of any
information flowing back from the future need not be a

supernatural or omniscient Informant. If we turn from Nostradamus's gibberish to his successes, nearly all can be explained by
transmission from someone in a time-frame later than his own,
who has a moderate knowledge of French history as far as
Napoleon III, and a slighter knowledge of British history, mostly
of the seventeenth century. We could imagine that team of time-
probing scientists preparing an attempt to reach back to the
French seer and, with that aim in view, deputing their best
communicator to do a little reading-up and collect promising
material to transmit.

Stapledon does suggest a way of interpreting some of the facts
that have emerged in this survey. His conception of the way in
which thoughts and actions might influence thoughts and actions
in an earlier time-frame can, I believe, be taken seriously. But his
science fiction cannot handle everything. It fails with closer and
more trivial matters, with personal premonitions and dream
prevision, where the fulfilment may be only a day or two away
and is a more or less private happening, which will not go on
record for the hypothetical scientists to pick up. If someone like
Dunne's subject E dreams of an elephant and, a week later,
unexpectedly sees an elephant, her experience will not go into a
history book for future Stapledonian scientists to discover it. They
will never know about it and her dream cannot have been caused
by backward-reaching activities on their part. Some far closer
Informant, acquainted with E, might be the source of the
anticipated elephant if the trans-temporal contact of minds could
be admitted at all. The shortcoming of the science-fiction
explanation is more evident still with warning dreams where, if
the dreamer takes preventive action, the threatened event never
happens.

A sceptic may dismiss prevision and prophetic dreams anyhow
and try to explain them all away, but there are sufficient grounds
for preferring a theory that makes room for them as Stapledon's
fiction does not. In any case, some of our documented prophecies
are not amenable to this treatment either. The voice in Isaiah 53 is
not the voice of an experimenter in the year 3000. In fact, none of
the case-histories really suggests sophisticated transmission from a

remote future. They can be lined up in columns, with the prophet or anticipator on the left, and the kind of Informant that would be adequate on the right. Here are nine:

Anticipator	*Informant*
1. Second Isaiah	An early Christian
2. John (author of Revelation)	Someone familiar with the outlines of Late Roman history
3. 'Malachy'	A reader of an account of the popes from 1800 onwards
4. Nostradamus	Someone moderately familiar with French history up to Napoleon III and some British history
5. Dante Alighieri	An orientalist
6. John Milton	A Babylonian scholar
7. Jacques Cazotte	A survivor of the French Revolutionary Terror
8. Morgan Robertson	Someone familiar with an account of the *Titanic* and her sinking
9. The author of the 1918 German horoscope	Someone familiar with German history between 1930 and 1950

I defer Fatima as raising exceptional issues.

On the one hand, such Informants would not be extraordinary and Stapledonian scientists need not be brought in. On the other, there is no way to envisage the trans-temporal contact of minds. None of these postulated persons would have been likely to try sending telepathic messages, backwards, forwards or laterally. The Jim-and-Jane analogy seems to break down if Jim is not using his phone. Yet the Jim-and-Jane situation still exists. It is more as if the whole process were haphazard – as if Informants wrote notes and left them lying about and Anticipators picked them up and made use of them. This would have to take place outside the normal temporal order. Note-writing and note-reading do not.

In the last decades of the twentieth century, time travel was beginning to be discussed not only seriously but, from the present point of view, relevantly. Scientists such as John Gribbin explained how it might be possible, and how objections might be overcome. In our own case-histories, we seem to have been encountering not so much purposive communication as information drifting backwards. Physicists have aired notions that may have a bearing. They have spoken, for instance, of hypothetical particles called tachyons that move faster than light. According to relativity, time would stop for a body reaching the speed of light, and for a body going faster it would run backwards.

One speculation is that tachyons might be produced by brain activity, so that thoughts could travel back in time, as the notion of the Informant requires. Gribbin even remarked that a future Informant sending you back a Dunne-type anticipatory dream might be simply yourself, a little older, a little way ahead.

While tachyons are unproved, the post-Einstein universe has aspects that point the same way as the interpretation of prophecy proposed here. Marcus Chown, who collaborated with Gribbin on two books, explains that different observers can have different 'times'. Hence . . .

It is possible to imagine two observers whose clocks tick at wildly different rates. In the time it takes one observer to get from Monday to Friday, the other goes only from Monday to Tuesday. Now imagine a bridge, or 'tunnel', between the two observers. Such a tunnel, which is permitted to exist by general relativity, is known as a 'wormhole'. By going down the wormhole, our observer can go back in time, from Friday to Tuesday.

Or, presumably, can transmit a message. A wormhole (viewers of *Star Trek* may recall them) is defined by Chown as 'a tunnel through space-time which connects widely spaced regions and provides a shortcut'. He ventures further, flirting with what he calls causality violation, which implies that an event can be caused by another event in the future, one that hasn't happened yet. From which it may be inferred that something which is going to happen next year could inspire a prophetic utterance today, foretelling it.

I cannot presume to discuss these mysteries. It is enough to notice the analogies. But I can think of a myth or metaphor that would, I believe, cover everything. I must emphasize that it *is* a myth or metaphor. My concern has been to establish facts, not build up to a theory. The facts that have come to light have taken us as far as the recurrent 'as if'. Whether that can be translated into a serious hypothesis, I do not know. It can, however, be translated into a myth or metaphor, although literal language, which almost unavoidably falsifies, is hard to escape.

Let us imagine the human brain projecting a sort of capsule with a tiny portion of its knowledge or thoughts. It can do this spontaneously without conscious action. Such capsules can drift outside time and space as we experience them or backwards and forwards in the temporal stream. To apply this image to our Informants, number 4 generates a capsule representing the historical smattering and nothing else; number 6 generates a capsule representing a résumé of *Enuma elish* and nothing else. Receptive individuals like Nostradamus and Milton can draw the capsules in at unconscious levels, and unpack and incorporate and develop them. The contents of capsules drifting back from Informants who are future to their recipients (whether near or distant in time) supply the basis for prophecies and anticipations.

Warning, causing preventive action, can also be covered in this way. Suppose someone like Dunne's subject E has a dream of a boat sinking in heavy seas with friends of hers on board. They live a long way off and are seldom in touch, and she knows nothing of any intended cruise, so this is not an anxiety dream. The cruise, in fact, has not yet been planned. But another friend a week hence, when the intention has taken shape and he knows of it, is going to generate an anxiety image of their boat sinking. That image, encapsulated, has drifted back to the dreamer, and before they get their cruise under way she can dissuade them from running the risk.

★

These extra-temporal mind-capsules may perhaps claim a certain respectability as science fiction, like Stapledon's communicators. They at least avoid making the phenomena dependent on magic or angels or mysterious powers. Moreover, if we think of them drifting forwards out of the past, as well as backwards out of the future, they offer a bonus with another vexed question, reincarnation. This is not, of course, the place to open up a whole new topic. I mention it only to indicate some questions it raises and to suggest that the mind-capsule notion could be relevant here too.

Despite its widespread vogue, reincarnation has manifest difficulties. The plain fact is that people don't remember past lives, and without that continuity it is hard to see how somebody in the reign of Elizabeth II can be the same person as somebody in the reign of Elizabeth I. In Hinduism and Buddhism reincarnation is a matter of religious belief. In the West, where it has to be argued for, its advocates rely on a medley of data. There are the feelings people have about some historical period, as if they belonged in it. There is the *déjà vu* experience, when they recognize places where they have never been before. There are apparent dream recollections of scenes in a far-off past. Much has been made of cases of hypnotic regression. Psychoanalysts have employed hypnotism to re-activate a patient's submerged childhood, and the patient may remember it and relive it, sometimes credibly. The point is that not all hypnotic subjects stop there. Some regress further and report memories of previous lives.

Most such evidence is of dubious value. One best-selling book about regression, *The Search for Bridey Murphy*, was refuted when it turned out that the patient's story of a previous life could have been put together from contacts in childhood. In other cases, such as a famous one when a woman built up narratives of persecution in medieval France, it may be impossible to prove that the knowledge was not derived from books read and forgotten. It is all very well to talk about 'checking', and Arthur Guirdham, the psychologist in the case, tried it conscientiously with quite interesting results. But the subject's reports can be confirmed only if records exist giving confirmation, and if they do, the subject *may* have seen these records or been told about them. Checking can seldom get further than probabilities. Nevertheless, the quasi-memories can be vivid and very occasionally they can be checked, genuinely checked. Also, they may assert themselves against resistance, as with Edgar Cayce.

The data are too sketchy and ill-defined to be solid evidence for reincarnation. They may be evidence for something like mind-capsules drifting into the present from individuals in the past, even individuals long dead. If a man thinks he was a juror at a Salem witch-trial in 1692 because he 'remembers' the court-room, that is no reason to infer that he actually was, however accurate the description he gives. But a real juror's experience, encapsulated, may have reached him and been absorbed into his memory banks, to surface in a dream or under hypnosis, indistinguishable from a memory of his own.

An author who edged towards what could be the reality about this was Robert Graves. In his historical novels, besides doing ordinary research, he employed a technique he called analepsis. It consisted partly in a general self-surrender to transcendence of time, partly in mental identification with one past character, such as the emperor Claudius, or Sergeant Lamb, a soldier in the American War of Independence. Graves did not imagine that he had actually been Claudius or Lamb. He believed that the rapport enabled him to recover thoughts and experiences of his character which were not in the historical records. When, as a supplementary exercise, he considered the Number of the Beast, he kept John in mind and arrived somewhat circuitously at Nero and Domitian, who were at least the right emperors to arrive at; and he saw that the Number could fit them both in different ways, although his argument was not mine.

To revert to prophecy, we now have a model for it. When the prophet, or anticipator, stands at a given point in time, there is an Informant up ahead – perhaps only days away, perhaps centuries – and information flows back to the prophet about something in between. From the Informant's standpoint it is past, and matter for record. From the recipient's standpoint it is future, and matter for anticipatory awareness. Dante and Milton do not prophesy, but Mount Purgatory and the War in Heaven show the same process at work, a flow of knowledge in future minds back to themselves. They have drawn it in as a prophet does and used it creatively. This trans-temporal process may sometimes, in a muted way, be conscious, although it has not hitherto been recognized for what it is. Anyhow, it happens. Whether or not any literal meaning can be given to mind-capsules, it very occasionally happens.

Does the model imply that everything is fated and fore-ordained? Certainly not. I have stressed more than once that the Informants, so far as their nature can be guessed at, are limited. With some of them, all that is transmitted is a personal experience, such as a dream. With others, it comes from books, but not many. No celestial libraries are needed. The world must always be infinitely greater than the trickle of source-material. If the model is judged fanciful, I can reply only by pointing to the facts, the case-histories. They are what matter. If anyone has another explanation to cover them, I shall be happy to consider it, as long as it doesn't consist in merely evading them.

I have deferred Fatima, one of the most impressive of the case-histories, because I have to recognize that it is exceptional. The unattractive piety that has often surrounded it cannot obscure it. The solar sign undoubtedly happened, as the hostile journalist was forced to admit, and it was seen by a huge crowd and by witnesses miles away. It was not a product of suggestion. It may have been an optical illusion due to some rare atmospheric freak, but this rare thing happened at the place predicted and on the day predicted and more or less at the time predicted. On top of that is the major prophecy to which the sign presumably gave authenticity. According to Lucia, the Lady foretold the spread of Communism — Russia's 'errors' — and its eventual termination through Russia's 'conversion' if the Church carried out the devotional practices she asked for. It makes little difference whether this part of the message was truly received in 1917 or was an afterthought. It was published far ahead of the Soviet débâcle, which hardly any observer or expert foresaw. The young Portuguese visionary, I repeat, knew better than almost any of them.

Or her mentor did. And here we confront a problem that does not arise in any of the other cases. Lucia's revelations were not attributed to a spirit or an anonymous voice. The Informant was seen and heard as Mary, coming from a heavenly region where the course of the twentieth century was known. Arguably, Lucia could only have accepted a mentor who appeared as a familiar figure, loved and revered and trusted, and known for having appeared elsewhere – at Lourdes for instance. But if the real source was different, if the message was wrapped up in fabricated apparitions, the performance was a blasphemous fraud by whatever agent was responsible. The believer, of course, can say: 'Yes, it's true, Mary appeared.' I am not sure what the alternative is – perhaps simply: 'I don't know what happened, but these apparitions are impossible.' On either showing we are left with the predictions, as extraordinary as any in this book.

Joachim of Fiore may be allowed a final word of summation. He is very important, but not as a prophet in a narrowly predictive sense. His specific forecasts were few and unsuccessful. His memorable achievement consisted, first, in enabling Christians to be hopeful about the earthly future, and second, in imagining how a better future would come about. His quantum leap to the Third Age, the Age of the Holy Spirit, expressed an insight that survived in later ideologies. When the Angelic Pope and the Second Charlemagne are excised as accretions, Joachim's fundamental vision remains. Rome, it is worth recalling, has never condemned it. The Catholic Church's heritage includes this prophecy of its own supersession, or rather transformation. In a body that has all too often been condemnatory, such forbearance is interesting.

It would be encouraging to think that Joachim's great prophecy really was predictive and true, that his hope was awakened or confirmed by imagery winging back to him from dwellers in a transfigured society – from the people of a time still future for ourselves, when that society will exist and the quantum leap to it, between ourselves and them, will be an accomplished fact.

Are there any conclusions? Yes, but it is dificult to state them without making concepts like the mind-capsules seem more literal than they can possibly be. Prophecy and kindred phenomena allow the supposition that bits of the human personality can be projected outside. The projections are carriers of knowledge and memories; their sources remain intact within the originating brain. Outside the organism, they are outside its conditions of time and space. They are mobile and can enter other brains before and after. When they drift backwards in time, their absorption into a past recipient creates an anticipatory awareness. There may be only a few at a given moment, there may be shoals. They may scatter, they may cluster.

On one question apart from prophecy this idea points to a negative answer. It weakens any support there may be for reincarnation. Feelings about historical periods, *déjà vu*, quasi-memories of previous lives in dreams or under hypnosis – all can be explained, in so far as explanation is needed, by the absorption of psychic fragments from past individuals that have drifted forwards into the present. This is not a refutation and it says nothing about the teachings of Hinduism or Buddhism, but it undermines the proofs favoured by Western believers. A memory that a believer cites in evidence may not be fantasy or fiction; it may be a real memory . . . but someone else's, someone perhaps who lived long ago. However, if discarnate psychic elements can subsist and transcend time and space, the case for immortality in some other sense becomes stronger. Or at least, the contention that bodily death must be total death becomes weaker. There is a new unknown in the situation.

This discussion has given 'prophecy' a more exact meaning. Vague fantasies of 'seeing the future' have been found wanting; the key conception that has emerged is 'transmission of information backwards in time' – to a recipient who is thus able to foresee things to come. I would like to stress that while certain scientific ideas do seem to relate to this conception, I arrived at it without knowing anything about them, simply on an appraisal of the data. The argument is in Chapter 10. My reading of such authors as John Gribbin came afterwards. But it showed that parallels exist. While few scientists would study prophecy for its own sake, it may be that facts of the kind assembled in this book – facts suggesting that 'transmission of information backwards in time' is a real phenomenon – could be of value in interpreting the post-Einstein universe.

With whatever aim, more cases of prophecy could doubtless be collected, and some would probably shed more light. What about experimental research? Deliberate transmission is a dubious notion. How would it be done? Even if someone had the ability to take the role of Informant, what about the past person aimed at? How would a recipient be identified, how monitored? I continue to salute Stapledon's soaring imagination in this area as in others, and maybe his last human species will be different, but we are the humble first species. The only experiment that might be worth trying would be a receptivity exercise. If psychic elements from the future (no matter how they should be conceived) are all around us and if communications can really come when given a chance, then perhaps the thing to do is to give them a chance, to silence the mental clamour that keeps them out and see what happens. Dante and Milton opened the door to inspiration, and it appears that knowledge from future minds infiltrated their poems in defiance of their own Christian traditions. To think of experiments is to think of tests and apparatus and generally doing things. Yet there might be a kind of experiment in which the watchword is simply 'Listen'.

One of the Bible's literary prophets did precisely that. Habakkuk could be the patron saint of such an experiment. For him, as for the rest, inspiration came from the Lord, and he knew as well as they did that the Lord could not be commanded. But he could be invited. Alone in the prophetic company, Habakkuk consciously invited him:

I will take my stand to watch
and station myself on the tower,
and look forth to see what he will say to me.

Other Informants, human as well as divine, might be invited similarly.

Appendix One

The Number of the Beast

The ramifications of 666 are not confined to the ones discussed in Chapter 4, although those probably cover everything that John himself intended. Unlike Greece, classical Rome gave numerical values to only six letters (M, for a thousand, came later), and they add up surprisingly:

D = 500
C = 100
L = 50
X = 10
V = 5
I = 1
_____
666

While this is undoubtedly neat, it cannot count as a solution. It points to Rome but does nothing to enhance comprehension of chapters that point to Rome anyhow. It does not make 666 the number of a name or a man, and John would hardly have tossed a Latin conundrum at readers used to Greek, Aramaic and, perhaps, Hebrew.

Robert Graves, nevertheless, noted the possibility of an acrostic. His first version of this was:

Domitianus
Caesar
Legatos

Xti (i.e. Christi)
Viliter
Interfecit

'Domitian Caesar basely killed the envoys of Christ.' For complicated reasons, he altered this, but there is no need here to pursue his explanation, which is in his book *The White Goddess*, chapter 19.

As observed, one method of arriving at 666, very probably the original, is to add together all the numbers from 1 to 36. These can be arranged in a magic square, with the rows, columns and long diagonals all having the same total, 111. For example:

6	32	3	34	35	1
7	11	27	28	8	30
19	14	16	15	23	24
18	20	22	21	17	13
25	29	10	9	26	12
36	5	33	4	2	31

Magic squares figure in Renaissance ocultism. Cornelius Agrippa, in *Occult Philosophy*, considers squares of different sizes. The numbers from 1 to 9 can form a 3 × 3 square with a constant of 15:

4	9	2
3	5	7
8	1	6

The numbers from 1 to 16 can form a 4 × 4 square with a constant of 34. Such a square, thought to have great magical potency, is in Dürer's engraving *Melancholia*:

16	3	2	13
5	10	11	8
9	6	7	12
4	15	14	1

Agrippa continues as far as a 9 × 9 square. He associates this series of seven magic squares with the seven planets of astrology. The 3 × 3 square goes with Saturn, the 4 × 4 square with Jupiter and so on. The 6 × 6 square as above, containing the numbers that add up to 666, is the square of the Sun. Hence, Agrippa connects 666 with the Sun, as does Irenaeus, by a totally different route.

I have no idea whether these planet–square correspondences could have been thought of early enough to have any bearing on Revelation. Agrippa knew some related Arabic numerology, but something neo–Pythagorean might be more to the point.

William Blake and Arthur

As outlined in Chapter 7, the prophecy of Arthur's return expresses a persistent pattern of hope. This was given poetic form by a unique genius who felt a conscious affinity with the prophets of Israel.

Hard as it is to decode the ideas of William Blake (1757–1827), they deserve consideration here, if only because of his attempt to get *behind* the Arthur mythos. A poet and artist little recognized in his time, Blake earned his living mainly as an engraver. He saw visions and was regarded by some as mad. He was not mad, but he *was* outside any cultural mainstream. His thinking owed something to such eccentrics as Richard Brothers, the first British-Israelite, John Varley, one of the few active astrologers in his time, and Owen Pughe, a disciple of Joanna Southcott. Pughe had unusual notions about British antiquity, druids and kindred matters, but Blake ranged far beyond these influences. His lyrical poems are well known but constitute only a fraction of his output. Over the years, in his abstruse Prophetic Books, he worked out an elaborate mythology of the human condition.

What he says, to sum it up with regrettable brevity, is this. The world was once united, enlightened, wise and creative. Then came a fall (not the biblical one), and humanity became divided outwardly and inwardly, sinking by stages from the spiritual heights into error, division, servitude and blindness. The fall, however, is not for all time. There will be a rebirth. Vision and unity will be recovered, and all that was lost will be reinstated. The pristine integrity of human nature will return.

Blake presents his drama through a group of symbolic characters. His final work *Jerusalem* (not the short poem often called so), which dates from 1804–20, is centred on the chief of these, Albion. 'Albion' is the ancient name of Britain. Blake's Albion is one of the Titans of Greek myth who stands for Britain and, on another level, for humanity as a whole. This is possible because of a theory of British primacy in world history: everything derives from Britain, so Britain – Albion – can stand for everything. Self-alienated from the divine vision, Albion sinks by degrees into a deathlike sleep, and that is the fall. He will wake up, and that will be the rebirth. The world's prophesied paradisal future has touches of likeness to Joachim's Third Age. It is unlikely, however, that Blake knew of him. The title of a fragmentary poem, *The Everlasting Gospel*, recalls the subversive Joachite tract that caused so much trouble, but Blake could have got it from Revelation 14:6 as the Joachite author did.

His most ambitious painting, now lost, was called 'The Ancient Britons' and took hints from Pughe. In an accompanying note, Blake refers to Albion and says: 'The stories of Arthur are the acts of Albion, applied to a prince of the fifth century.' Arthur, the glorious king who 'dies' but will return, embodies in his own time and place the overarching reality – the archetype – that Albion represents. Blake's myth-making corresponds to a fundamental insight. As has been shown, his schema of fall-and-resurrection is detectable in various ideologies, such as Rousseau's and Gandhi's, and even in Marxism as a fully developed theory, where an idyllic 'primitive communism' supposedly existed at the beginning, was destroyed by class tyrannies and will be restored on a higher level by the Revolution.

I discussed these topics fully in *Camelot and the Vision of Albion*. Since then I have re-thought the matter of Arthur, but it seems to me that the ideological portions of the book and its attempted elucidation of Blake remain valid.

Notes

Author and title headings refer to the Bibliography. Several of the reference works listed in it supply considerable material beyond what is indicated by citations in the Notes. I have used *Chambers Biographical Dictionary*, the *Dictionary of National Biography*, the *Encyclopaedia Britannica* and the *New Catholic Encyclopedia*.

Preface

For unsuccessful 'rational' forecasting see Rescher, Sherder and Wallechinsky. The quotations from Wilbur Wright and H.G. Wells are from Rescher, pp. 2 and 248; his remark on the unforeseen downfall of Communism is on p. 32. Sherder lists failures of 'Futurology' on pp. 169–78. Many other forecasts, mostly wrong, are in Wallechinsky pp. 10–105.

Nostradamus and Dunne are to be found in subsequent chapters. The anticipatory imagery mentioned here is in Dunne's *An Experiment with Time* pp. 99, 100–102. For the Maimonides Center experiment see Broughton pp. 95–9.

I have not attempted to discuss the 2012 forecast. See Adrian G. Gilbert, *The Mayan Prophecies* (Element Books, Shaftesbury, 1995).

Chapter 1. Priestesses and Star-gazers

There are convenient summaries of data in *Man, Myth and Magic*, articles 'Divination', 'Oracles'. On divinatory methods see also Flint pp. 218–19; Wallechinsky pp. 433–6.

Delphi: chiefly Hoyle. Topics as follows: Apollo pp. 9–10, 52–3, 55, 66; Delphi's centrality pp. 9–10, 24, 44–5; oracular procedure pp. 26, 34–7, 47, 49, 136–9; Hyperborean connection pp. 63–4, 67; Delphi as focus of Greek unity pp. 89, 134–6; artistic and cultural aspects pp. 84–90; advice to Greek colonists pp. 100–10, 125. Compare also Ashe (1) pp. 83, 108–9; Lindblom pp. 1, 26–8; Wallechinsky pp. 342–3. Robert Graves gives versions of Cassandra's story in *The Greek Myths*, section 158, p, q.

Delphic utterances: in the Croesus episode, Herodotus, *History*, I.46–55, 86–91; during Persian invasion, ibid., VII.140–43, 220 (the lines quoted are from the *Oxford Book of Greek Verse in Translation*, nos. 300, 301; A.D. Godley); to Julian, *Oxford Book of Greek Verse in Translation*, no. 627 (Sir William Marris); Sibyls: Bate pp. 8–10; also *Man, Myth and Magic*, article 'Sibyls'.

Sibylline Books: Bate pp. 11–14; Suetonius, ed. cit. p. 72.

Classical astrology: Barker p. 29; Boyde p. 250; Grant pp. 17, 29, 122; Suetonius, ed. cit. pp. 50, 111, 131, 142, 159, 244, 266, 355–7.

Virgil's Fourth Eclogue is quoted from the translation in the Loeb Classical Library, pp. 29–33. See also observations on it in Barker pp. 214–20; also in Michael Grant, *Cleopatra* (Panther, London, 1974), pp. 194–5 and note.

Seneca on new worlds: Grant p. 114.

Chapter 2. Prophetic Israel

Vespasian and Messianic prophecy: Suetonius, ed. cit. p. 324, in Life of Vespasian.

On scriptural material, besides the Bible itself, see the *Jerome Biblical Commentary*. In this chapter, I am perforce going over ground gone over previously in *The Land and the Book*, listed as Ashe (4); the reader will accept, I hope, that I made use of much biblical scholarship that it would be confusing to itemize here. Important works noted in the present connection are by Lindblom and Isserlin.

On Israelite origins: Isserlin pp. 48–64, 220–21.

Divine 'choosing' of Israel: Lindblom p. 336.

Convictions about the Land and the nature of God: Ashe (4) pp. 10–11, 41–4, 91–2; Lindblom pp. 332–3.

Rashi's justification of the conquest of Canaan: Ashe (4) pp. 72–3.

Indigenous and imported cults: Ashe (4) pp. 121–6; Isserlin pp. 234–7.

History of Israelite kingdoms: Isserlin pp. 65–92.

Lost Tribes theories: Ashe (4) pp. 187–9. A presentation of the British-Israelite theory at a time when some of its contentions were still holding is by H.N. Sargent, *The Marvels of Bible Prophecy* (Covenant Publishing Company, London, 1938).

Israel's prophets: Lindblom passim, especially pp. 65–70, 75–6, 87, 94–5, 102, 153.

Elijah: Ashe (4) pp. 158–66.

Literary prophets: Ashe (4) pp. 167–84; Lindblom pp. 105–8, 153–64, 210–13, 343.

The Remnant: Ashe (4) pp. 85, 89, 189–90, 199; Lindblom pp. 140, 367, 372.

Predictive prophecy and the rejection and anticipated renewal of Israel: Ashe (4) pp. 183, 198–9; Lindblom pp. 49, 50, 199–200, 218, 317–18, 373, 391–3, 414.

Ezekiel 38 and 39 and British-Israel interpretation: see Sargent, *op. cit.* pp. 196–7.

Pyramid measurements: *Man, Myth and Magic*, article 'Pyramid-ology'; Wallechinsky pp. 340–42.

Second Isaiah and conversion of Gentiles: Lindblom pp. 267 fn, 282, 400.

Post-Exile history and Antiochus: Ashe (4) pp. 225–37, 244–52.

Apocalypse and Messiah: Ashe (4) pp. 274–84; Lindblom p. 422.

Jewish Sibylline literature: Barker p. 218 fn; Bate pp. 18–29.

Hope of return, and Zionism: Ashe (4) pp. 10, 376–408.

Chapter 3. The Other Messiah

This book is not concerned with New Testament studies except in so far as they are relevant to its theme. In attempting a sketch of early Christianity, my object is simply to show why certain Old Testament passages were held to be prophetic in relation to it. I also ask whether any of the sayings attributed to Jesus should be regarded as prophecies. Such being the limitations, individual references to works of scholarship would again be out of place; but many of its findings are brought together in the *Jerome Biblical Commentary*, where these passages are examined. In the case of the fourth 'Servant Song' – the most important of them, both in itself and because of the questions it will be seen to raise – the *New Catholic Encyclopedia* gives an exposition of Christian ideas.

Chapter 4. Antichrist and Apocalypse

Nero, the fire and the Christians: Grant pp. 125–37, and Suetonius's *Life of Nero*.

The quotations are from the translation of Tacitus's *Annals* (XV) by Church and Brodribb, with minor changes.

Nero's successes in the East and Greece: Grant pp. 182–5, 188–9, 206.

His 'immortality' and expected return: Bate pp. 28–9, 37–9; Grant pp. 206–8.

Other ideas about Antichrist: Baring-Gould pp. 1–8; Cohn (2) pp. 33–6.

Pope Joan: Baring-Gould pp. 8–20.

The Revelation or Apocalypse of John: again, the *Jerome Biblical Commentary*. Swete's edition of this book, with Greek text and copious notes, is still valuable.

Joanna Southcott: articles in the *Dictionary of National Biography* and *Man, Myth and Magic*. There are slight disagreements about the box.

Number of the Beast: Irenaeus V.30.1–3; Swete pp. 174–6; Farrer pp. 158–9.

Solar flattery of Nero: Barker p. 350; Grant pp. 165, 189. The passage from Seneca is translated by Robert Graves in an appendix to his novel *Claudius the God*.

Later association of emperor with Sun: Barker pp. 89, 347–56, 362 fn 1, 489; Bowder pp. 7–8, 26–7, 35, 90, 102, 115, 155.

Position of Christians in the Empire and final persecution: Barker pp. 249–52, 273–4, 466; Bowder pp. 11–18.

Standard histories deal with the Empire in the fifth century and the sackings of Rome in 410 and 455. There is a good deal about the formation of successor states in John Morris, *The Age of Arthur* (Weidenfeld & Nicolson, London, 1973), although Morris's interpretation of events in Britain must be read with caution.

The association of the successors with the ten horns is due to H.B. Swete (*The Apocalypse of St John*, pp. 224–5)

Chapter 5. Merlin

Christian Sibylline literature: Barker, p. 218 fn; Bate pp. 32–6; St Augustine, *The City of God*, XVIII:23.

Tiburtina: Cohn (2) p. 31; McGinn pp. 70–76.

Methodius: Cohn (2) p. 32; McGinn pp. 70–76.

No scare in 1000; McGinn p. 88; compare Stephen Jay Gould, *Questioning the Millennium* (Vintage Books, London, 1998), pp. 82–5.

Augustine's attitude to prophecy: *The City of God*, V:7, IX:22 and elsewhere; Flint pp. 160–61.

Merlin Geoffrey of Monmouth (1) VI:17–19, VII:1–4 (the Prophecies), VIII:1, 10–12, 19; Loomis (ed.) chapter 8.

Merlin's transitional quality: see C.S. Lewis, *The Cosmic Trilogy*, (Pan Books, London, 1989), pp. 375, 557, 645–8.

Myrddin: Loomis (ed.) chapter 3.

Innocence of Welsh prophets: Gerald of Wales, *Description of Wales*, I:16.

Proliferation of 'Merlin' prophecies: Loomis (ed.) pp. 79, 352–4; McGinn pp. 180–85.

Mousehole episode: *Folklore, Myths and Legends of Britain* p. 135.

Other bogus Merlin material: Glass pp. 45–8 (credulous, as elsewhere).

Chapter 6. The Calabrian Abbot

St Hildegard: basic information in the *New Catholic Encyclopedia*. See also McGinn pp. 100–102.

Assessment of Joachim's system as 'the most influential', etc., is in Cohn (2) pp. 108–10, where its general nature is summarized.

The treatments principally consulted here are by Marjorie Reeves, *The Influence of Prophecy in the Later Middle Ages* and *Joachim of Fiore and the Prophetic Future*. See also a collection of essays under her editorship, *Prophetic Rome in the High Renaissance Period*. These are cited as R(1), R(2) and R(3). The first is an academic study which presupposes some knowledge of Joachim's ideas.

Joachim's life: R(1) pp. 3–15, 21–2; R(2) pp. 2–5, 22–4; McGinn p. 130. The meeting with King Richard: Gillingham pp. 156–7.

The three 'ages': R(1) pp. 131–2; R(2) pp. 6, 13–15; Cohn (2) p. 108.

Ecclesiastical attitudes: R(1) pp. 28–36; McGinn p. 127.

Possible influence on Dante: R(2) pp. 64–6.

St Francis and Franciscans in this connection: R(1) pp. 72–3, 105, 146–8; R(2) pp. 27–8, 30–47; Armstrong pp. 29–31, 83, 133, 183; Cohn (2) pp. 110–11.

The 'Eternal Evangel': R(1) pp. 59–61, 187–9; R(2) pp. 33–4; the *Roman de la Rose*, lines 11, 791–11, 896.

Guglielma of Milan: R(1) pp. 248–50.

Angelic Pope: R(1) pp. 47, 438; R(2) pp. 72–82; R(3) pp. 9–10, 17, 32–3, 80, 157–87, 373–6, 389–90.

Second Charlemagne: R(1) pp. 313–14, 320–31; R(2) pp. 60–70, 85–7; R(3) pp. 17, 104.

Frederick: Cohn (2) pp. 111–13; R(2) pp. 60–61.

Botticelli: R(1) pp. 436–7; R(2) pp. 92–3; R(3) pp. 21, 331–2.

Savonarola episode: R(1) pp. 434–40; R(2) pp. 88–92; R(3) pp. 21, 79–80.

Speculations in Age of Discovery: R(1) p. 360; R(2) pp. 116–21, 129; R(3) pp. 95, 282, 285.

Vaticinia: R(1) pp. 58, 193–4, 214–15; R(2) pp. 75–8; R(3) p. 12.

'Malachy': R(1) p. 461; R(2) pp. 109–10; Bander's edition (text with translation and commentary); Fisher pp. 36–9; Glass pp. 66–71; Wallechinsky pp. 383–4.

Ideological echoes: R(2) – Lessing pp. 167–8, Saint-Simonians p. 168, Comte pp. 168–9, Schelling p. 170, Garaudy p. 175; Cohn (2) p. 109.

George Eliot: *Romola*, ed. cit. pp. 6–7 (Proem); 18 (Book I, chapter 1); pp. 179–80 (Book II, chapter 21).

Chapter 7. The Return of Arthur

Bodmin incident: Loomis (ed.) pp. 53–4.

Arthur's departure: Geoffrey of Monmouth (1) XI:2.

Survival of famous persons: *Folklore, Myths and Legends of Britain*, pp. 486–9. 'Sebastianism' is noted in William C. Atkinson, *A History of*

Spain and Portugal (Penguin Books, London, 1973), pp. 159–60.

Geoffrey's Avalon: Geoffrey of Monmouth (2); Loomis (ed.) pp. 92–3.

The Majorcan romance: Loomis (ed.) p. 68.

Cave-legend: I summarized several versions of this in *The Traveller's Guide to Arthurian Britain* (Gothic Image, Glastonbury, 1997).

William of Malmesbury: Loomis (ed.) p. 64.

The Tudor myth and kindred mystiques: Ashe (3) pp. 103–5, 109–19, 126–33.

Shambhala and Gesar: Ashe (1) pp. 158–70.

Glastonbury: Ashe (2) passim; the Ringwode prophecy pp. 102, 109.

Chapter 8. Nostradamus: The Miscellany

Leoni gives an account of Nostradamus's life and publications, pp. 15–40, and surveys the work of commentators. Cheetham covers some of the ground in her Introduction.

Nostradamus's method of composition: Leoni pp. 107–8; his hope of a Second Charlemagne p. 110; his vocabulary p. 113 and see also Gould p. 321.

As stated, most of the interpretations are basically Leoni's; some of these are adapted from earlier ones by Le Pelletier and others. As a rule, the apparent fulfilments are matters of general history. The lines about Montmorency (IX.18) are noted by Gould (p. 325) and supported by Treasure (pp. 116–18). For the Portuguese–British relationship, X.100, see Atkinson's *History of Spain and Portugal* as cited in notes to chapter 7, pp. 189–90.

Relevant details of the conspiracy against James II, apparently the topic of IV.89, are given by Edward Gregg in *Queen Anne* (Routledge & Kegan Paul, London, 1980), pp. 35–6, 49, 59–60. The word *blond* certainly seems erroneous, but there is a miniature of William by the contemporary artist Willem Wissing in which his hair might be described as chestnut. A biographer of Thomas Jefferson remarks that his hair, which was red in his youth, was sometimes called fair.

In the light of Nostradamus's phrasing in IX.77, it is interesting that

Carlyle defines Louis's alleged crime as conspiring against Liberty (*The French Revolution*, Book II, chapter 7).

Chapter 9. Nostradamus: The Sequence

Here, as in Chapter 8, most of the interpretations are given, in substance, by Leoni. However, there is such a wealth of Napoleonic material that nearly all can be enhanced. The following references apply to some of the less familiar points.

Abolition of the Holy Roman Empire: Schom p. 424.

The 'million men' remark: Cronin p. 464; Schom, pp. 665–6; Herold pp. 344–5.

Napoleon's rise beginning at Toulon: Schom p. 22.

Use of the word 'satrap': Treasure p. 51.

Conflict with Directory: Schom pp. 88–9, 152–3; Herold pp. 74–5.

Haircut: Schom pp. 207–8; see also Aronson p. 54 and Cronin pp. 176–7, 182.

Bee as Napoleonic emblem: Aronson p. 89, Cronin pp. 247, 394–5.

Nocturnal round-up in Brumaire coup: Aronson pp. 51–2; Schom pp. 220–21.

Keith's expulsion from Genoa: *Dictionary of National Biography*.

Intimidation of Naples and Spain: Schom p. 303.

Short official garment as Consul: Cronin pp. 177–8. His long robe as Emperor is shown in paintings.

New Charlemagne: Schom pp. 335, 347, 423.

Ecclesiastical affairs: ibid. pp. 291, 458, 535, 554, 648–9.

Bernadotte's defection: Herold p. 341; Schom p. 605.

Rearguard action by Ney and Victor: Schom pp. 641–2.

Dream about bear: Schom p. 477.

Murat's desertion and subsequent vagaries: Aronson pp. 167–8, 189, 216–17.

For the regimental nickname Vein Openers, see Byron Farwell, *Queen Victoria's Little Wars* (Norton, 1985), p. 357.

St Helena: Schom pp. 766–8, 783.

Belief in the Class B items depends more on Cheetham's interpretations. The Varennes quatrain is approved by Cheetham and by Colin

Wilson (pp. 255–6), but Leoni points out the difficulties. Brewer's *Dictionary of Phrase and Fable* offers a meaning for the white stone, although it does not seem apt.

For would-be applications of Nostradamus's prophecies to post-Napoleonic times, see Fisher pp. 41–57, Wallechinsky pp. 352–3 and Cheetham passim. Regarding III.57, Loog's explanation and its result, see Cheetham p. 5 and Howe pp. 161–3.

Leoni makes a geographical distribution of the quatrains. It is very approximate but shows that the French-plus-British grouping that contains all the good ones, or nearly so, is a minority.

Chapter 10. How is it Done?

For ideas about foreknowledge in medieval philosophy (which have continued to be held since), see St Thomas Aquinas, *Summa Theologica*, Part I, Question 14, Article 13 (Does God know the future? Yes) and Part I, Question 57, Article 3 (Do angels know the future? No).

Some early observations are cited in Flint pp. 30–32, 90.

Katherine Maltwood's *Guide to Glastonbury's Temple of the Stars* was reissued in 1964 (James Clarke, Cambridge) and reprinted in 1982. The theory has been kept alive also by advocates such as Mary Caine.

Chapter 11. Dante and Milton: Unrecognized Sources

Dante's Earth: Boyde pp. 67–9, 96–8; Lewis pp. 140–44.

Dante's heavens: Boyde p. 138; Lewis pp. 96–8.

Purgatory: Boyde pp. 84–7, 109–11, 173; Jacoff (ed.) pp. 193, 205 n. 4; Sayers p. 89.

Location of Paradise: Boyde pp. 109–11, 182; Lewis pp. 144–5.

Rivers flowing through tunnels: Augustine cited by Aquinas, *Summa Theologica*, Part I, Question 102, Article 1. The motif reappears in a popular medieval work of pseudo-geography, *The Travels of Sir John Mandeville*, chapter 33.

Islamic legends: Asin pp. 111–17, 122–4.

Medieval attitude to originality: Lewis pp. 208–11.

Meru: Ashe (1) pp. 105–8, (2) pp. 227–9; Boorstin pp. 82, 84;

Mahabharata (trans. J.A.B. Buitinen, University of Chicago Press, 1973 etc.), vol. 2, pp. 533, 703.

Borobudur: Ashe (2) pp. 228–31; Chatterji pp. 113; *Encyclopaedia Britannica*, article 'Borobudur'; Grabsky passim.

Spiritual progress with narrative: Jacoff (ed.) p. 127.

Dante and classical authors: ibid. pp. 100–102.

Babylonian Creation Epic: Pritchard pp. 60–72.

Israelite rehandlings: Ashe (4) pp. 80–81, 278–9.

Angels' creation and fall: Boss p. xix; Boyde pp. 188, 245–6; Milton pp. 111, 313.

Humans as replacements: Flint p. 158 fn 70.

Milton on the indecisive battle: Milton p. 347.

Milton's views on the Son of God: ibid. pp. 88, 113, 205–7, 211, 267.

Angels as gods: ibid. pp. 234, 315.

The Chariot: Ashe (4) p. 204.

Chapter 12. Seers and Witches

Nixon: Fisher p. 207; Glass pp. 75–8; Gould pp. 316–17; Wallechinsky pp. 347–9.

Mother Shipton: *Folklore, Myths and Legends of Britain* pp. 96, 348; Glass pp. 132–9 (this author appears to believe in the forged prophecies); Gould pp. 317–18; Wallechinsky pp. 349–52; and the anonymous *Mother Shipton* booklet.

Peden: Gould p. 316; *Dictionary of National Biography*.

Thomas the Rhymer and the Brahan Seer: Fisher pp. 59–71; *Folklore, Myths and Legends of Britain* p. 542; Glass pp. 105–15; Wallechinsky pp. 436–7. For Peden, Thomas the Rhymer and the Brahan Seer, see further Ashe, *Encyclopedia of Prophecy*.

Tecumseh: Sugden pp. 246–51.

Prophecy inspired by evil beings: Augustine V:7, IX:22; Flint pp. 160–61. The quotation from *Malleus Maleficarum* is from Part 2, chapter 2.

Early witchcraft and the great witch-hunt: Cohn (1) passim; Flint pp. 62–3, 231.

Extent, attitudes, numbers involved: Sharpe pp. 5, 8–9, 21–2,

128–47, 237, 253. The text 'Thou shalt not suffer a witch to live' is
Exodus 22:18 in the King James Bible.

Development of the witches in *Macbeth*: Lewis p. 125.

Chapter 13. The Cazotte Prophecy

See Cazotte's *The Devil in Love* in the edition listed in the
Bibliography. In addition to a translation of the story, this contains
the short biography by Gérard de Nerval giving Nodier's childhood
reminiscence and La Harpe's narrative of the prophecy. The relevant
pages are 110–16.

Décote (pp. 341–52) assembles the testimonies of Mme d'Hautefeuille and others and adds comments such as Saint-Beuve's.
Lamothe-Langon, as it happens, is demolished as an authority on
anything in Cohn (1) pp. 132–8.

Nodier's opinion that it would have been easy to foresee the Terror
is quoted by Nerval in the work cited (pp. 116–17). This includes
Cazotte's later 'Revelation' (pp. 145–60), one of several items casting
doubt on his general acumen; Décote gives others. The earlier
fantasy about severed heads is on pp. 117–19.

Wallechinsky (pp. 385–7) has an uncritical account of the prophecy.
Wilson (p. 312) takes it up, stressing the corroboration, but I think
he exaggerates its extent.

Regarding the revolutionary cult of Reason, compare Schom p. 253.

Chapter 14. More Astrologers

Early Christian opposition to astrology: Flint pp. 20, 96.

Effect of the Magi: Flint pp. 53, 365, 368–70.

Medieval acceptance of astrology: Flint pp. 99, 128–30, 145; Lewis
pp. 103–4; Boyde p. 250.

Dee: Glass pp. 116–21.

Lilly: Gould pp. 315–16; Wallechinsky pp. 356–8.

Old Moore: Howe p. 22.

Varley: ibid. p. 31.

Predictive almanacs: ibid. p. 34.

Role of Theosophy: ibid. pp. 54–64.

Evangeline Adams: Wallechinsky pp. 363–6.

Newspaper astrology: Howe pp. 68–9.

Nicollaud: Howe pp. 68–9.

German revival: ibid. pp. 79–96.

Hanussen: Gill pp. 258–60; Koestler pp. 261–4.

His coaching of Hitler: Toland p. 229.

His prediction of Hitler's attaining power: Toland pp. 296–7, 1072. Hanussen's 1933 horoscope of the Führer is said to have forecast great success followed by failure after the breaking of the 'union of three', and the disappearance of his work during the spring of 1945 'in smoke and flame'. The union of three might, I suppose, be the Tripartite Alliance of Germany, Italy and Japan, which began definitely crumbling in 1943.

Reichstag fire: Gill p. 260; Toland p. 312. There is more about Hanussen's role in Peter Padfield, *Himmler* (Henry Holt, New York, 1990), p. 123.

Hanussen's murder: Gill p. 260; Toland p. 569.

Other Hitler horoscopes, 1931–4, and first Nazi attack on astrologers: Howe pp. 109–10; Toland pp. 275, 569.

Louis de Wohl: Howe pp. 205–10.

Krafft: Howe pp. 120–91, 220–32; Toland pp. 683, 691, 719; Wallechinsky pp. 377–9.

Horoscope of German Republic: Howe p. 159.

Hess's flight, alleged astrological motive and *Aktion Hess*: Howe pp. 192–203; Toland pp. 762–3.

The two horoscopes in spring 1945: Howe p. 240; Toland p. 971; Trevor-Roper pp. 107–8.

Successful astrologers and planetary correlations: Howe pp. 245, 248 (Gauquelin).

Chapter 15. Premonitions and Previsions

Aberfan: Fisher pp. 181–2. Some details are given in J.H. Brennan, *Occult Reich* pp. 15–16; published by Futura Books, London, in 1974, this is a speculative book on the paranormal in relation to Nazism, and I have not used it elsewhere.

Rush's dream: Joseph J. Ellis, *Founding Brothers* (Knopf, New York, 2001), pp. 220, 222, 225, 248.

Central Premonition Registry: Fisher pp. 182–4; Wallechinsky pp. 291–4.

Macklin: Fisher pp. 204–5; Glass pp. 194–6.

'Cheiro': Glass pp. 180–84; Wallechinsky pp. 366–8.

Johanson: Wallechinsky pp. 361–3.

Titanic: Fisher pp. 179–81; Wade pp. 42–3; Wallechinsky pp. 387–90; Whyte vol. 2 pp. 37–8, 314 fn, 328, 339, 356.

Cayce: Fisher pp. 75–85; Glass pp. 189–94; Wallechinsky pp. 371–4; Wilson pp. 166–8.

Dixon: Fisher pp. 87–97; Glass pp. 184–8; Wallechinsky pp. 392–4. Her mistaken abandonment of her own best prediction is described by Ruth Montgomery in *A Gift of Prophecy* (Bantam, New York, 1967), pp. 108–10.

Poor record of 'psychics': Fisher pp. 99–109; Wallechinsky pp. 403–6.

Fatima: Martindale passim, and article in the *New Catholic Encyclopedia*. Fisher (pp. 192–5) gives an account that is most inadequate but includes the spurious version of the 1960 message, persisting with the 'third world war' theme. Cardinal Ratzinger, who knew the real contents, indicated in 1996 that the message was not 'apocalyptic'.

Greeley's forecast: Wallechinsky p. 42.

Chapter 16. Answers?

Dunne's volunteers: Dunne pp. 256–79.

Louisa E. Rhine: Broughton pp. 18–22.

Bridey Murphy and Arthur Guirdham's case-history: Wilson pp. 512, 518–22.

For the scientific matter, see several books by John Gribbin, and Marcus Chown, *The Universe Next Door* (Headline, London, 2001).

Different 'times': Chown p. 43.

Wormholes: Chown p. 255.

Appendix 1. The Number of the Beast

Association of magic squares with planets: Nauert pp. 120, 276; *Man, Myth and Magic*, article 'Magic Squares'.

Appendix 2. William Blake and Arthur

Blake's mythology: Ashe (3) pp. 14, 51–2, 149–85.

Peter Ackroyd in *Blake* (Sinclair-Stevenson, London, 1995) gives some information on the three eccentrics mentioned here: pp. 174, 290–91, 328–32.

Bibliography

Armstrong, Edward A., *Saint Francis: Nature Mystic*, University of California Press, Berkeley, CA, 1973

Aronson, Theo, *The Golden Bees*, Corgi Books, London, 1975

Ashe, Geoffrey:
(1) *The Ancient Wisdom*, Macmillan, London, 1977
(2) *Avalonian Quest*, Methuen, London, 1982
(3) *Camelot and the Vision of Albion*, Heinemann, London, 1971
(4) *The Land and the Book*, Collins, London, 1965

Asin, Miguel, *Islam and the Divine Comedy* (trans. Harold Sunderland), John Murray, London, 1926

Augustine, St, *The City of God* (trans. Henry Bettenson), Penguin Books, Harmondsworth, 1984

Bander, Peter, *The Prophecies of St Malachy*, Tan Books, Rockford, IL, 1973

Baring-Gould, S., *Antichrist and Pope Joan*, Unicorn, Caerfyrddin, 1975

Barker, Ernest, *From Alexander to Constantine*, Clarendon Press, Oxford, 1956

Bate, H.N., *The Sibylline Oracles. Books III–V*, SPCK, London, 1918

Boorstin, Daniel J., *The Discoverers*, Vintage Books, New York, 1985

Boss, Valentine, *Milton and the Rise of Russian Satanism*, University of Toronto Press, Toronto, 1991

Bowder, Diana, *The Age of Constantine and Julian*, Paul Elek, London, 1978

Boyde, Patrick, *Dante: Philomythes and Philosopher*, Cambridge University Press, London, 1981

Broughton, Richard, *Parapsychology*, Rider Books, London, 1992

Cazotte, Jacques, *The Devil in Love*, Mansilio, New York, 1993 (for contents, see note on Chapter 13)

Chambers Biographical Dictionary, Edinburgh and New York, 1990 edition

Chatterji, B.R., 'The Hindu Kingdoms of Indo-China and Java' in *The Cultural Heritage of India* (vol. 3), Sri Ramakrishna Centenary Committee, Calcutta, 1937

Cheetham, Erika, *The Prophecies of Nostradamus*, Corgi Books, London, 1975

Cohn, Norman:
(1) *Europe's Inner Demons*, Paladin, London, 1976
(2) *The Pursuit of the Millennium*, Paladin, London, 1970

Cronin, Vincent, *Napoleon*, Collins, London, 1971

Décote, Georges, *L'Itinéraire de Jacques Cazotte*, Librairie Droz, Geneva, 1984

Dictionary of National Biography

Dunne, J.W., *An Experiment with Time* (3rd ed.), Faber, London, 1934

Eliot, George, *Romola*, William Blackwood edition of her works, vol. 6; original publication 1863

Encyclopaedia Britannica 1974 edition

Farrer, Austin, *The Revelation of St John the Divine*, Clarendon Press, Oxford, 1964

Fisher, Joe, *Predictions*, Sidgwick & Jackson, London, 1981

Flint, I.J., *The Rise of Magic in Early Medieval Europe*, Clarendon Press, Oxford, 1991

Folklore, Myths and Legends of Britain, Readers Digest Association, London, 1973

Geoffrey of Monmouth:
(1) *The History of the Kings of Britain* (trans. Lewis Thorpe) Penguin Books, Harmondsworth, 1966
(2) *Vita Merlini*: The Life of Merlin (ed. and trans. J.J. Parry), University of Illinois Press, Urbana, 1925

Gerald of Wales, *The Journey through Wales/The Description of Wales* (trans. Lewis Thorpe), Penguin Books, Harmondsworth, 1978

Gill, Anton, *A Dance between Flames*, John Murray, London, 1993

Gillingham, John, *Richard the Lionheart*, Weidenfeld & Nicolson, London, 1989

Glass, Justine, *The Story of Fulfilled Prophecy*, Cassell, London, 1969

Gould, Rupert T., *Oddities: a Book of Unexplained Facts*, Philip Allan, London, 1928

Grabsky, Phil, *The Lost Temple of Java*, Orion, London, 1999

Grant, Michael, *Nero*, Dorset Press, New York, 1989

Graves, Robert, *The Greek Myths* (2 vols), Penguin Books, Harmondsworth, 1960

Herold, J. Christopher, *The Age of Napoleon*, Penguin Books, Harmondsworth, 1969

Howe, Ellic, *Urania's Children*, William Kimber, London, 1967

Hoyle, Peter, *Delphi*, Cassell, London, 1967

Irenaeus, *Five Books against Heresies* (trans. John Keble), James Parker, London, 1872

Isserlin, B.S.J., *The Israelites*, Thames & Hudson, London, 1998

Jacoff, Rachel (ed.), *The Cambridge Companion to Dante*, Cambridge University Press, London, 1993

Jerome Biblical Commentary, The (ed. Raymond E. Brown, Joseph A. Fitzmeyer and Roland E. Murphy), Prentice-Hall, Englewood Cliffs, NJ, 1968

Koestler, Arthur, *Arrow in the Blue*, Collins with Hamish Hamilton, London, 1952

Leoni, Edgar, *Nostradamus and his Prophecies*, Bell Publishing Company, New York, 1982

Lewis, C.S., *The Discarded Image*, Cambridge University Press, London, 1970

Lindblom, J., *Prophecy in Ancient Israel*, Basil Blackwell, Oxford, 1962

Loomis, Roger Sherman (ed.), *Arthurian Literature in the Middle Ages*, Clarendon Press, Oxford, 1959

McGinn, Bernard, *Visions of the End: Apocalyptic Traditions in the Middle Ages*, Columbia University Press, New York, 1979

Man, Myth and Magic (ed. Richard Cavendish; 7 vols), BPC Publishing, London, 1970–72

Martindale, C.C., *The Message of Fatima*, Burns Oates and Washbourne, London, 1950

Milton, John, *Christian Doctrine (De Doctrina Christiana)* (trans. John Carey) in *Complete Prose Works of John Milton*, vol. VI, Yale University Press, New Haven, 1973

Mother Shipton, reprint of anonymous booklet, West Country Editions, Bath, 1976

Nauert, Charles G., Jr, *Agrippa and the Crisis of Renaissance Thought*, University of Illinois Press, Urbana, 1965

New Catholic Encyclopedia, Catholic University of America, Washington, 1967

Nostradamus *see* Cheetham, Erika; Leoni, Edgar.

Pritchard, James B. (ed.), *Ancient Near Eastern Texts Relating to the Old Testament*, Princeton University Press, Princeton, 1955

Reeves, Marjorie:
(1) *The Influence of Prophecy in the Later Middle Ages*, University of Notre Dame Press, 1993
(2) *Joachim of Fiore and the Prophetic Future*, Harper and Row, New York, 1977
(3) (ed.), *Prophetic Rome in the High Renaissance Period*, Clarendon Press, Oxford, 1992

Rescher, Nicholas, *Predicting the Future*, State University of New York Press, New York, 1998

Sayers, Dorothy L., *Introductory Papers on Dante*, Methuen, London, 1954

Schom, Alan, *Napoleon Bonaparte*, HarperCollins, New York, 1997

Sharpe, James, *Instruments of Darkness*, Hamish Hamilton, London, 1996

Sherder, William A., *The Fortune Sellers*, John A. Wiley and Sons, New York, 1998

Suetonius, *The Lives of the Twelve Caesars* (trans. Joseph Gavorse), Modern Library, New York, 1931

Sugden, John, *Tecumseh*, Henry Holt, New York, 1998

Swete, Henry Barclay, *The Apocalypse of St John*, Macmillan, London, 1907

Toland, John, *Adolf Hitler* (2 vols), Doubleday, New York, 1976

Treasure, G.R.R., *Cardinal Richelieu*, Adam and Charles Black, 1972

Trevor-Roper, Hugh, *The Last Days of Hitler*, Macmillan, London, 1947

Wade, Wyn Craig, *The Titanic: End of a Dream*, Penguin Books USA, New York, 1986

Wallechinsky, David, Amy Wallace and Irving Wallace, *The Book of Predictions*, William Morrow, New York, 1980

Whyte, Frederic, *The Life of W.T. Stead* (2 vols), Jonathan Cape, London, 1925

Wilson, Colin, *The Occult*, Hodder and Stoughton, London, 1971

Index

Columbus 14, 120, 215
communism viii, 141, 288, 304
Comte, Auguste 130
Condorcet, Marquis de 127,
    255, 256, 258, 262
Constantine 92
coup of Brumaire 177–8, 190
Creation, Milton 226–39
Cumaean Sibyl 8–10
Cyrus 5, 29, 36, 53

Daniel, Book of 32–5, 51–3,
    74, 77–8, 94
Dante Alighieri 214–25, 229,
    239–41, 293, 294, 307
  Informant 299, 303–4
  Jesus Christ 61
  Joachim of Fiore 114–15,
    130
  papacy 117
  witches 246
Dauphin 160, 170, 172
David, King 19, 20, 28, 36, 48
de Wohl, Louis 272
Dead Sea Scrolls 37
Dee, John 163, 212, 266
Deiphobe 8
Delphi 2–7
Devil (Satan) 33, 67, 76–87, 96
  Milton 228–9, 231–9, 240
  witchcraft 246, 248
Dickens, Charles 242, 243
divination 1–2, 11, 20–1
Dixon, Jeane x, 126, 284
Domitian 70, 74, 78, 79, 86–7,
    309
Don John 159, 171, 198–9
Doyle, Arthur Conan 204–5
dreams x–xi, 291–2, 293–4,
    298, 301

ancient Israel 21
  Napoleon 184
druids 100
Dunne, J.W. x–xi, 291–2, 298,
    301

Earth Goddess 2
Earthly Paradise 218–19, 224,
    233
Edward VIII 268
Egypt 16, 18, 20–1, 194
Elagabalus 90
Elijah 22–3
Eliot, George 130–1
Elizabeth I 138–9, 266–7
Enuma elish 226–9, 231, 233–9,
    240
Erythraean Sibyl 7–8, 98–9
Eternal Evangel 115–16, 129
evil 31
Exodus 18–19
Ezekiel 27–8, 33, 36, 216, 218,
    239, 240
Ezra 30, 32

'faithful remnant', Chosen
    People 23, 25–8
False Prophet 80–1, 96
Fatima prophecy 285–9, 304–5
France
  see also French Revolution
  Napoleon predictions 173–92
  Nostradamus emphasis 198,
    199, 209
  War of the Spanish
    Succession 167, 172
Franciscans 115–16, 126
French Revolution 140–1, 169,
    172, 173, 193, 255–65
Futurology vii, viii

Julius Caesar 11, 12, 59

Kennedy assassination 284
kerygma (Good News) 46,
    57–8, 63, 207
Krafft, Karl Ernst 198, 272–3

La Harpe, Jean de 255–65
Lailoken 101
Last Emperor 99, 109, 117–18
Leoni, Edgar 151, 154, 165,
    174, 192, 211
Lessing, Gotthold 129, 130
Lewis, C.S. 101, 215
life after death 31
Lilly, William 111, 244, 367
literary prophets, Israel 24–5
Loog, C.L. 197–8
Lost Tribes of Israel 20
Louis of Condé, Prince 158,
    171
Louis XIII 160, 167, 171
Louis XIV 165, 167, 168, 172
Louis XV 168, 172
Louis XVI 169–70, 172, 194–5
Lovecraft, H.P. 269
Lucia dos Santos 285–9, 304–5
Luke 44, 60–1

Macbeth 249, 250–4
Macklin, Cyril 279
Mahabharata 127–8, 221–2
Malachy 121–5, 202, 210, 299
Malleus Maleficarum 246–8, 250
Malory, Sir Thomas 137
Maltwood, Katherine 211–12
Marie Antoinette 170, 172,
    194–5, 257, 259
Mark 44, 60
Marx, Karl 131–2, 141

Marxism 113, 141, 312
Matthew 44, 48–9, 51, 59–60,
    62–3
Mayan prophecies xi
Menestrier 122
Merlin viii, 100–11, 112, 134,
    136, 138
    astrology 267
    Informant 205, 295
    Nostradamus comparison 155
Meru 221–5
Messiah
    Christian 43–65
    Jewish 16, 36–7, 38
Millennium 97, 196
Milton, John 214, 226–41,
    293–4, 299, 303–4, 307
mind-capsules 301, 302, 303,
    304, 305, 306
miracles 46, 47–8
Monaco siege 178
Mongolia 143–4
Monmouth, Duke of 164–5,
    171, 211
Montmorency execution 161,
    171, 210
Moore, Francis 267
Morgenthau Plan 276, 277
Morris, William 132
Moses 18–19, 21
Mother Shipton 243–5, 246,
    248, 267
mountain imagery 216, 217–24,
    239–40
Muhammad 1, 221
Murat, Joachim 177, 185, 191

nabi prophets 21–2, 23–4
nationalism 142–4
Native American prophets 245

336

Naylor, R.H. 268–9
Nazism 142, 144, 269–73
Neale, John 261
Nebuchadnezzar 26, 33
Nehemiah 30, 52–3
Nelson, Robert 279, 292
Nero 68–9, 70, 71
  astrology 12–13
  Beast analogy 79, 84–7, 94–5
Nerval, Gérard de 264–5
New Testament
  Book of Daniel 51–2
  Gospels 44–51, 58, 59–63,
    114
  Messiah 16
  Revelation 44, 72–85, 92–3,
    96–7, 201–2, 203
  Joachim of Fiore 113–14
  Milton interpretation 229–30
  the 'other' 205, 207–8
  Satan 228–9
  Thessalonians 66–7
  Trinity 113–14, 128
newspaper astrology 268–9
Nicollaud, Charles 197, 269
Nixon, Robert ('Cheshire
    Prophet') 242–3, 292
Nodier, Charles 255–6, 260–1,
    262–3
Nostradamus ix, 149–200, 201,
    202, 203–4, 293
  class B quatrains 157–8,
    192–5, 199
  German astrology 272–3,
    277
  Informant 294–5, 297–8,
    299, 301
  miscellaneous quatrains
    158–72
  Napoleon predictions 173–92

the 'other' 205, 206, 209–13
spirit invocation 245, 248
twentieth-century predictions
    196–8
number of the Beast 81–7, 93,
    97, 303, 308–10
Numbers 21, 38
numerology 86–7

Old Testament
  astrology 99
  divine inspiration 205–6
  Jesus Christ 47, 48–51,
    51–4
  Messiah 16–21
  prophets 21–38
  Satan 228–9
  Second Isaiah 29, 53–8,
    201–2, 206–7, 295, 299
  Sybilline matter 98
  Trinity 114, 128
omens 1
oracles, Greek 1–7
the 'other' 206–13, 294–5

paganism, Celtic 100
Palestine 16–17, 18–19, 29, 31,
    32, 280
papacy 72, 113, 115, 116
  Angelic Pope 116–17, 118,
    119, 120–3, 125, 131
  Napoleon relationship 181–2
  Nostradamus 165
  St Malachy 121–5
Partridge, John 267
Paul 44, 46, 50, 66–7, 69
Persian War (1727) 193–4
Peter 61, 63, 69, 87
Philippe, Duc d'Orléans 167–8
Plato 4, 14, 283